In Search of James Joyce

In Search of *James Joyce*

Robert Scholes

University of Illinois Press
Urbana and Chicago

Manufactured in the United States of America
1 2 3 4 5 C P 5 4 3 2 1

This book is printed on acid-free paper.

Library of Congress Cataloging-in-Publication Data

Scholes, Robert E.
In search of James Joyce / Robert Scholes.
p. cm.
Includes index.
ISBN 0-252-01913-X (alk. paper).—ISBN 0-252-06245-0 (pbk.)
1. Joyce, James, 1882–1941—Criticism and interpretation.
I. Title.
PR6019.O9Z79434 1992
823'.912—dc20 91-40000
CIP

This book is dedicated to the memory of

Herbert Joseph "Ted" Scholes

Actor, lifeguard, something in a steel mill, traveling salesman of patent medicines, lifelong entrepreneur. Of English and Irish family, born and raised in a dismal section of Philadelphia with an Indian name, he could and did quote Kipling by the yard. He told funny stories about his father getting drunk and falling into the Christmas tree. He took me to my first big league ball game at Ebbetts Field in Brooklyn and died while they were tearing it down. I got a chair from the wreckers and still have it, rusting in the garage. He used to send me to Sunday mass while he stayed home in bed. On his death bed he had a pious reconversion to Catholicism—not missing any bets, I thought—with the result that at the wake I got into a quarrel with a priest over my father's corpse. This old father—old artificer—prepared me well for the study of James Joyce. For this and for his unfailing wit and enduring kindness to me, I offer these belated thanks.

Contents

Introduction

Midway through the journey of my academic life I found myself trying to write a book called *In Search of James Joyce.* This is not that book, for I did not write it. I have kept that title, however, partly in rueful acknowledgment of what I failed to accomplish, but mainly because a search for James Joyce is precisely what this collection of essays has come to represent. The unwritten book would have been different: more unified, more complete. Why did I never write that book? What happened—to the extent that I understand it—is that, by the time I had sufficient perspective on Joyce to write a book devoted to his work but not idolatrous, there were other books that it seemed more important to write. I wrote them and have no regrets. Still, I kept being drawn to Joyce: writing about him on various occasions; teaching his work in one context or another.

Two decades ago, when I chose this title for that other book, I rather thought that my search would end with the discovery of its object, that my book would present a Joyce who had never been delineated so richly and accurately in a critical study. As I say, this is not that book. Rather, it is the record of a search begun almost by chance and continued with some reluctance for thirty years, during which time I kept returning to Joyce with new critical tools but never succeeded in pinning him down. It is, in a sense, the record of a quest that failed because its grail turned into an object among other objects as its pursuer lost some of his innocence. Over the decades my attitude toward Joyce and his work gradually changed, until, finally, I have come to be interested in many of the very writers his name and fame eclipsed, writers who did not embrace the modernism he and those most closely associated with him have come to represent. But that, as we say, is another story and perhaps another book.

About such books as this the question is properly asked, Are they indeed worth reading? A collection of essays unified only by their object and by the person who wrote them, neither of which remained the same during the time period in which they were written—what claims can be made for such a text? I would like to claim neither too much nor too little for what the reader may find here. You will not find a progressively deeper penetration into the heart and mind of James Joyce—or of Robert Scholes, for that matter. You will find, however, a record of prolonged engagement with the riddle of Joyce, in which two narratives gradually become apparent: a narrative of changes in critical methods in literary study over three decades and a narrative of the cooling of a youthful infatuation into something more like an ironic respect. Both the changes in method and the changes in attitude reveal new aspects of Joyce—or perhaps different Joyces. And this is the major claim I am able to make for these essays. In their shifts and dodges and misprisions they offer glimpses into Joyce as valid and as penetrating as most others—and especially into the earlier work of Joyce: his youthful essays and poems, his stories, and his autobiographical novel.

Each essay reprinted here was, as Wallace Stevens said of graver matters, "the cry of its occasion." Some of them have continued to be read by students of Joyce, in various collections that are still in print. Some have remained slumbering in back issues of scholarly journals. Because I see their value in the perspectives they offer, I have not tried to resolve these into a single "correct" view of Joyce. I have let stand their youthful ardor as well as their pedantic flourishes, though I have tried to situate each one and explain its occasion. Presented in this way, they constitute a record of academic fashions in criticism, to some extent, as well as episodes in the affair of a critic with an author. To the extent that these dimensions of the text are valuable, it seems to me, their value depends on the typical quality of the matters recorded rather than on some special and unique quality in them. Let me begin, then, by trying to describe the academic situation from which they emerged and to locate myself within it.

My generation of graduate students in English was mostly male and largely innocent of its own cultural construction. Most of us, finishing graduate school at the end of the 1950s, had been originally trained as New Critics, oriented to poetry rather than fiction or drama, and we believed, with almost touching simplicity, in the absolute value of literary study as an end in itself. My decision to do graduate work at Cornell was motivated (in addition to the fact that the school would have me) by the faculty's willingness to let me emphasize the novel in my studies. My move away from the poetical and toward narrative texts was perhaps a sign that I was already impatient with New Critical boundaries. This impatience, which had all the feel of a personal impulse, turned out to be symptomatic of a larger shift taking place in American and European critical discourse at that time, as the study of what was later called "narratology" became for a decade or so an important dimension of literary study.

It is my awareness that a whole series of what seemed to be personal and fully volitional moves of this sort were in fact typical of many others like myself that gives me confidence in the usefulness of this record as something beyond the merely personal. Such an awareness has also led me to be somewhat skeptical about the feelings of freedom and choice that accompany such shifts of intellectual posture. On the other hand, elements in my personal history—of difference from and resistance to the larger changes in critical mood or fashion—suggest that each of us is more than a cog in a large critical machine, or perhaps that the machine is blessedly inefficient. At any rate, the narrative structure that fits neatly over my life as a literary scholar finds me beginning as a somewhat rebellious New Critic and moving through structuralism and semiotics toward cultural criticism. What makes this narrative slightly different from that of our critical discourse as a whole is that my work, though aware of deconstruction, has never made the deconstructive swerve.

Looking back through the essays in this book, I can find reasons to account for my personal trajectory. I was a rebellious New Critic for the same reasons that I have not embraced deconstruction: that is, I seem always to have had, even when not fully aware of it, a hermeneutic desire to understand the Joycean text (and many another text) as an act of communication from an author to a reader. I have sought to read Joyce's work as the work of James Joyce, a real person who lived a certain life and hoped to communicate important things through his writing. This does not mean that I assumed a complete and perfect intention on Joyce's part, which could be deciphered in this or that story or poem; it does mean that I refused to give up the fiction of intentionality as a necessary criterion or protocol of reading. On the other hand, studying Joyce taught me early on that the notion of a bounded and complete "work" would have to be abandoned. Joyce produced not discrete works but a Joycean text to which he kept adding from his first written word to his last. Like Balzac, he was writing a great human comedy, in which characters crossed textual boundaries, and the text of his life was forever enmeshed with the text of his work.

I had been interested in literary theory from an early date, perhaps because of the teaching of René Wellek and the art historian George Kubler in my undergraduate days at Yale, or perhaps for deeper and more idiosyncratic reasons. In graduate school my interest in theory was fed by working with professors who took theory seriously and were careful to situate their own literary approaches: W. R. Keast, M. H. Abrams, R. S. Crane, and William M. Sale, Jr. When dissertation time approached, my theoretical work had convinced me that any mere interpretations or opinions of mine would be of little interest, so I asked my mentor, William Sale, if he knew of any humble and useful task I might perform, such as editing a text or something of that sort. He and Arthur Mizener responded by asking me if I would like to catalog Cornell's newly acquired Mennen Collection of the papers of James Joyce. I asked Professor Sale if this would be a dissertation. He replied tersely that it would be a book—as indeed it became, after a couple of years of work.

The Mennen Collection consists of material that had been kept by Joyce's brother Stanislaus, which meant that it was full of useful and interesting material about Joyce's life and work until 1920, when the brothers' lives diverged. Working on this material, placing and dating manuscript fragments and letters, identifying correspondents, and performing other menial tasks gave me the fullest appreciation of how an author's work grows out of a life and a culture. It also left me especially knowledgeable about the background of Joyce's early work, so that my critical attention to Joyce has tended to focus mainly on that. I have never, for instance, become a "Wakean," which, if I had done my work at Buffalo, say, instead of Cornell, might have been inevitable. As it is, much of my writing on Joyce was done during the sixties and was fueled directly by my work on the Cornell collection. In the seventies and eighties I ranged more widely but always found myself coming back to Joyce, though these returns were contextualized in different ways.

Working on Joyce, as it turned out, positioned me well to undertake larger studies in narrative literature and in modernism as a mode of cultural production. Studying Joyce also forced me to become more of a comparatist, though I have never caught up with his own linguistic mastery. Having prepared myself to teach and study English literature from the Restoration to modern times, I never intended to be a Joyce specialist, and, indeed, I have never quite become one. But I am grateful to those who directed me to my first Joyce project—and to Joyce himself, for providing so much stimulation and aesthetic energy. These essays deserve a collection of this sort only because Joyce has remained so alive in his texts as to repay many times over the various kinds of attention I have given them. One reason we still read Joyce, I believe, is that his gift for language itself, which was there from the beginning but continued to develop and expand, is of an order that links him to other virtuosos of the language, including Shakespeare. Another reason is that Joyce never gave up trying to use his gift for language to encompass more and more of his world and its history. He soon gave up realism as a technique, but he never gave up representation as his goal. He was a maximalist to the end, as concerned as Rabelais to transcribe the stuff of his world in words. I hope my respect—and, at times, my enthusiasm—for Joyce's enterprise remains perceptible through the necessary pedantries of these academic essays and the inevitable cooling of my first idolatrous infatuation with his writing.

[1]

Stephen Dedalus: *Eiron* and *Alazon*

[1961]

This is the first essay on Joyce that I published. It is governed by two impulses: to rescue *Portrait* from the New Critical need to see it as a work that is ironic at the expense of Stephen Dedalus; and to somehow incorporate the critical theorizing of Northrop Frye into the reading of literary texts. When I studied *Portrait* in graduate school, my teachers always insisted on the book's irony, as if it were a thing settled once and for all. In my own reading of the text, however, especially as this was modified by my study of Joyce's life and background, I felt that Stephen was presented in a manner that was far from being primarily ironic. At the time, I did not fully understand the way irony was coupled to New Critical values, which were then taken to be the only correct way of evaluating literature. Because irony was felt to ensure "aesthetic distance," it was essential to find it actively present in the greatest texts, since without it they would not be so great. For Joyce to be great, he had to be ironic—especially about a character based so elaborately on his own life. I, too, wanted him to be great—my idolatry is embarrassingly visible throughout the essay—but I kept finding evidence that Joyce was presenting Stephen in a manner that was not simply deflationary. Frye's notion of two character types, *eiron* and *alazon,* seemed to offer a way to challenge the dominant view of Stephen as the victim of his author's irony. This terminology is dated now, just as deconstructive terminology will seem dated in a few more years, but I still find the view of Stephen presented here (barring the idolatry of Joyce) to be a persuasive one—or, at any rate, a position that should be taken into account by readers of Joyce.

Critics of James Joyce's *A Portrait of the Artist as a Young Man* tend to divide themselves into two factions. One group insists that the novel is "romantic," the other that it is "ironic." Because of the peculiar biases of contemporary criticism these two words amount, respectively, to blame and praise. In this essay I do not take issue with those who hold that "romantic" equals "immature" and "thin" while "ironic" equals "mature" and "rich"—much as I might like to—but suggest that all those who insist that Joyce's *Portrait* be fixed in either of these two formulations are guilty of a kind of willful myopia.

A recent spokesman for the ironic view of *Portrait* has been William York Tindall. In *A Reader's Guide to James Joyce* he writes:

> A value of Joyce's method is that Stephen exposes himself while Joyce, at that little distance, exposes Stephen. The difference between their views of the same thing constitutes an irony so quiet that it escapes many readers, who, reducing two to one, take Stephen at his own estimate. To miss Joyce's estimate, however, is to miss half the meaning and all the fun. That Stephen, less admirable than he thinks, is not Joyce seems proved again by Joyce's irony. "I have been rather hard on that young man," Joyce told his friend Frank Budgen, emphasizing the last words of his title. (p. 64)

There are a number of things wrong with Mr. Tindall's observations here. First, Joyce was talking to Budgen not about *Portrait* but about *Ulysses.* Second, what Budgen actually records him as saying is, "I haven't let this young man off very lightly, have I? Many writers have written about themselves. I wonder if any one of them has been as candid as I have?" (*James Joyce and the Making of Ulysses,* Bloomington, Ind., 1960, p. 51). Far from emphasizing the separateness of himself and Stephen, Joyce emphasizes their identity. The passage which he and Budgen had been discussing is in itself instructive:

> You were going to do wonders, what? Missionary to Europe after fiery Columbanus. Fiacre and Scotus on their creepystools in heaven spilt from their pintpots loudlatinlaughing: Euge! Euge! Pretending to speak broken English as you dragged your valise, porter threepence,

> across the slimy pier at Newhaven. *Comment?* Rich booty you brought back; *Le Tutu,* five tattered numbers of *Pantalon Blanc et Culotte Rouge,* a blue French telegram, curiosity to show:–Mother dying come home father.[1]

At this point Joyce looked up and made his remark about not letting Stephen off lightly. It is essential for us to add one point to Joyce's observation–neither is Stephen letting himself off lightly. All these absurdities and many more are revealed to us not by a detached narrator but through Stephen's own interior monologue. He addresses himself in the second person as his own best critic, being better supplied with embarrassing details than any other critic can possibly be, and being terribly acute–"Kinch, the knifeblade." Though Joyce and Stephen are in many respects identical, Stephen himself is divided into two voices, one of them the accusing critic.

Illustrations of this from *Ulysses* could be multiplied endlessly, but they would not appease those critics who accuse Joyce of "romanticism" in *Portrait.* They would point out (as Denis Donoghue does in the *Sewanee Review,* 68, 2, p. 256) that *Ulysses* and *Portrait* are two different books. Mr. Donoghue, for example, grants *Ulysses* greatness but denies *Portrait* major stature because it is marred by lyricism, romanticism, and a "softness of focus" which is related to Joyce's refusal to "evoke as much judgment as apprehension." He concludes this part of his argument by stating that "drama or rhetoric should have warned Joyce that Stephen the aesthetic *alazon* needed nothing so urgently as a correspondingly deft *eiron;* lacking this, the book is blind in one eye" (p. 258). This statement takes us to the root of the problem of Stephen's character in *Portrait,* and we may well begin by considering Stephen Dedalus as *alazon.*[2]

The Greek word *alazon* means "imposter, someone who pretends or tries to be something more than he is. The most popular types of *alazon* are the *miles gloriosus* and the learned crank or obsessed philosopher" (Frye, p. 39). Clearly, Stephen Dedalus has some qualities of the learned crank or obsessed philosopher about him. He is a member of the tribe *alazon,* but he is not explained by a reference to the learned crank any more than Falstaff could be accounted for by a reference to the *miles gloriosus.* We see the connection, but we see a lot more also. In the case of Stephen Dedalus the concept of the *eiron* is as important as that of the *alazon.*

"The *eiron* is the man who deprecates himself, as opposed to the *alazon.* Such a man makes himself invulnerable, and, though Aristotle disapproves of him, there is no question that he is a predestined artist, just as the *alazon* is one of his predestined victims" (Frye, p. 40). Frye's statement is enormously suggestive when applied to Joyce's *Portrait.* Joyce, whose strategy is silence, exile, and cunning, is clearly the artist as *eiron.* His "victim," then, or subject is naturally the *alazon.* Thus we have Stephen Dedalus as *alazon.* But Stephen is an artist himself–and not just *an* artist but *the* artist–that is, both Joyce himself, the artist who made *Portrait,* and the artist in general, all artists. If Joyce's *Portrait* is to do justice to *the* artist, we must have Stephen himself as both *eiron* and *alazon.*

This double view of Stephen is exactly what we have seen operating in the passage from *Ulysses* quoted above. What must be determined now is whether the same view can be found in *Portrait.* I believe not only that it can be found there, but that by tracing Joyce's work through three successive drafts of the story we can observe him engaged in solving the problem of achieving it.

The first version of *Portrait* was a narrative essay of some two thousand words, written in January 1904 when Joyce was twenty-one years old, and called "A Portrait of the Artist" (published in the *Yale Review,* 49, 3, p. 360). On page 2 of the manuscript the narrator recounts an event in the life of the young artist:

> He ran through his measure like a spendthrift saint, astonishing many by ejaculatory fervours, offending many by airs of the cloister. One day in a wood near Malahide a labourer had marvelled to see a boy of fifteen praying in an ecstasy of Oriental posture. It was indeed a long time before this boy understood the nature of that most marketable goodness which makes it possible to give comfortable assent to propositions without ordering one's life in accordance with them. The digestive value of religion he never appreciated.

The Malahide incident here is presented in illustration of the boy's deep religious feeling. But this is clearly a case of Joyce's taking his *alazon* at his own face value. The absence of irony in the treatment almost requires the reader to become an *eiron* and puncture the smugness of the narrator-hero.

Joyce used the incident again in chapter 22 of *Stephen Hero* (New Directions, 1955, p. 156). In this version the incident is not narrated directly but comes to the mind of Stephen at an appropriate moment, as he compares his own past religious beliefs with those of a pious young lady:

> He thought of his own spendthrift religiousness and airs of the cloister, he remembered having astonished a labourer in a wood near Malahide by an ecstasy of oriental posture and no more than half-conscious under her charm he wondered whether the God of the Roman Catholics would put him into hell because he had failed to understand that most marketable goodness which makes it possible to give comfortable assent to propositions without in the least ordering one's life in accordance with them and had failed to appreciate the digestive value of the sacraments.

This chapter of *Stephen Hero* was written in April 1905, a little more than a year after the early "Portrait." In this treatment of the Malahide incident, Stephen accepts his own past behavior uncritically and Joyce accepts Stephen's. Again, the *alazon* is taken at his own evaluation. But by having Stephen recollect his past behavior Joyce had provided an appropriate situation for Stephen to contemplate and criticize himself. Nine years later when he came to rewrite this scene for the third time in his final version of *Portrait,* he was able to make significant use of this kind of opportunity for Stephen's self-criticism.

In the third version Stephen recalls the Malahide incident in a very different connection. He has been thinking about his friend Cranly's possible duplicity and his frequent outbursts of rudeness:

> Stephen had forgiven freely for he had often found this rudeness also in himself. And he remembered an evening when he had dismounted from a borrowed creaking bicycle to pray to God in a wood near Malahide. He had lifted up his arms and spoken in ecstacy to the sombre nave of the trees, knowing that he stood on holy ground and in a holy hour. And when two constabulary men had come into sight round a bend in the gloomy road he had broken off his prayer to whistle loudly an air from the last pantomine. (p. 273)

Here the incident is designed not to illustrate the youthful Stephen's true religiosity in contrast to the marketable goodness of others, but as an instance of rude behavior. Cranly's rudeness reminds him of his own. Thus, in retrospect, Stephen appears at greater disadvantage in this scene than in the earlier versions. But that he sees himself in this manner indicates a kind of understanding and self-criticism which he was not endowed with in the earlier drafts of this incident. He has become *eiron* as well as *alazon.*

Significantly, the passage introduces one of Stephen's most critical self-dissections. He misquotes Nashe, and in the midst of an effusive lyrical reflection is interrupted by a louse on his neck. In a display of the "learned crank" sort of knowledge he then remembers that Cornelius a Lapide had said that lice were not created by God with the other animals on the sixth day but were born of human sweat. In the next moment, just as he is torn with the self-pity occasioned by the disparity between his soaring mind and his "ill clad, ill fed, louse eaten" body, he realizes that he has quoted Nashe incorrectly after all and that his mind is not so superior to his body as he had assumed: "He had not even remembered rightly Nashe's line. All the images it had awakened were false. His mind bred vermin. His thoughts were lice born of the sweat of sloth" (p. 275). The *alazon* deplores the fact that a brilliant mind should be tied to a vermin-ridden body. The *eiron* observes that his mind is lousy too, and drives the analogy home with one of the very bits of crank-learning which the *alazon* has just displayed.

The protean rapidity with which Stephen modulates in this passage from the learned *alazon* to the caustic *eiron* is in part Stephen's defense and in part the measure of his genius. It is also the measure of Joyce's genius. In Stephen he presents a kind of Romeo and Mercutio in one character: the *eiron* and *alazon,* each with his shield before the breast of the other. The modifications in the title of Joyce's *Portrait* through its three drafts support the argument that he gained perspective on Stephen between the first and the last. Budgen reports that Joyce once told him that some readers forgot in reading the book the last four words of the title. In Joyce's own first version it apparently had not occurred to him to add those four words. That he did add them ten years later suggests that he became more aware of his hero's youthfulness. The critics who find *Portrait* highly ironic insist that these words—"as a young man"—are intended to alert us to the irony. This is probably true, but they also serve another function. They prepare us to expect and make allowances for a certain amount of callowness in the protagonist. The title, not so simple to interpret as the ironic critics believe, is ambivalent, supporting even as it discloses, just as Stephen's self-criticisms simultaneously expose and make amends for his failings. It can, in fact, be shown that though Joyce's awareness of Stephen's youthfulness increases through the three versions of the book, Stephen himself is much more mature in the last version. He gains maturity not only through his increased self-critical ability but through Joyce's endowing him with learning and judgment which he himself had not acquired at the same stage of development. Stephen, as we have him in the last version, is still a year younger than Joyce was when he wrote the first version of *Portrait,* but already Stephen seems too mature, his perspective on himself too developed, to produce such a rhapsodical bit of self-justification as Joyce did in his first self-portrait.

In *Ulysses,* Stephen is a year older than in *Portrait.* He has traveled: "Fabulous artificer, the hawklike man. You flew. Whereto? Newhaven-Dieppe, steerage passenger. Paris and back. Lapwing. Icarus. *Pater, ait.* Seabedabbled, fallen, weltering. Lapwing you are. Lapwing he" (p. 208). He has flown; now he is grounded; his perspective on himself is necessarily sharper than a year earlier. Also Joyce's technique has developed to facilitate the ironic self-scrutiny of Stephen. In *Portrait* the dialogue between *eiron* and *alazon* inspired by the quotation from Nashe had to be managed entirely in the third person, as Joyce narrated Stephen's thoughts in a fairly conventional manner. But in *Ulysses* the interior monologue provides a much more flexible medium for the narration of such an internal conflict. The two voices are heard distinctly, the monologue actually becoming an interior dialogue, as the *eiron* accuses the hapless *alazon:* "You were awfully holy, weren't you? You prayed to the Blessed Virgin that you might not have a red nose. You prayed to the devil in Serpentine avenue that the fubsy widow in front might lift her clothes still more from the wet street. *Osi, certo!* Sell your soul for that, do, dyed rags pinned round a squaw." The *alazon* replies in a kind of masochistic repentance and horrified fascination, "More tell me, more still!" And the *eiron* continues:

> On the top of the Howth tram alone crying to the rain: *naked women!* What about that, eh?
> [*Alazon:*] What about what? what else were they invented for?
> [*Eiron:*] Reading two pages apiece of seven books every night, eh?

To the last charge the *alazon* can reply only, "I was young" (p. 41).

This, of course, is the point. The reply is lame, but it is important. As Stephen grows he becomes more responsible for his actions and more open to criticism. He also becomes a better critic of himself. Thus Joyce has not "reassessed" Stephen in *Ulysses.* The self-criticism which is noticeable in the last section of *Portrait* (as in the Malahide and Nashe passages quoted above) is simply extended into the later book, facilitated by the interior dialogue technique, and made more incisive by Stephen's new, "grounded" perspective. The sharper note, appropriate to Stephen's fallen status and increased maturity, would have been inappropriate in *Portrait.* But the presentation of Stephen as both *alazon* and *eiron* is not new; rather it is an extension and development of Joyce's technique in the later sections of *Portrait.*

In the earlier parts of *Portrait* Stephen is less exposed to irony than in the later ones. The reason for this should be obvious. The younger the artist is, the less open he is to the charge of immaturity. His age is its own defense. This suggests another reason why Joyce added the last four words to the title of his final version of *Portrait.* In the first version the artist enters college in the second paragraph, and most of the narrative is devoted to this stage of his life. In *Stephen Hero* the University College chapters made up about half of the original novel and almost all of the text we now have. In the final version, four of the five chapters are devoted to Stephen's precollege life. In each version the portion allotted to Stephen's early years is significantly expanded. Stephen's youth forces the portrait of him to be "romantic"—up to a point. When he is mature enough to excite criticism he receives it—from himself. And, though his self-criticism in *Ulysses* is more severe than in *Portrait,* it still has the same effect of short-circuiting external criticism, maintaining Stephen in a fairly sympathetic light, though the light increases in intensity in proportion to Stephen's growing maturity.

When Stephen leaves Dublin at the end of *Portrait,* he is, in a sense, being exiled from a city which has rejected him, which has no place for him in civil, clerical, or even domestic life. In this sense Stephen has affinities with the traditional figure of the *pharmakos,* or scapegoat. Northrop Frye has observed that we meet *pharmakos* figures, among other places, "in stories of artists whose genius makes them Ishmaels of a bourgeois society" (*Anatomy,* p. 41).

It is Stephen's "genius" that makes him an Ishmael, and this genius is precisely what is demonstrated by his ability to play *eiron* to his own *alazon,* to see his own failings and attack them more successfully than Cranly or Lynch or any other character is able to. But Stephen is not a pure *pharmakos.* His exile is in part that paradoxical thing, a voluntary exile, and his departure is partly a triumphal escape, so that he exhibits many of the qualities of what Mr. Frye calls the "*pharmakos* in reverse"—the character who, "with the sympathy of the author or audience, repudiates... a society to the point of deliberately walking out of it" (*Anatomy,* p. 48). By insisting that his exile is voluntary, Stephen forces our acceptance of it as mainly a triumph rather than a catastrophe. His concluding statement is not the traditional "farewell my homeland" of the departing exile, but a welcome to life. He is not leaving a world but entering one.

In terms of Joyce's intention to create a portrait of the artist as a *young* man, this is a perfectly sound note on which to end. To wish, as Mr. Donoghue seems to, that someone was around to deflate Stephen in the midst of his "Welcome, O life" declaration is a somewhat perverse devotion to irony for its own sake. It amounts to insisting that Mercutio return to the stage and indulge in some bawdy remarks during the balcony scene. Yet, to maintain, as one "ironic" reader of the novel does, that Joyce in this passage is exposing the implausibility of Stephen's ambitions and the poverty of his alienation from life seems just as perverse as to insist that Stephen has been allowed to rant without sufficient critical scrutiny. Actually, Stephen's self-critical perspective is not lost even in this most "romantic" moment. In these last lines the *eiron* is not missing but for the moment is reconciled to and blended with the *alazon.* Stephen has just written down in his diary his mother's criticism of him: "She prays now, she says, that I may learn in my own life and away from home and friends what the heart is and what it feels." Far from rejecting this view, he endorses it and adopts it as his own: "Amen. So be it. Welcome, O life!" In reading these words one should remember what Joyce has so carefully documented: that far from being an *alazon,* blind in one eye, Stephen sees as the artist must, with two eyes, as *eiron* and *alazon,* a single vision. And for this vision he pays the price of exile and obtains the reward of escape, out of life and into life, simultaneously.

Notes

1. Budgen, p. 51, and *Ulysses* (Modern Library, 1934), p. 43 (all references to *Ulysses* in this essay are to this edition).

2. For various definitions of critical terms, I rely heavily on Northrop Frye's *The Anatomy of Criticism* (Princeton, N.J., 1957).

[2]

Textual Matters

[1962, 1964, and 1965]

Three separate items follow which deal with textual and editorial matters. I hesitated over including them in this book, since they mainly address a situation that has been changed by my own edition of *Dubliners,* hyperbolically called "definitive" by the publishers, which is still in print. But I finally decided to include them because the debate over Joycean texts seems very much alive at the present time, due to the work of John Kidd in his remorseless critique of the 1986 edition of *Ulysses* edited by Hans Gabler and others. During the recent debates I was asked how I had decided what format to follow for the use of dashes to introduce direct discourse in *Dubliners.* Somewhat to the dismay of purer theoretical bibliographers, I replied that I simply took the format finally accepted by Joyce in the published *Ulysses* and followed it for *Dubliners* because I could find no clear justification for any other format and saw no need to multiply variations in the published texts. As the following essays make clear, Joyce wanted some alternative to quotation marks but had not really worked out exactly what he wanted when *Dubliners* was published by Grant Richards–who, in any case, did not let Joyce have his way in the matter.

As I believe will be apparent in these essays, I have put some real work into textual and bibliographical studies–enough to entitle me to an opinion about current debates over Joyce's texts and other bibliographical matters. My view, which emerges most clearly in my brief review of the Viking edition of *Portrait,* is that textual critics tend to overemphasize the positivistic dimension of their craft, seeking certainties where they are not to be found. The "final intention of the author" is often a fiction for textual editors as well as for literary interpreters; and last thoughts may be final simply because the author was not given time for others, not because they are best. When an author's reputation has actually been made in texts held to be "imperfect," bibliographers should at least acknowledge that textual perfection may be less important than they would like it to be. In preparing editions we need to follow the author's wishes, so far as they can be determined; but they can never be determined so fully as to obviate the need for literary judgment on the part of editors. These essays are reprinted here partly as a contribution to current debates but also because my discussions of Joyce's revisions reveal important things about his intentions and his craftsmanship, things I learned only by performing the harmless drudgery required of the textual scholar.

Some Observations on the Text of *Dubliners:* "The Dead"

Complaints about the texts of standard editions of James Joyce's works are fairly common, but they are usually directed at *Ulysses* and *Finnegans Wake* rather than at Joyce's earlier works. Yet the standard American editions of *Dubliners,* from the first edition of B. W. Huebsch to the Modern Library, and the standard English editions, from the first edition of Grant Richards to Jonathan Cape, are among the most un-Joycean texts of all Joyce's printed works—for reasons which become apparent when the prepublication printing history of the book is considered.

The present study is based primarily on a detailed examination of the manuscript and printing history of "The Dead." This story has been selected because of its length and importance in *Dubliners* and because the manuscript and printed versions available for its textual study are more complete than those available for the consideration of the other stories in *Dubliners.* Examinations of the textual histories of other stories in the collection indicate, however, that what is true of "The Dead" is also true of them, and that generalizations made on the basis of a study of "The Dead" will be valid for *Dubliners* as a whole.

The main outlines of the printing history of *Dubliners* have been recounted by Gorman and Ellmann in their biographies of Joyce and in the bibliography of Slocum and Cahoon.[1] In 1905 Joyce offered a manuscript of twelve stories to Grant Richards. In February 1906 Richards accepted the book for publication, and Joyce sent him a thirteenth story, "Two Gallants." In April the book went to the printer. When the printer objected to certain words and passages in the stories as indecent, a long controversy ensued between Richards and Joyce, with the result that Richards declined to publish the book and returned Joyce's manuscript. Probably the whole book was never set up in type for this impression. Two printed pages of proof survive, in the Houghton Library at Harvard, and they exhibit some peculiarities which make one suspect that no honest attempt to set up the whole edition was ever made. The two pages are from the beginning of "Two Gallants," the story which Joyce added to the collection after the manuscript was in Richards's hands. Joyce's instructions were that this story should be inserted between "After the Race" and "The Boarding House," where it now stands as the sixth story in all modern editions (letter: Joyce to Richards, 22 Feb. 1906, at Harvard). But the surviving proofs of the story are numbered 12 and 13, indicating that it was certainly not the sixth story printed, and they do not follow consecutively—there is a gap of approximately one page in the text between the first page (numbered 12) and the second (numbered 13).[2] In the margin of page 13 is the notation "we cannot print this," the printer's initials, and the date—17 April 1906. Joyce himself commented on the peculiarity of beginning the process of printing his book with the sixth story (letter: Joyce to Richards, 16 June 1906, at Harvard).

Whatever mysterious machinations went on, it is most unlikely that any more than a few pages of proof were ever typeset in this first attempt at *Dubliners*. By the time Joyce's negotiations with Richards had reached a dead end in October 1906, the manuscript had been expanded to fourteen stories by the inclusion of "A Little Cloud" (letter: Joyce to Richards, 9 July 1906, at Harvard). In the next year Joyce wrote the final story, "The Dead,"[3] but it was not until April 1909 that he succeeded in interesting another publisher in *Dubliners*. Joseph Hone of Maunsel and Co., Dublin, agreed to look at the manuscript (letter: Hone to Joyce, 18 Apr. 1909, at Cornell) and in

September 1909 Joyce was writing to Richards that Messrs. Maunsel hoped to bring out his book early in the coming spring (letter: Joyce to Richards, 4 Sept. 1909, at Cornell).

The book was announced by Maunsel for the spring of 1910 and Joyce received and corrected proofs in June of that year.[4] But even as the proofs were being corrected the now-familiar pattern of attempted censorship began again. Messrs. Maunsel objected to passages in "Ivy Day in the Committee Room"; Joyce did not make the requested changes in proof; and publication of the stories was delayed (letters: Roberts to Joyce, 7 June 1910 and 9 Feb. 1911, at Cornell). Sometime before the final collapse of negotiations on Joyce's visit to Dublin in September 1912, an edition of 1,000 copies is believed to have been run off—probably in July 1912.[5] But when Maunsel finally refused to publish the book and Joyce tried to purchase the sheets from John Falconer, the printer (so that he could publish them himself under the imprint of the Liffey Press), the sheets were reported destroyed by the printer.[6] Joyce always said that his book was "burned" (See *Gas from a Burner,* for example), but if 1,000 copies of the sheets of *Dubliners* were actually destroyed, the deed was undoubtedly accomplished by the easier and less wasteful process of guillotining.

Despite the destruction of the edition, this Dublin setting of *Dubliners* is of considerable importance to those interested in Joyce's text, for Joyce obtained—"by a ruse," he said[7]—a set of proofs from this edition, which subsequently became the printer's copy for the first published edition of his book (see Slocum and Cahoon, A8 and Joyce's letters to Richards of 24 Jan. and 4 Mar. 1914, at Harvard).

Joyce's difficulties in finding a publisher continued until November 1913, when he again approached Grant Richards. Richards accepted the book for the second time late in January 1914 (letter: Joyce to Richards 27 Feb. 1914, at Cornell; the contract is at Yale) offering Joyce the same royalty agreement as in 1906; and Joyce accepted the contract (later referred to by J. B. Pinker as a "terrible document"; see letter: Pinker to Joyce, 7 May 1915, at Cornell). In April 1914 Joyce read proof on the Richards edition (letter: Joyce to Richards, 8 May 1914, at Harvard) expecting to have a chance to read revised copy before publication. In May he learned that he was not going to have a second chance at the proofs, and he sent Richards a list of corrections to be forwarded to the printer (letter: Joyce to Richards, 14 May

1914, at Harvard). Most of these corrections have never been made to this date in any edition. (Joyce's list is printed as an appendix to this study.) In June 1914 Dubliners was finally published.

A detailed study of the textual history of "The Dead" must rest on six documents:

A. fragments of a holograph manuscript with printer's notations, in the Slocum Collection at Yale;
B. a complete manuscript–partly typed but completed in the hand of an amanuensis–in the Cornell collection;
C. an almost complete set of galley sheets from the Dublin printing, in the Slocum Collection;
D. an almost complete copy of a late stage of the destroyed Dublin edition–sewn but not bound–in the Slocum Collection;
E. a complete set of page proofs of the Grant Richards edition, 1914, in the Slocum Collection;
F. the first edition itself (copy used for this study is in the Slocum Collection).

The interrelationships of these six documents are fairly complex but they can be traced with considerable certainty. Document A bears the notations of the Irish printer and was the copy text for the Maunsel (Dublin) printing.[8] If it were complete there would be no need to consult document B at all. But since A is fragmentary its relationship to B must be established in the hope that B can tell us something reliable about the missing parts of A. Fortunately the relationship is not difficult to work out. B is undoubtedly a faithful (though inexact in a few instances) copy of A. The occasional misreadings of the typist, like "Malius" for "Malins" and "wooed" for "waved" can be directly related to misleading handwriting in the holograph manuscript. Some of the typist's and amanuensis's mistakes, such as "parent" for "gaunt" and various omissions of letters and words, have been corrected in Joyce's hand to conform (in places where this is verifiable) to the holograph manuscript.[9] But apparently changes were made in the holograph manuscript after copy B was taken from it, since various alterations, written in red ink on the holograph, are not reflected in the copy. For example, Joyce changed the name of Gretta Conroy's first love from "Fury" to "Furey" in the extant pages of the holograph but allowed "Fury" to stand throughout B. We must infer that the red-ink changes postdate the copy and that some of the other changes which were apparently made before the Dublin galleys were printed would probably show up as red-ink changes if the missing pages of the holograph could be located. Thus Joyce undoubtedly corrected the words of the song "The Lass of Aughrim" in this manner, after learning the true version from Nora Barnacle's mother, who sang it to him on his trip to Galway in August 1909 (letters: James to Nora Joyce, 26 and 31 Aug. 1909, at Cornell).

The corrected holograph manuscript, document A, became the printer's text for the Dublin (Maunsel) edition (see note 8). The relationships among the various texts can be illustrated most clearly by tracing one passage through all its stages. This passage (pp. 255, 256 of the Modern Library edition [hereafter ML]; p. 227 of Jonathan Cape, 1954 [hereafter JC]) is unfortunately among the missing parts of document A, but it was corrected by Joyce in document B,[10] and apparently no red-ink changes were made in A after B was copied. The passages are designated here by lowercase letters corresponding to the uppercase designations (above) of the documents from which they are taken. The variants among these will be discussed later.

b-1 (manuscript in the hand of the amanuensis, corrected by Joyce, pp. 20–21)

> Nobody answered this question and Mary Jane led the table back to the legitimate opera. One of her pupils had given her a pass for *Mignon.* Of course, it was very fine, she said, but it made her think of poor Georgina Burns. Mr Browne could go back farther still to the old Italian companies that used to come to Dublin, Tietjens, Trebelli Ilma de Murzka, Campanini, the great Giuglini, Revelli, Aramburo. Those were the days, he said, when there was something like singing to be heard in Dublin. He told too of how the top gallery of the Old Royal used to be packed night after night, of how one night an Italian tenor had sung five encores to *Let me like a soldier fall,* introducing a high C every time, and of how the gallery boys would sometimes in their enthusiasm unyoke the horses from the carriage of some great *prima donna* and pull her themselves through the streets to the hotel. Why did they never play the grand old operas now, he asked, *Norma, Lucrezia Borgia?* Because they could not get the voices to sing them: that was why.

—O, well, said Mr Bartell D'Arcy, I presume there are as good singers to day as there were then—
—Where are they? asked Mr Browne defiantly—
—In London, Paris, Berlin, said Mr Bartell D'Arcy warmly.
I suppose Caruso, for example, is quite as good, if not better than any of the men you have mentioned.—

c-1 (from galley 8 of the Maunsel printing, 1910)

Nobody answered this question, and Mary Jane led the table back to the legitimate opera. One of her pupils had given her a pass for *Mignon.* Of course, it was very fine, she said, but it made her think of poor Georgina Burns. Mr. Browne could go back farther still to the old Italian companies that used to come to Dublin—Tietjeus, Trebell's, Ilma de Murzka, Campanini, the great Gingliui, Revelli, Aramburo. Those were the days, he said, when there was something like singing to be heard in Dublin. He told too of how the top gallery of the Old Royal used to be packed night after night, of how one night an Italian tenor had sung five encores to *Let me like a soldier fall,* introducing a high C everytime, and of how the gallery boys would sometimes in their enthusiasm unyoke the horses from the carriage of some great *prima donna* and pull her themselves through the streets to her hotel. Why did they never play the grand old operas now, he asked—*Norma, Lucrezia Borgia?* Because they could not get the voices to sing them: that was why.

—O, well,—said Mr. Bartell D'Arcy,—I presume there are as good singers to-day as there were then.—

—Where are they?—asked Mr. Browne, defiantly.

—In London, Paris, Berlin,—said Mr. Bartell D'Arcy, warmly. I suppose Caruso, for example, is quite as good, if not better than any of the men you have mentioned.—

d-1 (from page proofs of the Maunsel printing, 1910, pp. 260–61)

Nobody answered this question and Mary Jane led the table back to the legitimate opera. One of her pupils had given her a pass for *Mignon.* Of course, it was very fine, she said, but it made her think of poor Georgina Burns. Mr Browne could go back farther still to the old Italian companies that used to come to Dublin—Tietjens, Trebelli, Ilma de Murzka, Campanini, the great Giuglini, Revelli, Aramburo. Those were the days, he said, when there was something like singing to be heard in Dublin. He told too of how the top gallery of the old

Royal used to be packed night after night, of how one night an Italian tenor had sung five encores to *Let me Like a Soldier Fall,* introducing a high C every time, and of how the gallery boys would sometimes in their enthusiasm unyoke the horses from the carriage of some great *prima donna* and pull her themselves through the streets to her hotel. Why did they never play the grand old operas now, he asked—*Norma, Lucrezia Borgia?* Because they could not get the voices to sing them: that was why.

—O, well,—said Mr Bartell D'Arcy,—I presume there are as good singers today as there were then.—

—Where are they?—asked Mr Browne defiantly.

—In London, Paris, Vienna,—said Mr Bartell D'Arcy warmly.—I suppose Caruso, for example, is quite as good, if not better than any of the men you have mentioned.—

e-1 (page proofs from the Richards first edition, 1914, pp. 246–47)

Nobody answered this question, and Mary Jane led the table back to the legitimate opera. One of her pupils had given her a pass for *Mignon.* Of course, it was very fine, she said, but it made her think of poor Georgina Burns. Mr Browne could go back farther still, to the old Italian companies that used to come to Dublin—Teitjeus, Trebell's, Ilma de Murzka, Campanini, the great Gingliui, Revelli, Aramburo. Those were the days, he said, when there was something like singing to be heard in Dublin. He told too of how the top gallery of the old Royal used to be packed night after night, of how one night an Italian tenor had sung five encores to *Let me like a Soldier fall,* introducing a high C every time, and of how the gallery boys would sometimes in their enthusiasm unyoke the horses from the carriage of some great *prima donna* and pull her themselves through the streets to her hotel. Why did they never play the grand old operas now, he asked, '*Norma, Lucrezia Borgia?* Because they could not get the voices to sing them: that was why.'

'O, well,' said Mr Bartell D'Arcy, 'I presume there are as good singers to-day as there were then.'

'Where are they?' asked Mr Browne defiantly.

'In London, Paris, Berlin,' said Mr Bartell D'Arcy warmly. 'I suppose Caruso, for example, is quite as good, if not better than any of the men you have mentioned.'

f-1 (from the Richards first edition, 1914, pp. 246–47)

Nobody answered this question and Mary Jane led the table back to the legitimate opera. One of her pupils had given her a pass for *Mignon.* Of course it was very fine, she said, but it made her think of poor Georgina Burns. Mr Browne could go back farther still, to the old Italian companies that used to come to Dublin– Tietjens, Ilma de Murzka, Campanini, the great Trebelli Giuglini, Ravelli, Aramburo. Those were the days, he said, when there was something like singing to be heard in Dublin. He told too of how the top gallery of the old Royal used to be packed night after night, of how one night an Italian tenor had sung five encores to *Let me like a Soldier fall,* introducing a high C every time, and of how the gallery boys would sometimes in their enthusiasm unyoke the horses from the carriage of some great *prima donna* and pull her themselves through the streets to her hotel. Why did they never play the grand old operas now, he asked, '*Dinorah, Lucrezia Borgia?* Because they could not get the voices to sing them: that was why.'

'O, well,' said Mr Bartell D'Arcy, 'I presume there are as good singers to-day as there were then.'

'Where are they?' asked Mr Browne defiantly.

'In London, Paris, Milan,' said Mr Bartell D'Arcy warmly. 'I suppose Caruso, for example, is quite as good, if not better than any of the men you have mentioned.'

Some of the differences between b-1 and c-1 are of indeterminable significance. The change from "the hotel" to "her hotel," for example, may be due to a mistake made in the preparation of B, a red-ink change in A, or a compositor's change in the preparation of C. But other differences allow us to make inferences with almost absolute certainty. The various changes in the spelling of proper names are undoubtedly due to the compositor's inability to read Joyce's holograph accurately in those instances where he could not guess at the correct spelling on the basis of his own knowledge. We have seen how the typist of document B had trouble with the proper name "Malins," reading a *u* for the *n.* The compositor of C had the same trouble here (and also earlier when he misread the Irish phrase *"Beannacht libh"* as *"Beaunacht libh"*–as it appears in galley 7). In this case he has read "Tietjeus" for "Tietjens," "Trebell's" for "Trebelli," and "Gingliui" for "Giuglini." Passage d-1 from the final Maunsel printing includes the correction of all these misspellings and some other changes of the sort which would have been made only by Joyce. "Berlin" in b and c (and presumably in the missing part of a) becomes "Vienna" in d, and "Old

Royal" becomes "old Royal." Texts C and D are impressed from the same setting of type,[11] though C is in the form of unpaged slip galleys and D is in the form of numbered pages, apparently in the last stage of preparation before sewing and binding.[12] We cannot now tell how many states of this impression existed between the galleys and the final printing, but numerous corrections were made and incorporated into state D. In "The Dead" alone 300 commas were removed between C and D; over 30 hyphens were removed, the hyphenated constructions being modified to either one or two words; and a substantial number of textual changes were made. (The most important of these will be considered below.)

When the Dublin impression of *Dubliners* was destroyed by Maunsel's printer, Joyce, as we know, obtained a set of proofs which became the copy-text for Grant Richards's printer. The normal assumption would be that Joyce would take the last and most correct text, in this case text D. But this was not a normal situation. The text he was able to get, he got "by a ruse"; and it was certainly not text D. A glance at passages c-1, d-1, and e-1 will show that e contains the same absurd misspellings which we found in c, and that the third on the list of operatic cities is once again Berlin. This can mean only that the printer's copy for E must have been much closer to C than to D.

There are several reasons why we must be satisfied with saying that the printer's text in this case is *close* to C rather than simply inferring that C *was* the copy-text. Joyce and Richards in their correspondence unmistakably refer to pages rather than galley sheets;[13] and a few parts of E seem closer to D than to C (as when Mr. Browne's skin, "dark yellow" in galley 3 of C, becomes "swarthy" on p. 268 of D and remains so on p. 225 of E). In these cases we cannot be sure whether the corrections to C have been incorporated in some other set of page proofs—a hypothetical, partially corrected C1—or whether Joyce has introduced corrections by hand in a set essentially the same as C but in pages rather than galleys. We can note, however, that wherever substantive changes occur between C and E, they are marked by a culling out of commas in the surrounding passages; and wherever D indicates that corrections should have been made in C which were not, in fact, made before E was printed, the surrounding area remains heavily punctuated in E (as in C), and the commas are finally culled out in the first edition itself, state F.

The whole problem of punctuation in the text of *Dubliners* is an important and interesting one. This problem can be divided into two main aspects—the punctuation of direct discourse and the use of the comma. Joyce was habitually a light punctuator. The textual history of *Dubliners* indicates that he was twice forced to go through his text, once in the Irish printing and again in the English, removing what he considered an excess of editorial or compositorial punctuation, culling out more than 300 commas from "The Dead" between C and D, and over 225 between E and F, after having eliminated more than 50 between C and E. He preferred not to use a comma before the conjunctions *and, but,* and *for.* This practice has occasionally resulted in confusion. Compare, for example, the following sentences from the six texts:

a-2 (p. 18) "Probably in the school they had gone to as girls that kind of work had been taught for one year his mother had worked for him as a birthday present a waistcoat. . . . "

b-2 (p. 10) same as a-2

c-2 (galley 4) "Probably in the school they had gone to as girls that kind of work had been taught for one year; his mother had worked for him as a birthday present a waistcoat. . . . "

d-2 (p. 273) same as a-2 and b-2

e-2 (p. 230) same as c-2

f-2 (p. 230) "Probably in the school they had gone to as girls that kind of work had been taught for one year. His mother had worked for him as a birthday present a waistcoat. . . . "

Here, Joyce in his manuscript avoided using the standard comma before the phrase "for one year," which would have made it clear that "for" in that case was a conjunction and not a preposition. An officious compositor in setting text C changed Joyce's sentence, wrongly breaking it after "for one year" instead of before it. Joyce corrected this change so that D reads as A and B do in this passage, but E naturally follows C. Finally the reading was emended even further in the wrong direction in F (by a compositor or editor) and so it stands in our modern editions (ML 238; JC 212). This is one of the corrections Joyce sent Richards in lieu of a second proofreading, apparently having missed it—as he missed many others in his haste—on the first reading (see Appendix).

Joyce's views on the subject of the punctuation of direct discourse were even less orthodox than his views on the comma. He strongly objected to the use of the inverted comma or quotation marks, and expressed these views to Grant Richards in February 1906 and again in March 1914. As Joyce's views on the subject are very strong, and since the published volume of his letters prints this passage in a somewhat garbled form, the passage is reprinted here in the notes.[14] In the Irish printing of *Dubliners* Joyce nearly succeeded in having his usage in the matter of quotations followed accurately. Passage b-1 above illustrates Joyce's habitual method of punctuating quotations in the *Dubliners* manuscripts. A dash introduces every paragraph which is either in part or wholly direct discourse, and another dash concludes each such paragraph. (In his later works he dropped the concluding dash.) But c-1 (above) shows that the Irish compositors did not follow Joyce entirely. They used the dash as if it were a quotation mark, trying to surround every directly quoted speech with dashes which exclude the narrator's statements: "–O, well,–said Mr. Bartell D'Arcy,–I presume . . . ," etc. This peculiar blend of Joycean and normal usage is not a strictly Irish development. One finds, for example, both techniques combined rather confusingly in the fifth chapter of the Modern Library edition of *A Portrait of the Artist as a Young Man.* At any rate, the heavy use of dashes in C remains unchanged in the final Irish text D. Either Joyce was satisfied or the compositor stood firm.

Grant Richards, however, insisted on normal English usage; thus in text E the dashes are replaced by inverted commas. We can even note in e-1 (above) how, at the end of the long first paragraph, the English compositor clumsily converted indirect into direct discourse through mistaking the dash used as colon in c-1 for a dash introducing a quotation. This stands as direct discourse in the modern English text (JC) even though the use of the conditional past tense is clearly an indirect mode of rendering what would be present tense in direct discourse; but the modern American text (ML) even more confusingly closes with quotation marks which have no mate opening the quotation anywhere in the paragraph. The main point of all this interest in the method of presenting direct discourse is that no edition of *Dubliners* has ever been printed which follows the usage desired by Joyce, though he was able to enforce his views on these matters in the books which followed *Dubliners.*

Passage f-1 (above) indicates the way in which Joyce corrected text E and also it reveals that his correction was not perfect. He rearranged the operatic passage and corrected the spelling; Berlin he again replaced, this time by Milan instead of Vienna as in d-1; and for *Norma* he substituted the more recondite *Dinorah;* but he missed the erratic capitalization of *"Let me like a Soldier fall"* and the introduction of the awkward direct discourse at the end of the first paragraph. That he did not pick up all the mistakes is not surprising. He had promised Grant Richards to return corrected proof two days after receipt (Joyce was still in Trieste at the time), and he expected to have a chance to correct revised copy (letters: Joyce to Richards, 8 and 14 May 1914, at Harvard). Also, by this time he had corrected *Dubliners* countless times and the human law of diminishing returns had undoubtedly begun to affect him. The more one reads over the same work, the less one sees of what is actually on the page. And, finally, he must have been mainly preoccupied with his new work, *A Portrait of the Artist as a Young Man,* which he was engaged in completing for the *Egoist,* the London periodical which had started publishing the novel in February 1914 (see Ellmann, p. 364). All these factors combined readily account for the lack of thoroughness of Joyce's corrections of text E for the Grant Richards first edition of *Dubliners* in 1914.

Now we may turn to ten of the improvements which Joyce had made in the Irish text of "The Dead" between C and D which he never reintroduced in the English edition, and which consequently have been omitted in all modern printings of the book. These improvements were made only in proof; and, therefore, when Joyce was unable to obtain a late state of the Irish printing he had no record of these changes. In all cases cited below, text F substantially follows C and E, the modifications made in D having been lost when C1 became the printer's text for E.

Change 1

Text F. 'Well, I'm ashamed of you,' said Miss Ivors frankly. 'To say you'd write for a paper like that . . . '

Text D. "paper" changed to "rag" (cf. ML 240; JC 214)

Change 2

Text F. 'The fact is,' said Gabriel, 'I have just arranged to go–'

Text D. "just" changed to "already" (ML 242; JC 215)

Note that changes 1 and 2 serve to make Miss Ivors a bit more outspoken in her attack and to make Gabriel's refusal of her request that he join in a trip to the west of Ireland seem a bit less impromptu.

Change 3

Text F. '. . . What row had you with Molly Ivors?'
'No row. Why? Did she say so?'
'Something like that. . . . '
'There was no row,' said Gabriel moodily. . . .

Text D. "row" changed to "words" in all instances and "was" changed to "were" (ML 245; JC 217–18)

Change 4

Text F. Her son-in-law was a splendid fisher. One day he caught a beautiful big fish and the man in the hotel cooked it for their dinner.

Text D. Her son-in-law was a splendid fisher. One day he caught a fish, a beautiful big big fish: and the man in the hotel boiled it for their dinner. (ML 245; JC 218)

In change 4 Mrs. Malin's personality is rendered more vividly; the mode of preparation of the fish made more specific.

Change 5

Text F. 'And do you mean to say,' asked Mr Browne incredulously, 'that a chap can go down there and put up there as if it were a hotel and live on the fat of the land and then come away without paying anything?'

Text D. —And do you mean to say,—asked Mr Browne incredulously,—that a fellow can go down there and put up there as if it were a hotel and then come away without paying a farthing?—(ML 258; JC 229)

In change 5, text D, "anything" becomes "farthing." But note that "chap" in text F is not a relapse after a change to "fellow" in D, but a new change introduced between E and F, probably for the same reason that "farthing" was introduced between C and D—to make Browne's speech more concrete and Browne, therefore, more vivid.

Change 6

Text F. The table burst into applause and laughter at this allusion.
Text D. "allusion" changed to "sally" (ML 262; JC 233)

Change 7

Text F. 'Someone is fooling at the piano, anyhow,' said Gabriel.
Text D. "fooling" changed to "strumming" (ML 266; JC 236)

Both 6 and 7 seem to be attempts to find words more in keeping with the mood or tone of the passages they are in.

Change 8

Text F. 'Yes, sir,' said the cabman.
'Make like a bird for Trinity College.'
'Right, sir,' said the cabman.
Text D. In the cabman's second speech "said" is changed to "cried." (ML 269; JC 239)

Another change in the interest of vividness, "cried" expresses the cabman's relief at finally getting a direction he understands.

Change 9

Text F. A ghastly light from the streetlamp lay in a long shaft from one window to the door.
Text D. "ghastly" changed to "ghostly" (ML 278; JC 247)

This is a most important correction. Text B reads "ghostly," C "ghastly," probably due to a misreading of A by the compositor of C. Joyce made the correction in D but did not pick it up again in his proofreading of E. The slightly eerie connotations of "ghostly" with its suggestion of Ibsen's play *Ghosts* (a spiritual ancestor of Joyce's story) are much more appropriate for this scene than the more horrible connotations of "ghastly."

Change 10

Text F. '. . . He gave me back that sovereign I lent him and I didn't expect it really. It's a pity he wouldn't keep away from that Browne because he's not a bad fellow really.'
Text D. the second "really" changed to "at heart" (ML 279; JC 248)

These ten changes represent only the obvious substantive changes made in the text of "The Dead" by Joyce and subsequently lost. Texts D and F also vary through compositorial errors introduced in E which passed unnoticed into F and thence into modern texts. The simply ungrammatical "The peals of laughter which followed Gabriel's imitation of the incident *was* interrupted . . . " (ML 268; JC 238, my italics) is just an error—B, C, and D all reading "were." And there are other similar problems. A study I have now in progress of the other stories in *Dubliners* indicates that many other substantive changes have been lost from the text. But a textual study of "The Dead" alone is enough to establish the fact that we are reading one of our most precise and careful writers in editions which can be greatly improved, which can be made both more correct and more Joycean.

Appendix

When Joyce learned that he was not going to have a second opportunity to read proof on the first edition of *Dubliners,* he prepared the following list of corrections and sent them to Grant Richards for action. Unfortunately, the corrections were not made. Some of the more obvious errors in punctuation and grammar have been detected and eliminated in later editions, but over twenty of these corrections have never been made in a printed text of *Dubliners.* In addition to matters of correctness, matters of tone and pace are attended to in this list. The most important correction noted here is undoubtedly that for page 265, which transfers back to Gretta Conroy a speech mistakenly given to her husband by the compositor of the Grant Richards edition. This list of unmade corrections plus the as yet untotaled number of lost improvements (such as those for "The Dead" discussed above) should certainly be taken into account when a new edition of *Dubliners* is prepared.

The list which follows is exactly as Joyce made it, with page and line references to the first edition. Page and line references to current American and English editions have been added in parentheses after Joyce's corrections, ML referring to Modern Library, JC to Jonathan Cape, 1954. Whenever the correction has been made in the modern editions, this fact is noted in parentheses.

DUBLINERS
Misprints

page	11:	line	26:	for	imbecile!'	read	imbecile! (corrected–ML9:29/JC 9:16)
"	34:	"	8:	"	gauntlet	"	gantlet (ML 34:9/JC 30:2)
"	56:	"	6:	"	form's	"	form' (ML 59:17/JC 50:20)
"	65:	"	30:	"	umbrella	"	sunshade (ML 66:15/JC 59:11)
"	68	"	27:	"	grocer's hot	"	hot grocer's (ML 69:15/JC 61:30)
"	86:	"	5:	"	roystered	"	roistered (ML 87:8/JC 77:29)
"	88:	"	28:	"	notice	"	notices (ML 90:4/JC 80:16)
"	89:	"	11:	"	doorways	"	doorway (ML 90:20/JC 80:28)
"	95:	"	11:	"	hand,	"	hand (ML 96:31/JC 86:14)
"	104:	"	8:	"	*Blast* (italics)	"	Blast (plain) (ML 106:8/JC 95:8)
"	105:	"	1:	"	hairless	"	hairless that (ML 106:27/JC 2195:23)
"	111:	"	26:	"	first	"	first, (corrected ML 114:2/JC 102:9)
"	135:	"	2:	"	produce	"	product (ML 138:7/JC 123:16)
"	140:	"	6:	"	League	"	league (ML 143:16/JC 128:7)
"	142:	"	31:	"	Park	"	park (ML 146:14/JC 130:24)
"	158:	"	10:	"	sir,	"	sir' (ML 162:26/JC 145:3)
"	158:	"	11:	"	Mr. Henchy,'	"	Mr. Henchy, (ML 162:26/JC145:3)
"	158:	"	19:	"	drank	"	drunk (ML163:4/JC–corrected–145:12)
"	162:	"	16:	"	and	"	'and (corrected–ML 167:7/JC 148: 27)
"	162	"	23:	"	him,	"	him (ML 167:15/JC 149:4)
"	164	"	25:	"	coward,	"	coward (ML 169:21/JC 151:9)
"	170	"	20:	"	gentlemen.	"	gentlemen, (ML 175:26/JC 157:3)
"	190	"	29:	"	footpath,	"	footpath (ML 197:9/JC 175:8)
"	200	"	27:	"	D'ye	"	Do you (ML 207:22/JC 184:17)
"	203	"	3:	"	Munno	"	Mmmno (ML 210:3/JC 186:20)
"	215	"	2:	"	Manmon	"	Mammon (corrected–ML 222:8/JC 197:23)
"	215	"	10:	"	this	"	his (corrected ML 222:17/JC 198:2)
"	230	"	24:	"	year. His	"	year his (ML 238:31/JC 212:18)
"	265	"	13:	"	he	"	she (ML 274:28/JC 244:14)
"	268	"	24:	"	too.	"	to. (corrected–ML 278:11/JC 247: 11)

Notes

I wish to express my gratitude to the Houghton Library of Harvard University and the Cornell University Library for allowing me to make use of their important unpublished Joyce materials in preparing this study, and especially to the Yale University Library for giving me complete freedom to quote from the invaluable manuscripts and proofs of *Dubliners* at Yale. I am also grateful to the Committee on Research Grants of the University of Virginia and the Richmond Area Fund for financial assistance with this project.

1. Herbert Gorman, *James Joyce* (London, 1949), pp. 145-58, 169-76, 195, 211-17, 219-21; Richard Ellmann, *James Joyce* (New York, 1959); John J. Slocum and Herbert Cahoon, *A Bibliography of James Joyce* (New Haven, 1953), A8.

2. Slocum and Cahoon, A8, suggest that the story was "expanded" in the 1914 edition, but it seems more likely that it was abbreviated by the printer in 1906. The two pages do not blend coherently; the speakers' roles become interchanged in the second page of the 1906 page proof, indicating omission of a page. In all other respects the text is substantially that of the later editions.

3. See Ellmann, chap. 15, for the genesis and background of this story.

4. The galley proofs of "The Dead" (at Yale) are dated by the printer "June 19/10." Roberts's letters to Joyce of 30 April and 7 June 1910 (at Cornell) indicated that the first set of proofs was mailed to Joyce on 7 June. See also Slocum and Cahoon, A8.

5. Slocum and Cahoon, A8, find no reason to doubt that 1,000 copies were actually printed and they are probably correct. In a letter of 9 August 1912 (at Cornell) Roberts suggested that Joyce try to get Grant Richards to take over the sheets printed by Falconer of Dublin.

6. The end of *Dubliners* is told simply and graphically by Charles Joyce in a letter to Stanislaus Joyce, 11 September 1912 (at Cornell). Less than a week before, his letter of 6 September had been full of hope for the prospects of *Dubliners* being published by himself and his brothers as the Liffey Press.

7. Letter: James to Stanislaus Joyce, 2 September 1912 (at Cornell). I speculate on the nature of the ruse in Marvin Magalaner, ed., *A James Joyce Miscellany,* 3d series (Carbondale: Southern Illinois University Press, 1962), in an essay on Joyce's broadsides.

8. Since "The Dead" had not been written when Richards first had *Dubliners* partially printed in 1906, and since the 1914 edition was set from proofs rather than manuscript, the only printer who could have made notations on the Yale manuscript of "The Dead" is the Irish printer.

9. See the Cornell manuscript (typed and handwritten by an amanuensis), pp. 2, 9; Yale manuscript, pp. 3, 16. Corrections in Joyce's hand in the Cornell typescript/manuscript are on pages 1, 20, 21, 35, 38, 39, 42, 44, 45, 49, 55, and 56.

10. The passage contains a word missed by the amanuensis in copying (apparently) and supplied by Joyce (p. 21).

11. The two impressions have been compared on the Hinman collating machine at the University of Virginia.

12. The pages have neat, uniform margins; the leaves have been handsewn. This text is probably the only survivor of the 1,000-copy Irish edition.

13. Richards, in his letter of 23 March 1914 (at Cornell), informed Joyce that pages 3-4 and 13-14 of "The Sisters" had been lost; Joyce, in his letter of 26 March (at Harvard), replied that he was supplying typed copies of the missing pages.

In the same letter Joyce asked Richards to return the title page of the Dublin printing.

14. Letter: Joyce to Richards, 4 March 1914 (at Harvard): "As regards to the inverted commas the Irish compositors are not to blame. I myself insisted on their abolition; to me they are an eyesore. I think the page reads much better with the dialogue between dashes. But if you are persuaded of the contrary I agree to waive the point and let the inverted commas replace the dashes. But I think you ought not to reject my suggestion at once. I think the commas used in English dialogue are most unsightly and give an impression of unreality."

Further Observations on the Text of *Dubliners*

This essay is a continuation of a study begun in *Studies in Bibliography*, 15 (1962). In the first essay, on the basis of an examination of the various manuscripts and proofs of one story, "The Dead," I attempted to establish a rationale for the textual criticism of *Dubliners*. In brief, and without the supporting evidence, the rationale is this: The first complete printing of *Dubliners* was done by the firm of Falconer in Dublin in 1910 for a projected edition to be published by Maunsel and Company. This printing went through three states: (1) a set of galleys, printed from Joyce's holograph manuscript but including many compositorial "improvements" in punctuation (including about 1,000 additional commas); (2) a set of early page proofs, somewhat more correct than the galleys; (3) a set of printed pages (referred to as a "late stage" of the printing in these studies but almost certainly the final stage, ready for the binder) thoroughly corrected by Joyce and containing some new improvements to the text made by him in proofreading.

When the Dublin publisher and printer finally refused to publish the book, Joyce obtained a set of the early page proofs (the second state described above), which became the printer's copy for the actual first edition published by Grant Richards in 1914. There are two states of the printing of this edition. The Edinburgh printer, the Riverside Press, eliminated the galley stage and provided a set of page proofs for correction. Having been set from the quite incorrect early page proofs of the abortive Dublin printing, these proofs required considerable correction. They were sent to Joyce, who made his corrections hastily, expecting to see another set of proofs. When the other proofs were not sent to him, he forwarded a set of corrections which he hoped would be made. It was not until two years later that he discovered that not only had the 30 additional corrections not been made but that 200 of the original corrections indicated on the page proofs had not been made either. The second state of the Grant Richards edition is the first edition itself. Modern reprint texts of *Dubliners* differ from this only by a few proofreader's corrections and some new compositor's errors introduced into the text.

For this second study of the text of *Dubliners* I have examined and collated all the available manuscript and proof versions of all the stories not treated in my first study—that is, all but "The Dead." Since the materials available for study vary from story to story, each will be treated separately below, after a discussion of the general problems which will face the future editor of *Dubliners*.

General Problems

One of the major problems for the future editor of *Dubliners* will be the punctuation of the text. He will certainly want to return to Joyce's own desired punctuation of direct discourse (dashes instead of quotation marks); but will he want to follow Joyce's habitual manuscript procedure and place a dash both before and after a paragraph in which direct discourse appears, or will he adopt the procedure of the published versions of *Portrait* and *Ulysses* and use the opening dash only? I am inclined to favor the latter, as representing Joyce's final procedure—but the question is certainly arguable. The use of commas will present another problem of considerable complexity, owing to the bizarre prepublication printing history of the book. The compositor of the Maunsel (Dublin) printing added about 1,000 commas to Joyce's text. In "A Mother," for example, where we have a full set of galley proofs to examine, we find that the galleys have 87 more commas than the manuscript from which they were set. The Grant Richards page proofs for the first edition (which were set from page proofs of the Maunsel printing) show that 70 commas were removed between the galleys and the Richards page proofs, and we find that 12 more were expunged for the first edition itself. But some of the total of 82 expunged commas were present in Joyce's manuscript, and a number of compositorial commas which were not in the manuscript have been allowed to stand in the text. Should the editor go back to manuscript or allow the final version to stand, as having been proofread by Joyce and therefore carrying his approval? We cannot be sure which readings in the first edition are among the 200 corrections Joyce wanted to make, but the existence of 200 errors certainly undermines our confidence in the first edition. Still, Joyce was given to continual revising in proof, a habit which prevents us from accepting with absolute confidence a manuscript reading over a reading in the first edition. Each case will have to be decided individually by an editor who is deeply familiar with Joyce's habits of punctuation and is willing to proceed eclectically, relying on his judgment.

There will also be problems in substantive readings for the future editor of *Dubliners.* The question of "lost" improvements in the late stage of the Maunsel (Dublin) text has been considered in my earlier essay (and some additional material of this kind will be presented below) but there are questions even more complex than this which the editor will have to face. The final manuscript of "Ivy Day in the Committee Room," for example, which was the printer's copy for the Maunsel (Dublin) printing, bears a number of marginal corrections in Joyce's hand. Some of these marginal corrections appear in the page proofs and finally in the first edition; others seem never to have been printed. (They might, however, have been incorporated into the final Dublin state, of which, for this story, there is no known copy.) Here again, and in other similar cases, the editor will have to rely on his critical judgment and decide whether Joyce thought the better of his marginal improvement and deliberately omitted to include it in the printed text, or he simply lost track of it, and now the editor must execute Joyce's long-delayed intention. All this suggests a generalization about the problems of an editor in relation to bibliographical theory. It seems that no theory of textual transmission, however carefully and thoroughly worked out, will absolve the editor from using his judgment and his critical faculty. He will have to take risks. In the present instance we have an unusual amount of material available. What would we not give to have two manuscripts and two proof texts for one of Shakespeare's plays (as we have them for "Ivy Day in the Committee Room")? But even such a miraculous acquisition as this would probably leave the text of the play a long way from settled.

Individual Stories

"The Sisters"

Date of composition: This was the first story of *Dubliners* to be written. It appeared in the *Irish Homestead* on 13 August 1904. Joyce revised it slightly in June 1905 for submission to Grant Richards, and revised it extensively before submission to Maunsel in April 1909.

Texts available: (1) published *Irish Homestead* text; (2) 1905 manuscript; (3) revised manuscript, used for Maunsel printing; (4) late stage of Maunsel page proofs; (5) Grant Richards page proofs; (6) first edition.

The development of the final text: This aspect of "The Sisters" has been treated thoroughly by Marvin Magalaner in *Joyce: The Man, the Work, the Reputation* (1962), pp. 82–87; and *Time of Apprenticeship* (1959), pp. 74–86.

Lost improvements to the Maunsel text: The two major changes from manuscript in the late stage of the Maunsel text which were not picked up in the Richards text seem of slight importance:

a. "We crossed ourselves and came away." (first edition, p. 16; Viking Compass edition, p. 14; Jonathan Cape, 1954, p. 13)
   "We blessed ourselves and came away." (late Maunsel, p. 10. The manuscript reads "crossed." This change must have been made in the late Maunsel only.)
b. ". . . she filled out the sherry. . . . " (FE 16; VC 15; JC 13)
   ". . . she poured out the sherry. . . . " (late Maunsel only, p. 10)

"An Encounter"

Date of composition: The ninth in order of composition, this story was completed by mid-September 1905.

Texts available: (1) manuscript for Maunsel printing; (2) late stage of Maunsel printing; (3) Richards page proofs; (4) first edition.

The development of the text: The manuscript and page proofs show that Joyce continued correcting and improving right up to the end, but most of these changes are small—a word or two at most. The eyes of the peculiar stranger were "sage-green" in the manuscript and only acquired their more sinister "bottle-green" hue in the Irish proofs. This improvement was not lost in the Richards text, but a few were and are listed below.

Lost improvements to the Maunsel text:

a. "... some wretched fellow that writes these things for a drink." (FE 22, VC 20, JC 19)
"... some wretched scribbler that writes these things for a drink." (late Maunsel, p. 20. The priest's condemnation of the author of *The Apache Chief* is intensified and related more specifically to the writing in the story.)

b. "... used slang freely, and spoke of Father Butler as Old Bunser." (FE 24, VC 22, JC 21)
"... used slang freely and spoke of Father Butler as Bunsen Burner." (late Maunsel, p. 23. Mahony's nickname for the priest is given more point.)

c. "... a jerry hat with a high crown." (FE 27, VC 24, JC 24)
"... a jerry hat with a very high crown." (late Maunsel, p. 26. This is not strictly an improvement, since it is the reading of the manuscript also. The "very" drops out of the text in the Richards page proofs, probably accidentally, and never gets back in.)

d. "The man asked me how many I had." (FE 29, VC 25, JC 25)
"The man asked me how many had I." (late Maunsel, p. 27. As in (c) just above, this is the manuscript reading also, apparently transposed by the compositor in setting the Richards page proofs.)

"Araby"

Date of composition: The eleventh in order of composition, this story was completed in September 1905.

Texts available: (1) late stage of the Maunsel printing; (2) Richards page proofs; (3) first edition.

The development of the text: Though the absence of manuscript evidence makes speculation somewhat conjectural, this story seems to have satisfied Joyce as completely as any, for there are no major variations among the three texts available. One punctuation change apparently introduced by the compositor for the Richards edition should probably be corrected:

"It would be a splendid bazaar, she said she would love to go." (FE 36, VC 31, JC 32)
"It would be a splendid bazaar, she said; she would love to go." (late Maunsel, p. 38)

Lost improvements to the Maunsel text: None.

"Eveline"

Date of composition: The second in order of composition, this story was first published in *The Irish Homestead* on 10 September 1904.

Texts available: (1) published *Irish Homestead* text; (2) late stage of the Maunsel printing; (3) Richards page proofs; (4) first edition.

The development of the text: Joyce revised fairly extensively between the *Irish Homestead* and the Maunsel versions, and continued tinkering with an odd word or two right up to the first edition. The changes from the *Homestead* text are mainly of two kinds. In revising the narration of Eveline's reverie he sometimes replaced words or phrases not quite appropriate for her with more suitable material, and he sometimes added material for the sake of its naturalistic or symbolic point. Consider the examples below. The first consists of an entire paragraph from the *Homestead* version and the late Maunsel version.

> Home! She looked round the room, passing in review all its familiar objects. How many times she had dusted it, once a week at least. It was the "best" room, but it seemed to secrete dust everywhere. She had known the room for ten years--more–twelve years, and knew everything in it. Now she was going away. And yet during all those years she had never found out the name of the Australian priest whose yellowing photograph hung on the wall, just above the broken harmonium. He had been a friend of her father's–a school friend. When he showed the photograph to a friend, her father used to pass it with a casual word, "In Australia now–Melbourne."

> Home! She looked round the room reviewing all its familiar objects which she had dusted once a week for so many years, wondering where on earth all the dust came from. Perhaps she would never see again those familiar objects from which she had never dreamed of being divided. And yet during all those years she had never found out the name of the priest whose yellowing photograph hung on the wall above the broken harmonium beside the coloured print of the promises made to the Blessed Margaret Mary Alacoque. He had been a school friend of her father's. Whenever he showed the photograph to a visitor her father used to pass it with a casual word:
>
> –He is in Melbourne now.–

Irrelevant matter is pruned away. The word "secrete," which is inappropriate to the thought processes of Eveline, is removed, and the

Blessed Margaret Mary Alacoque is inserted. When we learn that this saint paralyzed herself with self-inflicted tortures but was cured miraculously when she vowed to dedicate herself to a holy life, we can see that Joyce is not merely adding to the naturalistic description of the home of Eveline but presenting the reader with a symbolic parallel to her own life of emotional paralysis. In other revisions the speech of the edgy Miss Gavan is sharpened a little and we are given more detail on Eveline's past relationship with her father. Compare the following two passages:

> Even now—at her age, she was over nineteen—she sometimes felt herself in danger of her father's violence. Latterly he had begun to threaten her, saying what he would do if it were not for her dead mother's sake.

> Even now, though she was over nineteen, she sometimes felt herself in danger of her father's violence. She knew it was that that had given her the palpitations. When they were growing up he had never gone for her, like he used to go for Harry and Ernest, because she was a girl; but latterly he had begun to threaten her and say what he would do to her only for her dead mother's sake.

Here we have not only the interesting addition of the palpitations and the father's past brutality but a significant change in the syntax of the last clause. The formal "were it not for her dead mother's sake" gives way to the "only for her dead mother's sake" in which we can catch the living rhythm of the father's speech. Though the account is narrated rather than dramatized and the discourse indirect rather than direct, the narrative takes its color from the idiom of the characters rather than from any narrative personality. Through countless little changes of this kind, Joyce carefully eliminated his own personality from *Dubliners,* as he developed a system whereby the events and characters presented in the narrative rather than any assumed narrative persona determine the diction and syntax of the narrative prose. This elimination of the narrator as a personality does away with the need for consistent narrative idiom and paves the way for the experiments of Joyce's later fiction.

Lost improvements to the Maunsel text: None.

"After the Race"

Date of composition: The third in order of composition, this story was first published in *The Irish Homestead* on 17 December 1904.

Texts available: (1) published *Irish Homestead* text; (2) late stage of the Maunsel printing; (3) Richards page proofs; (4) first edition.

The development of the text: Though this story saw fewer revisions than either of the others which appeared first in *The Irish Homestead,* Joyce did make quite a few changes in it for the Maunsel printing. The most heavily revised passage occurs midway through the story, in the paragraph describing Segouin's dinner. For comparison, here is the passage, first as it was in the magazine, then as it became in the late stage of the Maunsel text.

> The five young men dined in a small comfortable room by candlelight. They talked a great deal and with little reserve.

> The young men supped in a snug room lit by electric candle lamps. They talked volubly and with little reserve.

Joyce's intention here in electrifying the lighting was probably to add to the impression of meretriciousness which is one of this story's chief characteristics. In a similar revision he altered "That night the city wore the air of a capital" to "That night the city wore the mask of a capital." An *air* does not imply the deliberate desire to deceive which a *mask* does. And, finally, he pointed up Jimmy Doyle's desire to be deceived in the closing paragraph, by adding the material which follows the comma: "He knew that he would regret in the morning but at present he was glad of the rest, glad of the dark stupor that would cover up his folly." Joyce also made a number of other minor changes, improving a word here and there. Some of these did not find their way into the Richards text and are noted below.

Lost improvements to the Maunsel text:

a. "Each blue car, therefore, received a double measure of welcome . . . . " (FE 49, VC 42, JC 44)
   "Each blue car, therefore, received a double round of welcome . . . . " (late Maunsel, p. 57)
b. ". . . in the face of a high wind. . . . " (FE 51, VC 44, JC 46)
   ". . . in the teeth of a high wind. . . . " (LM 59)

"Two Gallants"

Date of composition: The thirteenth in order of composition, this story was finished and sent to Grant Richards to be added to the original twelve on 23 February 1906.

Texts available: (1) fragment of setting for Richards, 1906; (2) late stage of Maunsel page proofs; (3) Richards page proofs; (4) first edition.

The development of the text: Being a late story, this one probably was not revised so extensively as some of the early ones. We have two nonconsecutive pages from the typesetting made for Grant Richards on 17 April 1906 which differ in no significant way from the later text.

Lost improvements to the Maunsel text:

a. "The notes of the air sounded deep and full." (FE 64, VC 54, JC 58)
   "The notes of the air throbbed deep and full." (LM 76)
b. " 'Let's have a look at her, Corley,' he said." (FE 65, VC 54, JC 58)
   "–Let's have a squint at her, Corley–he said." (LM 76)
c. "Then he walked rapidly along beside the chains at some distance. . . . " (FE 66, VC 55, JC 59)
   "Then he walked rapidly along beside the chains to some distance . . . " (LM 77)
d. "The girl brought him a plate of grocer's hot peas. . . . " (FE 68, VC 57, JC 61)
   "The girl brought him a plate of hot grocer's peas. . . . " (LM 80. This change seems less significant than the others, but it is the only one which appears on Joyce's list of late corrections. Possibly the others had been made on the proofs and were among the 200 which were ignored by the printer.)

"The Boarding House"

Date of composition: The fifth in order of composition, this story is dated 1 July 1905 on the only surviving manuscript. Joyce mailed a copy to his brother, Stanislaus, on 12 July.

Texts available: (1) 1905 manuscript; (2) late stage of Maunsel page proofs; (3) Richards page proofs; (4) first edition.

The development of the text: This story was extensively rewritten between the 1905 manuscript, which was signed "Stephen Daedalus" and apparently intended for the *Irish Homestead,* and the Dublin printing of 1910. Several aspects of the rewriting warrant commentary. In one respect the rewriting parallels that of "Eveline" discussed above. In eight significant substantive changes the intent is obviously to make the language more colloquial, more appropriate to the events being narrated than to the more lofty tone of the narrative persona, "Stephen Daedalus." Thus, "obliged to enlist himself" becomes "had to become"; "attacked his wife" becomes "went for his wife"; "started a boarding house" becomes "set up a boarding house"; "an amateur boxer" becomes "handy with the mits"; "she had been specific in her enquiries and Polly had been decided in her answers" becomes "she had been frank in her questions and Polly had been frank in her answers"; plain "Lyons" becomes "Bantam Lyons"; "the loss of his job" becomes "the loss of his sit" (colloquial for *sit*uation); "had a bit of money put by" becomes "had a bit of stuff put by." In other revisions, Joyce is busy at the usual phrase sharpening, and in one case he is at some pains to make his irony less heavy-handed. The last sentence, originally reading "She remembered now what she had been waiting for: this was it" becomes "Then she remembered what she had been waiting for."

But the major revision to the early version of this story consists of an insertion some ten lines long. The nature of the insertion throws light on an interesting aspect of Joyce's technique. Joyce is often praised or blamed (depending on the critic's predilections) for the ambivalence or ambiguity of his fiction. When the artist refuses to provide any authoritative commentary, the critics tell us, we are free to believe whatever we want, and to seek for authorial intention is to commit one of the graver critical fallacies. But to this observer it seems that Joyce gives us our heads expecting us to use them. The insertion in question illustrates how we are to proceed. In the original version there was room for some quibbling about the extent to which each of the two principals was seducer or seducee. The added ten lines provide no commentary, but they give us the bit of evidence we need to resolve the problem with considerable certainty.

> Then late one night as he was undressing for bed she had tapped at his door, timidly. She wanted to relight her candle at his for hers had been blown out by a gust. It was her bath night. She wore an open combing jacket of printed flannel. Her white instep shone in the opening of her

furry slippers and the blood glowed warmly behind her perfumed skin. From her hands and wrists too, as she lit and steadied her candle a faint perfume arose.

Lost improvements to the Maunsel text:

a. ". . . the loss of his job." (FE 78, VC 65, JC 70)
". . . the loss of his sit." (LM 92)

A manuscript reading which should probably be restored: "There must be reparation made in such cases" is the manuscript reading for a line which all the printed texts have as ". . . in such case" (VC 64, JC 70). The error presumably crept in during the Irish printing and was never picked up. If Joyce had wanted the singular he would probably have used the standard "in such *a* case," but there is no evidence that he wanted any change from the manuscript.

"A Little Cloud"

Date of composition: The fourteenth in order of composition, this story was written in the first part of 1906 and mailed to Grant Richards in July of that year.

Texts available: (1) late stage of Maunsel page proofs; (2) Richards page proofs; (3) first edition.

The development of the text: Like "Two Gallants," which was also written after the first dozen stories had been submitted to Richards, this one probably required almost no revision for the Maunsel printing. Joyce expressed great pleasure in it in October 1906 while he was still working on revisions for some others.

Lost improvements to the Maunsel text: The one change is so slight as hardly to deserve the word improvement, but Joyce made it, probably feeling the word expressed Mrs. Chandler's attitude more accurately.

a. ". . . a regular swindle to charge ten and elevenpence for it." (FE 100, VC 83, JC 91)
". . . a regular swindle to charge ten and elevenpence for that." (LM 118)

"Counterparts"

Date of composition: The sixth in order of composition, this story was written almost simultaneously with "The Boarding House," and finished by 12 July 1905.

Texts available: (1) the 1905 manuscript, nearly complete; (2) late stage of the Maunsel page proofs; (3) Richards page proofs; (4) first edition.

Development of the text: Like "The Boarding House" this story was revised considerably before the Maunsel printing. The most interesting revisions are those for the long pub scene. Here Joyce added considerable color and life just by making more specific the expressions used for drinks. Thus "a drink" becomes "a half one"; "a drink" becomes "tailors of malt, hot"; "drink up" becomes "polish off that"; "said they would have theirs hot" becomes "told Tim to make theirs hot"; "hot specials" becomes "whiskeys hot"; and "one more" becomes "one little smahan more." Here, as in other revisions, the narrative indirect discourse is enriched by the phraseology of the speakers, and the effect is one of dramatization as the narrator adopts more of the speech of his characters. There are many other revisions in individual words and phrases, but the most interesting is a long passage almost entirely rewritten. In the manuscript the episode of the girl in the pub reads as follows:

> Farrington said he wouldn't mind having the far one and began to smile at her but when Weathers offered to introduce her he said "No," he was only chaffing because he knew he had not money enough. She continued to cast bold glances at him and changed the position of her legs often and when she was going out she brushed against his chair and said "Pardon!" in a Cockney accent.

This was one of the passages Grant Richards objected to as likely to cause trouble, and especially he objected to the girl's changing the position of her legs. Joyce leaped to the defense of his text, invoking the "Areopagitica" and insisting that without details such as this, "*Dubliners* would seem to me like an egg without salt." But when he came to revise his text after losing his argument with Richards he took it upon himself to expunge the offensive legs, discovering that he could do all he wanted to with arms and eyes. The vastly improved (if censored) passage reads as follows in the late Maunsel text:

> Farrington's eyes wandered at every moment in the direction of one of the young women. There was something striking in her appearance. An immense scarf of peacock blue muslin was wound round her hat and knotted in a great bow under her chin; and she wore bright yellow

> gloves, reaching to the elbow. Farrington gazed admiringly at the plump arm which she moved very often and with much grace; and, when after a little time she answered his gaze, he admired still more her large dark brown eyes. The oblique staring expression in them fascinated him. She glanced at him once or twice and, when the party was leaving the room, she brushed against his chair and said *O, pardon!* in a London accent. He watched her leave the room in the hope that she would look back at him but he was disappointed.

In the revised version we are not told so bluntly what Farrington is thinking, but we are brought much closer to his point of view. Naturalism has given way to impressionism in the passage. Even the girl's accent seems different when seen from Farrington's perspective rather than the narrator's. Where the narrator and reader heard Cockney, redolent of slums and sordidness, Farrington hears London, as exotic to him as Araby to the little boy of the earlier story. The reader can form his own opinion of that blue and yellow color combination, and he can judge the woman by the way she brushes against Farrington, but he is not told that her glances are "bold." One is tempted to come to the conclusion, however reluctantly, that if Joyce had taken some of Richards's advice instead of battling him on principle at every point, he might have saved himself a lot of grief and not done *Dubliners* any harm.

Lost improvements to the Maunsel text:

a. "Funds were getting low. . . . " (FE 115, VC 95, JC 105)
   "Funds were running low. . . . " (LM 136)
b. " . . . said with stupid familiarity. . . . " (FE 117, VC 96, JC 107)
   " . . . said with loutish familiarity. . . . " (LM 138)

"Clay"

Date of composition: The fourth in order of composition, this story seems to have cost Joyce more pains than most. In November 1904 he began a story, "Christmas Eve," which he abandoned half finished, apparently because the idea for another, "Hallow Eve," had superseded it. (The manuscript of "Christmas Eve" has been found and the fragment published in *The James Joyce Miscellany,* 3d ser., 1962.) "Hallow Eve" was completed and sent to Stanislaus Joyce for possible publication in *The Irish Homestead* in January 1905. James Joyce may have done some revision on the story at this point. It was in his mind much and mentioned frequently in his correspondence during the next few months, while the fifth and sixth stories were not written until July. By September the title had been changed to "The Clay." In November 1906 Joyce was working on the story again, adding the name of the laundry where Maria works. At some later date he must have reconsidered the title again, dropping the article from it.

Texts available: (1) late stage of Maunsel page proofs; (2) Richards page proofs; (3) first edition.

Development of the text: Until some manuscripts are found we will have to be content with the knowledge that Joyce worked on the story carefully, though we do not know the nature or direction of his improvements. The last change he made, as noted below, suggests that he added some of the details which make Maria appropriately witchlike, a cloak being the proper garment for a witch.

Lost improvements to the Maunsel text: On two occasions, Maria's garment is described as a "raincloak" in the late Maunsel text rather than as a "waterproof" which is the reading of the modern editions.

"A Painful Case"

Date of composition: The seventh in order of composition, this story was first written in July 1905, its original title being "A Painful Incident." A draft was sent to Stanislaus for copying in August of that year. A second manuscript exists, dated 15 August 1905. In August 1906 Joyce wrote that he had three paragraphs, and then five pages, to add to the story, but the August 1905 manuscript was printer's copy for the Maunsel printing, and there are no lengthy revisions which seem to have been inserted in this text, though this text is longer than the earlier manuscript. The most likely possibilities are these. First, the manuscript dated August 1905 may have been actually written in 1906. This is likely, not so much because Joyce might have misdated it accidentally, though this is possible, but because he often placed the date of original composition on a work which he revised much later. "Tilly" in *Pomes Penyeach* is backdated in this way, and *Portrait* carries both the date of the first draft and that of the last. A second possibility is that the revisions to the story were simply never inserted. This seems to me the least likely alternative.

Texts available: (1) heavily revised first manuscript; (2) second manuscript with few revisions, dated 15 August 1905; (3) portion of the late stage of the Maunsel printing; (4) Richards page proofs; (5) first edition.

The development of the text: Joyce's revisions have been covered thoroughly by Marvin Magalaner in *Time of Apprenticeship* (1959), pp. 87–96.

Lost improvements to the Maunsel text: None.

"Ivy Day in the Committee Room"

Date of composition: The eighth in order of composition, this story was completed in all its essentials in a draft dated 29 August 1905, but Joyce continued making minor revisions until the first edition was printed.

Texts available: (1) manuscript dated 29 August 1905; (2) a later manuscript used as copy-text for the Maunsel printing; (3) an *intermediate* stage of the Maunsel printing; (4) Richards page proofs; (5) first edition. The *intermediate* stage of the Maunsel printing consists of pages rather than galleys, but retaining the period in "Mr." and other indications that it is not the "late stage" of proof which is available for most of the other stories in *Dubliners.* This is the only sample yet discovered of the state of the text which was postulated as a hypothetical C_1 in my study of the text of "The Dead." This is the state of the Maunsel printing from which the Richards edition was set. Such errors as "Parke's" for "Parkes" and "revenge" for "renege" made by the Irish compositor in setting from Joyce's holograph manuscript are repeated in the Richards page proofs and finally corrected in the first edition. No doubt if a late stage of the Maunsel text were available we should find the corrected reading there too. This copy of the intermediate state of the Maunsel printing was not itself copy-text for the Richards, for it contains numerous corrections in Joyce's hand which were not made in the Richards page proofs. A virtually uncorrected set of proofs must have been sent to Richards.

The development of the text: The future editor of *Dubliners* will find himself confronted with an embarrassing complexity of riches in the form of authorial revisions to various states of the text of this story. The second manuscript, printer's copy for the Maunsel typesetting, contains marginal revisions, some of which were included in the Maunsel proofs and some of which were not, possibly because they were made in the manuscript after it was used by the compositor. The Maunsel proofs contain holograph corrections, some of which appear in the Richards proofs, most of which do not. Some of the overlooked corrections from both of these sources are inserted in the first edition and some are not. In one case Joyce, who fought so bitterly against Grant Richards for every word of his text, provides a marginal alternate reading for a disputed passage, apparently leaving the decision to an editor or compositor, whoever cared to make it. After the intermediate stage of the Maunsel edition had been set, Joyce went through it, eliminating all the attempts he had made to reproduce the sounds of Irish speech (e.g., "Owl'" gives way to "old"). He apparently decided that it was inartistic to rely on such nineteenth-century devices, and that he would depend on grammar and syntax alone to make his speech Irish. Of course, the Richards compositor did not have the benefit of these corrections, so the same culling out had to be performed between Richards page proofs and the first edition. Joyce seems to have started early to indulge in the practice of making heavy revisions in proof, much to the distress of all his publishers. Here are some of the major changes and problems related to the text of "Ivy Day."

a. On his entrance, Father Keon's voice is described in the modern editions as "a discrete, indulgent, velvety voice" (VC 126, JC 141). In the first manuscript the sentence continued, "which is not often found except with the confessor or the sodomite." In the second manuscript the clause is crossed out, in the interests of either decency or subtlety.

b. In the second manuscript Joyce inserted the word "lousy" before the expression "hillsiders and fenians." This should probably be added in the modern texts (VC 125, JC 139). He also substituted "Bantam" for "Lyons" (VC 130, JC 146) in the phrase "Of course Lyons spots the drink first thing"—a change which parallels one in "The Boarding House."

c. For a passage relating to Edward VII Joyce provided an alternate reading in the second manuscript:

passage: "He's fond of his glass of grog and he's a bit of a rake, perhaps, and he's a good sportsman. . . . "

alternate: "He can take a glass of grog like an honest Christian and, I grant you, he may have [ ] a wild lad in his day and he's a good sportsman." (missing word Joyce's oversight)

The alternate, it seems, was not needed. This, of course, was one of the passages which Joyce and his publishers disputed about so violently.

d. One sentence was added in the margin of the second manuscript but never printed. It should probably be added to the modern texts. It is a delightful thing in itself and it adds to the characterization of the ubiquitous Bantam Lyons, which seems to have been one of Joyce's general intentions in his revision of these stories. After " . . . a fit man to lead us" insert "Do you think he was a man I'd like the lady who is now Mrs Lyons to know?" The man in question is Joyce's hero, Parnell (VC 132, JC 148).

Lost improvements to the Maunsel text: Since we do not have the late stage of this text, there are none, but the manuscript changes discussed above should be noted. Perhaps we should also note here one error which has crept into the American text although the first edition was correct. The phrase "schoolboy of hell" (VC 123) should be "shoeboy of hell." This is not too important, but one critic has already based a clever interpretive paragraph on the misreading. *Caveat lector.*

"A Mother"

Date of composition: The tenth in order of composition, this story was finished by late September 1905.

Texts available: (1) manuscript used as printer's copy for the Maunsel edition; (2) galley proofs, the first stage of the Maunsel edition; (3) Richards page proofs; (4) first edition.

Development of the text: Joyce made a number of revisions of the *mot juste* variety between the galleys and the Richards text. This kind of revision is typical of all his corrections to *Dubliners* and is probably the least significant.

Lost improvements to the Maunsel text: Without the late stage of the Maunsel text no lost revisions can be found.

"Grace"

Date of composition: The twelfth in order of composition, this story was called "the last" by Joyce, as it completed his original plan for twelve stories in four groups of three. He began it in October 1905 and finished it sometime before the twelve stories were sent to

Grant Richards in December of that year. But during his stay in Rome the following year he did additional research in the Biblioteca Vittorio Emmanuale for the theological parts of the story.

Texts available: (1) manuscript used for Maunsel printing, very clean copy, probably not 1905 version; (2) Richards page proofs; (3) first edition.

The development of the text: Between the manuscript and the Richards page proofs, and, to a lesser extent, between the proofs and the first edition Joyce made a number of minor revisions. In two of the larger of these we can see him eliminating the superior prose of the narrator in favor of plainer locutions, more suited to the subject matter: "Nor was she an utter materialist for she also believed (to a certain extent) in the banshee and in the Holy Ghost" becomes "Her faith was bounded by her kitchen but, if she was put to it, she could believe also in the banshee and in the Holy Ghost"; and "a confirmed inebriate" becomes "an incurable drunkard." Other revisions are of the *mot juste* variety.

Lost improvements to the Maunsel text: None. No late Maunsel available.

"The Dead"

See "Some Observations on the Text of *Dubliners:* 'The Dead,'" *Studies in Bibliography* 15 (1962), 191–205.

Note

The author of this study wishes to thank the libraries of Yale and Cornell universities for their indispensable cooperation, the Committee on Research Grants of the University of Virginia for assistance with expenses for typing and films, and the American Council of Learned Societies for a Grant-in-Aid which enabled these researches to be pursued in New Haven and Ithaca during summer 1962.

Book Review: *A Portrait of the Artist as a Young Man,* by James Joyce*

The first question inevitably asked about a "definitive text" such as this is, "Did they really change anything important?" The answer to this question depends on what one thinks is important. If "important" means that the new text should require a new interpretation of the entire work, the answer is, "No, they did not change anything really important." But if it is important to have some 200 new or modified words in the text, and many more corrections of accidentals, then the new edition brings with it changes that may indeed be called important. What I propose to do by way of reviewing the new edition is first to discuss the rationale for the text as presented in Chester Anderson's unpublished dissertation, and then to illustrate from and comment upon the actual modifications in the text, as revealed by a collation of a copy of the twentieth printing (1962) of the "old" Viking Compass text and a first printing of the "new" (1964). A careful collation of the two texts was made by Joan C. Scholes for this occasion.

The manuscript materials relevant to the text of *Portrait* are these:

1. A fair-copy manuscript, in Joyce's hand, virtually complete, now in Dublin's National Library.
2. A typescript made from the manuscript in Trieste in 1913–14 which became the printer's copy for the serialized version of the novel in *The Egoist.* The typescript is unfortunately lost, having been destroyed by Harriet Weaver, according to custom, after the *Egoist* printing was complete. (She explained this in a letter to Chester Anderson, dated June 24, 1961.)

After the *Egoist* serialization, tear sheets from that magazine, with corrections by Weaver, Ezra Pound, and Joyce, were used as printer's copy for the first American edition of 1916. The original fair-copy manuscript was temporarily separated from Joyce during some of his

*The definitive text, corrected from the Dublin holograph. New York: Viking Press, 1964.

changes of habitation and was finally sent by him to Weaver for safekeeping. In 1951 she gave it to the National Library. After the Trieste typescript was made from it, the manuscript was not consulted again in the preparation of any edition until the present time. The first English edition (1917) used sheets from the first American. The first English edition with English sheets (1918) was based on the previous edition but incorporated some corrections from a list of errors drawn up by Joyce. All subsequent English editions have been based on the 1918 text. All subsequent American editions have been based on the 1916 text.

In the course of this history the text has degenerated through the usual introduction of compositorial errors and other inevitable processes, and the new edition undertakes to correct such defects. But Anderson contends–and his evidence is overwhelming–that the major textual damage was done early: between the manuscript and the Trieste typescript in fact, mainly through the typist's quite understandable omission of many phrases of a repetitive nature. Quite simply, the typist's eyes sometimes skipped from a word to the identical word on another line–a phenomenon most of us have encountered often enough. Thus Anderson's task has been primarily to restore lost Joycean words to the text by the simple expedient of returning to the manuscript reading. A secondary task has been the restoration of Joycean punctuation (which tends to be lighter than standard) by comparing the manuscript with the various printed versions and Joyce's list of corrections–a comparison which reveals the extent of Joyce's continuing struggle against the "house style" of various printing establishments.

This is only the crudest outline of Anderson's thoroughly researched textual effort. The seriously interested reader should consult his 1962 Columbia University dissertation for the full and fascinating details. And now, before considering some of the emendations (or, better, restorations) I wish to say a word about the behavior of the Viking Press in the matter of this text. Because of its high continuing sales, especially in college bookstores, *Portrait* is a most valuable literary property. The behavior of the Viking Press with this property must be contrasted with the behavior of Random House with its valuable Joycean property, *Ulysses.* Random House recently reissued *Ulysses* in a supposedly definitive text, but with no indication of how the edition was prepared or by whom. The text seems primarily remarkable for the fact that it has worked a bitter and unnecessary hardship on Joyce's serious readers by rendering obsolete all those commentaries and guides, including the indispensable word index, which were keyed to the pagination and lineation of the old text. The nature of the new Random House text does not seem to have required any substantial revision of these matters. The old page and line numbering could have been followed easily. Random House simply behaved in a careless and high-handed way, abusing their stewardship of Joyce's great work. Viking, on the other hand, has behaved admirably. Though a commercial press, with commercial interests and responsibilities, Viking has found it consistent with good business to do the right thing by Joyce's text, and in doing so has won itself substantial good will in the academic world. In Chester Anderson, Viking picked the right editor; in making the necessary changes the press made a real effort to stay as close as possible to the original pagination and lineation; and the rationale for the edition, the division of editorial labor, has been made clear in a brief textual note at the end of the book. In the textual note we are informed that the final arbiter of emendations has been Richard Ellmann, and we learn something of Anderson's procedure and the credit that is due him. One suspects that Ellmann's presence was invoked by Viking in part ritualistically, for the sake of his prestige in matters Joycean, but one feels also that it is not a bad idea for a literary and a textual critic to collaborate in this manner. However scientific textual criticism and bibliography may hope and pretend to be, some editorial decisions will always be essentially literary, matters of art rather than science, and only the literary critic will be able to make them. In the present case, literary criticism, in the guise of Ellmann, has clearly exerted only the mildest of restraining influences on textual impetuosity. Of the 264 words which Anderson said should be restored to the printed text, virtually all seem to have been accepted. On the whole, this book exemplifies a rare and encouraging kind of cooperation between textual and literary criticism, and even more important, between the academic community and a commercial publishing house.

For the interested reader, here are some typical restored readings, with some commentary on their significance.

1. Old text (p. 23)
   —We must pack off to Brother Michael because we have the collywobbles!

He was very decent to say that. That was all to make him laugh.

New text (p. 22)

—We must pack off to Brother Michael because we have the collywobbles! Terrible thing to have the collywobbles! How we wobble when we have the collywobbles!

He was very. . . .

(Now we know what the prefect said that Stephen recognized as a kind but feeble attempt to cheer him up.)

2. Old (p. 45)

That was a sound to hear but if you were hit then you would feel a pain. The pandybat made a sound too but not like that. The fellows said it was made of whalebone and leather with lead inside: and he wondered what was the pain like. There were different kinds of sounds.

New (p. 45)

. . . There were different kinds of pains for all the different kinds of sounds.

(The correction of this sentence changes Stephen's thought from an inane banality to a sensitive perception.)

3. Old (p. 61)

Though he had heard his father say that Mike Flynn had put some of the best runners of modern times through his hands Stephen often glanced at his trainer's flabby stubble-covered face. . . .

New (p. 61)

. . . glanced with mistrust at his trainer's flabby stubblecovered face. . . .

(The corrected sentence makes better sense, clarifying our understanding of Stephen's attitude. Incidentally, the removal of the hyphen from "stubblecovered" is typical of many restorations of Joycean punctuation, which tends to avoid hyphens and to be sparing of commas.)

4. Old (p. 73)

Against the walls stood companies of barbells and Indian clubs;

the dumbells were piled in one corner: and in the midst of countless hillocks of gymnasium shoes and sweaters and singlets in untidy brown parcels there stood the stout leatherjacketed vaulting horse waiting its turn to be carried up on the stage and set in the middle of the winning team at the end of the gymnastic display.

New (p. 73)

. . . vaulting horse waiting its turn to be carried up on the stage. A large bronze shield, tipped with silver, leaned against the panel of the altar also waiting its turn to be carried up on the stage and set in the middle of the winning team. . . .

(A trivial clarification, no doubt, but now we can see that the horse is part of the gymnastic display itself and the shield, which we had not known about, a more appropriate element in the victory tableau.)

5. Old (p. 83)

Then in the dark and unseen by the other two he rested the tips of the fingers of one hand upon the palm of the other hand, scarcely touching it lightly. But the pressure of her fingers had been lighter and steadier. . . .

New (pp. 82–83)

Then in the dark and unseen by the other two he rested the tips of the fingers of one hand upon the palm of the other hand, scarcely touching it and yet pressing upon it lightly. But the pressure of her fingers. . . .

(Even a few more words bearing on Stephen's attitude toward Emma and his relationship with her should be a matter for critical gratitude. It is a bit clearer now, that here Stephen is surreptitiously, avoiding the gaze of Heron and Wallis, trying to recreate the handclasp or touch of Emma.)

6. Old (p. 173)

A rim of the young moon cleft the pale waste of skyline, the rim of a silver hoop embedded in gray sand. . . .

New (p. 173)

A rim of the young moon cleft the pale waste of sky like the rim of a silver hoop embedded in gray sand. . . .

(This slight adjustment makes a fine simile ring clear and true after being muffled for years in that vague phrase "waste of skyline.")

7. Old (p. 232)
   Did that explain his friend's listless silence, his harsh comments, the sudden intrusions of rude speech with which he had shattered so often Stephen's ardent wayward confessions? Stephen had forgiven freely for he had found this rudeness also in himself.
   New (p. 232)
   . . . Stephen had forgiven freely for he had found this rudeness also in himself towards himself.

(Though the correction is small it is important. In the passage which follows, Stephen's curious experience in Malahide is narrated. In a wood he had prayed, "knowing that he stood on holy ground and in a holy hour," but when two constabulary men appeared he had broken off his prayer and whistled an air from "the last pantomime." We can now see clearly that this Malahide episode (which was employed differently in the first draft of *Portrait* and in *Stephen Hero*) is used here to indicate Stephen's awareness of some of his own weaknesses. He senses that the "ardent, wayward" element in himself is an excess of a kind which provokes rudeness, both in others and "in himself towards himself," and he accepts this as a part of the order of things. Cranly's "rudeness" may be merely the counterpart of the rudeness Stephen displayed when he abandoned his ardent pose on the approach of the Malahide constabulary in favor of a safer (and more vulgar) display of enthusiasm. On the other hand, as the passage progresses, Stephen weighs the possibility that Cranly's current behavior may not be merely this kind of understandable rudeness but a new embarrassment occasioned by Emma's particular greeting of Cranly and his new interest in her. In a narrative as complex and delicate as this, even the restoration of two words can help elucidate a difficult passage.)

The seven restorations which have been presented here are typical of many others which might have been reproduced as well. Phrases have been added which clarify or amplify a number of sentences, especially in the sermon on hell and the aesthetic discussions, and many smaller restorations and corrections have been made which result in clearer readings or more specific assignment of speeches to particular characters. The job was necessary and has been well done. At the small risk of ending a favorable review on a sour note, I must list here corrections for a few misreadings which have been introduced into the new text:

		for	*read*
p. 22,	line 26	perfect	prefect
73	7	an	and
73	11	to as to	so as to
171	23	wonder mortal	wonder of mortal

[3]

Joyce and the Epiphany: The Key to the Labyrinth?

[1964]

I wrote this essay hoping to see it appear in *PMLA,* where it was rejected on the advice of William Noon, S.J., who advised me to stay out of criticism and stick to bibliography, for which I seemed to have some aptitude. This rankled, and it led to some public squabbling between us that I deeply regret and for which I apologized to him during his last illness. He replied that I was not the only one to blame—that "it was the Old Adam in us both." Others might blame competitive pressures in late capitalist society. As for the essay itself, it continues the explorations begun in my first essay on Stephen Dedalus, but it is a quarrelsome essay, full of what Bill Noon called the Old Adam, or the anxieties of a young critic trying to make his mark. The argument, however, still seems to me mainly right, though the tone is unfortunate.

Ever since the manuscript of *Stephen Hero* turned up in the Harvard library, the term "epiphany" has been an important concept in the criticism of Joyce's works. In 1941, Harry Levin, working with the manuscript, came upon Stephen Daedalus's theory of the epiphany and, doing the natural thing, he applied the theory to Joyce's work as a whole.[1] Since then countless students and critics have turned their attention to this aspect of Joyce. Theodore Spencer, in the preface to his edition of *Stephen Hero;* Irene Hendry, in a well-known essay, reprinted in *Two Decades of Joyce Criticism;* Hugh Kenner; William York Tindall; and S. L. Goldberg are only the most obvious names in this group. Since Levin's discovery of the concept, forty of Joyce's own epiphanies have been found, and twenty-two of them have been published by Oscar Silverman; the rest are in manuscript at Cornell.[2] Every discussion of the epiphany which I have seen is derived from Harry Levin's original discussion of the term. Later critics have elaborated on the term, refined it, located and categorized numerous passages in Joyce which they call epiphanies. But they have essentially treated the term in the same way—as a key to the labyrinth of Joyce's work. Where Mr. Levin says that *Dubliners* is a collection of epiphanies, Mr. Tindall says that each story "may be thought of as a great epiphany, and the container of little epiphanies, an epiphany of epiphanies."[3]

It may be suggested that this does not help very much in the understanding of Joyce's work, but it may be argued in defense that it does not hurt much either. Epiphany-hunting is a harmless pastime and ought probably to be condoned, like symbol-hunting, archetype-hunting, Scrabble, and other intellectual recreations. But recently two formidable critics have raised the question of the epiphany in Joyce to a higher sphere. I refer to Hugh Kenner and S. L. Goldberg, who make the epiphany crucial to our whole view of *A Portrait of the Artist as a Young Man,* and especially to our view of the character of Stephen Dedalus in that work and in *Ulysses.*[4] The argument turns on the presence of the theory of the epiphany in the aesthetic of Stephen Daedalus in *Stephen Hero* but not in that of his descendant Stephen Dedalus in *Portrait.* Assuming that the theory of the epiphany is crucial to Joyce's own aesthetic, these critics find in its absence from Stephen's aesthetic in *Portrait* a clue to Joyce's attitude toward Stephen in that work and, consequently, to the attitude we as readers should take toward Stephen. Mr. Kenner finds Stephen's aesthetic in *Portrait* deliberately weakened by Joyce so as to expose Stephen as a sham artist: "the crucial principle of epiphanization has been withdrawn." Mr. Goldberg finds Stephen's aesthetic in *Portrait* deliberately weakened by Joyce so as to expose Stephen as a shallow human being. For Mr. Goldberg the epiphany has a "moral" quality because it links art to life; thus, Stephen's failure to include it in his aesthetic theory in *Portrait* indicates that Joyce has limited Stephen's "understanding of art just as he limits his understanding of life." Mr. Goldberg further complicates his case by insisting that in *Ulysses* Stephen "seems to revert to the more satisfactory, though still vaguely formulated, insight expressed in *Stephen Hero.* To understand what the notion of epiphany properly means—a meaning that Stephen now, but only now, tacitly assumes—we must turn to the remaining aspects of the Thomist theory of knowledge." Mr. Goldberg suggests that the notion of the epiphany has been withdrawn from Stephen in *Portrait* and "tacitly" returned in *Ulysses.* Which means, I am afraid, that he can find no mention of the theory in either *Portrait* or *Ulysses* but chooses, in order to implement his own interpretation of the works, to smuggle the notion back into one but not the other. He complains about critics who want to "save" Stephen's aesthetic in *Portrait* "by interpreting it in the light of—or rather, by conflating it with—ideas from outside the *Portrait.* Some want to add the notion of 'epiphany' from *Stephen Hero* to give a moral content to claritas. . . . " But Mr. Goldberg finds it necessary to "save" Stephen in *Ulysses* by the same kind of ingenious conflation.

In this essay, I wish to raise the question of whether the concept is worth all the importance attached to it by Joyce's critics; whether it is indeed a key, and if so, a key to what. In the process of dealing with these questions I hope to clarify to some extent what Joyce himself understood by the term: what it means in *Stephen Hero,* and what the forty extant samples of Joyce's own epiphanies indicate that it must have meant for Joyce. These questions are all, obviously, interrelated. The only specific definition of epiphany in Joyce's writings, including those unpublished manuscripts which are available for inspection, is that given in *Stephen Hero.* It is there that we must begin.

Most students of literature will be familiar with this definition, but I must quote it again here in the interests of exactness. In *Stephen Hero* Joyce uses two narrative devices to acquaint the reader with Stephen's theory. First the narrator presents Stephen's thoughts on the subject in the context in which he first conceived the notion of epiphany:

> He was passing through Eccles' St. one evening, one misty evening, with all these thoughts dancing the dance of unrest in his brain when a trivial incident set him composing some ardent verses which he entitled a "Vilanelle of the Temptress." A young lady was standing on the steps of one of those brown brick houses which seem the very incarna-

> tion of Irish paralysis. A young gentleman was leaning on the rusty railings of the area. Stephen as he passed on his quest heard the following fragment of colloquy out of which he received an impression keen enough to afflict his sensitiveness very severely.
>
> The Young Lady–(drawling discreetly)... O, yes... I was... at the... cha... pel...
>
> The Young Gentleman–(inaudibly)... I... (again inaudibly)... I...
>
> The Young Lady–(softly)... O... but you're... ve... ry... wick ... ed...
>
> This triviality made him think of collecting many such moments together in a book of epiphanies. By an epiphany he meant a sudden spiritual manifestation, whether in the vulgarity of speech or of gesture or in a memorable phase of the mind itself. He believed that it was for the man of letters to record these epiphanies with extreme care, seeing that they themselves are the most delicate and evanescent of moments.[5]

Following this we see Stephen explain the concept to Cranly, relating it to the three stages in aesthetic apprehension which he has derived from Aquinas. The epiphany is associated with the third and final phase of aesthetic apprehension. After the wholeness and symmetry of the object are apprehended, its radiance is apprehended:

> –Now for the third quality. For a long time I couldn't make out what Aquinas meant. He uses a figurative word (a very unusual thing for him) but I have solved it. *Claritas* is *quidditas.* After the analysis which discovers the second quality the mind makes the only logically possible synthesis and discovers the third quality. This is the moment which I call epiphany. First we recognise that the object is *one* integral thing, then we recognise that it is an organised composite structure, a *thing* in fact: finally, when the relation of the parts is exquisite, when the parts are adjusted to the special point, we recognise that it is *that* thing which it is. Its soul, its whatness, leaps to us from the vestment of its appearance. The soul of the commonest object, the structure of which is so adjusted, seems to us radiant. The object achieves its epiphany.[6]

The heart of this definition, in both its contexts, I take to be the notion that an epiphany is a *spiritual* manifestation. Joyce was certainly aware of the use of the term in Christian tradition for the showing forth of Christ to the Magi and for other spiritual manifestations, and was probably aware of its use to designate that climactic moment in Greek drama when a god makes his appearance to resolve the action. The *spiritual* nature of the phenomenon is emphasized in the second context in *Stephen Hero* as well as in the first. "Its soul, its whatness, leaps to us from the vestment of its appearance. The soul of the commonest object, the structure of which is so adjusted, seems to us radiant."

In the discussion with Lynch which replaces the discussion with Cranly as the vehicle for the presentation of aesthetic theory in *Portrait,* we arrive ultimately at a moment analogous to the moment in *Stephen Hero* when *claritas,* or radiance, was explained as the achievement of epiphany:

> —The connotation of the word—Stephen said—is rather vague. Aquinas uses a term which seems to be inexact. It baffled me for a long time. It would lead you to believe that he had in mind symbolism or idealism, the supreme quality of beauty being a light from some other world, the idea of which the matter was but the shadow, the reality of which it was but the symbol. I thought he might mean that *claritas* was the artistic discovery and representation of the divine purpose in anything or a force of generalization which would make the esthetic image a universal one, make it outshine its proper conditions. But that is literary talk. I understand it so. When you have apprehended that basket as one thing and have then analysed it according to its form and apprehended it as a thing you make the only synthesis which is logically and esthetically permissible. You see that it is that thing which it is and no other thing. The radiance of which he speaks is the scholastic *quidditas,* the *whatness* of a thing.[7]

Here the notion of the actual thing being merely a symbol of some ideal thing is specifically rejected by Stephen. He indicates that, though he once held that view, he no longer does. The concept of the epiphany, the spiritual manifestation, is not beyond Stephen; he is beyond it. The thing in itself is now enough for him. He has worked himself free of Platonic idealism, in theory at least. Joyce must have gone through the same process. But when we try to move from Stephen's aesthetic to Joyce's we are on very shaky ground. Nearly all of Joyce's own statements on aesthetics antedate the final writing of *Portrait* by many years. In fact, almost all the extant writings on this subject antedate *Stephen Hero* as well. Probably Joyce lost interest in it. A rejection of idealism leads ultimately to a rejection of aesthetics itself, which deals not with things but with ideas.

We can be certain, however, that Stephen is more of an idealist in

Stephen Hero and more of a realist in *Portrait.* Which position is superior, I must leave to the aestheticians. Still, certain other aspects of the theory of the epiphany in *Stephen Hero* should be examined. The sample epiphany we are given should not be ignored, nor should the specific terms of the definition. We are given a snatch of overheard dialogue as a sample, and two forms of epiphany are specifically designated. Both the sample and the forms may be related to Joyce's own practice in writing his epiphanies.

We are told that the epiphany may take either of two forms: (a) vulgarity of speech or gesture, and (b) a memorable phase of the mind itself. We will find, on examination, that Joyce's own epiphanies readily fall into one or the other of these two categories, but before turning to Joyce's practice we should examine the theory more closely. The assumptions which underlie the dual formula for epiphanization are interesting. Form (a) involves observation of phenomena external to the observer. Form (b) involves observation of phenomena within the observer's mind. The observer assumes that the external phenomena will be "vulgar" and that the internal phenomena will be "memorable." The assumption that the observer (the "man of letters," as he is termed) is superior to his environment is built into the concept itself. Stephen in *Stephen Hero* is not only much closer to the symbolist movement in his neo-Platonic insistence on spiritual manifestations; he is also much closer to fin de siècle aestheticism than Stephen in *Portrait.* In a word, the earlier Stephen is much more a man of the nineteenth century than the later Stephen.

If the separation of the observer and the world is clear in the theory of the epiphany, other aspects of the theory are far from clear. The achievement of epiphany seems to depend on the eye of the observer, but the *object* achieves *its* epiphany. One aspect Stephen does not consider is the reaction of the observer to an epiphany. Does it work any change in him? Is he wiser because of it? We do not know. Nor do we know the relationship of the epiphany to art, and this is a great question. Any object—a person, a clock, a mind—can achieve epiphany. The phenomenon is in no way related to the creative process. Even the recording of the phenomenon can be done by a "man of letters." No artist is required. In *Portrait* Stephen carefully distinguishes the process of aesthetic apprehension from artistic creation. And he says, with a certain amount of humility, "When we come to the phenomena of artistic conception, artistic gestation, and artistic reproduction,

I require a new terminology and a new personal experience."[8] The intention here seems to be to project three stages of creation parallel to the three stages of apprehension. But Stephen does not feel competent enough yet as a creative artist to deal with these stages. He needs "a new personal experience." He suggests, however, in his discussion of the final phase of apprehension, that this last phase may be in the mind of an artist the first phase of creation: "This supreme quality [*quidditas,* the *whatness* of a thing] is felt by the artist when the esthetic image is first conceived in his imagination."

By making Stephen aware of his limitations, Joyce has, in effect, strengthened Stephen's hand. Moreover, the aesthetic theory in *Portrait* is in fact much clearer than that in *Stephen Hero.* This is so partly because of the clarification of the relationship between creation and apprehension and partly because of the elimination of the troublesome and confusing theory of the epiphany. For Joyce's critics, however, the very sketchiness of the theory has been an asset. They have been able to make whatever they wanted of it. They have even been able to consider it what it never was in Stephen's theory, and certainly not in Joyce's mind, a principle of structure in fiction. One may sympathize with them in this attempt. But when devotion to the theory goes so far that its absence from *Portrait* is held against Stephen, it is time to call for a return to sanity. If Joyce himself took the theory seriously after 1904 we would almost certainly have some mention of it in his letters or notebooks or conversations. Certainly, as his behavior over *Ulysses* and *Finnegans Wake* shows, he was not backward about giving clues to sympathetic readers for the understanding of his works. But the epiphany seems never to have been in his recorded thoughts except in *Stephen Hero,* a manuscript with which he was dissatisfied and which he never meant to publish. The term, it is true, appears once in *Ulysses,* in a passage which ought to embarrass epiphanizing critics more than it has in the past. On Sandymount strand Stephen recalls his early literary pretensions, among which were his epiphanies:

> Reading two pages apiece of seven books every night, eh? I was young. You bowed to yourself in the mirror, stepping forward to applause earnestly, striking face. Hurray for the God-damned idiot! Hray! No-one saw: tell no-one. Books you were going to write with letters for titles. Have you read his F? O yes, but I prefer Q. Yes, but W is wonderful. O yes, W. Remember your epiphanies on green oval

> leaves, deeply deep, copies to be sent if you died to all the great libraries of the world, including Alexandria? Someone was to read them there after a few thousand years, a mahamanvantara. Pico della Mirandola like. Ay, very like a whale. When one reads these strange pages of one long gone one feels that one is at one with one who once. . . . [9]

The epiphanies themselves for the most part bear out Stephen's condemnation of them. They are trivial and supercilious or florid and lugubrious, in the main. Their chief significance is in the use Joyce often made of them in his later works. Twenty-two of them which are in manuscript at the University of Buffalo have already been published. Twenty-five are in manuscript at Cornell and have not been published, except for seven which are the same as those at Buffalo. These forty epiphanies fall readily into the two categories which Joyce outlined in *Stephen Hero:* vulgarities of speech or gesture, and memorable phases of the mind itself. I cannot examine all the epiphanies in detail here, but I will make one or two assertions about their use and attempt to illustrate these assertions. First, more of the known epiphanies are used by Joyce in *Stephen Hero* than in *Portrait,* and more in *Portrait* than in *Ulysses.* Second, Joyce's use of the epiphanies became freer and more creative progressively. I believe I can illustrate this tendency by examining Joyce's subsequent use of two epiphanies. The first, number 14 in the Buffalo volume published by Oscar Silverman, is used in both *Stephen Hero* and *Ulysses.* The three versions are as follows:

1. Epiphany

> Two mourners push on through the crowd. The girl, one hand catching the woman's skirt, runs in advance. The girl's face is the face of a fish, discoloured and oblique-eyed; the woman's face is small and square, the face of a bargainer. The girl, her mouth distorted, looks up at the woman to see if it is time to cry; the woman, settling a flat bonnet, hurries on towards the mortuary chapel.

2. *Stephen Hero*

> Two of them who were late pushed their way viciously through the crowd. /A girl, one hand catching the woman's skirt, ran a pace in advance. The girl's face was the face of a fish, discoloured and oblique-eyed; the woman's face was square and pinched, the face of a bargainer.

> The girl, her mouth distorted, looked up at the woman to see if it was time to cry:/ the woman, settling a flat bonnet, hurried on towards the mortuary chapel.[10]

3. *Ulysses*

> Mourners came out through the gates: woman and a girl. Leanjawed harpy, hard woman at a bargain, her bonnet awry. Girl's face stained with dirt and tears, holding the woman's arm looking up at her for a sign to cry. Fish's face, bloodless and livid.[11]

The changes in the *Stephen Hero* version are the minimum necessary to accommodate the present-tense epiphany to the past-tense narrative. In the *Ulysses* version, however, the scene has to be accommodated not merely to narrative prose but to the mental processes of Leopold Bloom. Thus, "leanjawed harpy, hard woman at a bargain" is not merely description but Bloom's shrewd appraisal of character. The incident itself has been subordinated to Bloom's view of it, the prose pared down to the essential minimum required to indicate Bloom's apprehension. The manuscript of *Stephen Hero* bears Joyce's selecting crayon marks through the part of the passage he borrowed for re-use. The original "spiritual manifestation" through vulgarity of gesture has become a very tiny building block in a very large edifice. An essentially artless recording of actuality has been given a place in a work of art by the shaping imagination of its creator. It has become more meaningful in relation to Bloom than it ever was in its own right. But it is no longer an "epiphany"; it has become an incident. We can observe a similar process at work in Joyce's use of the following epiphany in *Portrait:*

1. Epiphany

> Faintly, under the heavy summer night, through the silence of the town which has turned from dreams to dreamless sleep as a weary lover whom no carresses move, the sound of hoofs upon the Dublin road. Not so faintly now as they come near the bridge: and in a moment as they pass the dark windows the silence is cloven by alarm as by an arrow. They are heard now far away—hoofs that shine amid the heavy night as diamonds, hurrying beyond the grey, still marshes to what journey's end—what heart—bearing what tidings?[12]

2. *Portrait*

> *April 10.* Faintly, under the heavy night, through the silence of the city which has turned from dreams to dreamless sleep as a weary lover whom no caresses move, the sound of hoofs upon the road. Not so faintly now as they come near the bridge: and in a moment as they pass the darkened windows the silence is cloven by alarm as by an arrow. They are heard now far away, hoofs that shine amid the heavy night as gems, hurrying beyond the sleeping fields to what journey's end—what heart?—bearing what tidings?[13]

Here, though there are changes, they are insignificant. The former epiphany has become the entry for April 10 in Stephen's diary. But the significant difference lies in the context. It was the essence of epiphany in Joyce's youthful theory and practice that it had no context. Each was a little independent gem of vulgarity or "a memorable phase of the mind itself." The sample we have here is of the latter kind. But it is now in a context. It is followed immediately by another diary entry: "*April 11.* Read what I wrote last night. Vague words for a vague emotion. Would she like it? I think so. Then I should have to like it also." Stephen here is given by Joyce the advantage of some of his own ten or more years of maturity since the epiphany was first recorded. Stephen is critical of it himself but prepared to accept it if "she" (presumably E. C.) likes it. The epiphany here is no longer a "spiritual manifestation" but a piece of prose, subject to criticism like any other. And it is functioning dramatically in an artistic context, revealing character, attitude, and emotion. Another fragment, recorded by young James Joyce in his "man of letters" phase, has been rescued from the "green oval leaves, deeply deep," and been put to work by an older James Joyce, a literary artist. From that last phase of apprehension which makes the object radiant and coincides with artistic conception, this object has passed through ten years of gestation to its final reproduction in *A Portrait of the Artist as a Young Man.*

What then, finally, is to be the use of this term *epiphany* in Joyce criticism? I would suggest a very limited use. The phrase should designate those little bits of prose which Joyce himself gave the name to, as we find them in their raw and inartistic state. As a term to be used in the criticism of Joyce's art itself, I would like to see it abandoned entirely. To those who first discovered the term in *Stephen Hero* it must have seemed indeed to be the key to the labyrinth of

Daedalus. But the way to the labyrinth, like the descent to Avernus, is an easy journey. It is only the return which presents difficulties. In André Gide's *Theseus* the fabulous artificer tells the aspiring hero that the most dangerous aspect of the labyrinth is not the difficulty of the passage nor the Minotaur himself, but the headiness of the vapors of the place, which make its tenants reluctant to return. Icarus himself, in Gide's story, has succumbed to these vapors and, though rescued physically, he is a dead thing, his mind wandering in mazes of metaphysics. I should like to suggest that both Joyce and Stephen entered this Platonic darkness at one time via the key of the epiphany, and that they both emerged, tempered by their trials. It is the critics who love those heady vapors so much that they refuse to emerge. To them, I can say only, "Come up, come up, you fearful Jesuits."

Notes

1. Harry Levin, *James Joyce* (New York: New Directions, 1960), especially pp. 28-31.
2. Silverman's volume was published in 1956 by the Lockwood Memorial Library of the University of Buffalo. The Cornell items are listed in my catalog of the Cornell Joyce Collection, published by Cornell University Press, items 15, 17, and 18.
3. William York Tindall, *A Reader's Guide to James Joyce* (New York: Farrar, Straus and Cudahy, 1951), p. 11.
4. See Hugh Kenner, *Dublin's Joyce* (Bloomington: Indiana University Press, 1956), chap. 9, "The School of Old Aquinas"; and S. L. Goldberg, *The Classical Temper* (New York: Barnes and Noble, 1961), chaps. 2 and 3, especially pp. 63, 71.
5. James Joyce, *Stephen Hero* (New York: New Directions, 1955), pp. 210-11.
6. Ibid., p. 213.
7. James Joyce, *A Portrait of the Artist as a Young Man* (New York: Modern Library, 1928), pp. 249-50.
8. Ibid., pp. 245-46.
9. James Joyce, *Ulysses* (New York: Modern Library, 1934), p. 41.
10. *Stephen Hero,* p. 167. I have used slashes here to indicate that part of the passage subsequently crossed out by Joyce with crayon, as indicated in this edition.
11. *Ulysses,* p. 100.
12. In manuscript at Cornell, item 17d in my catalog. The misspelling *carresses* may be the fault of Stanislaus Joyce, from whose copy this is taken.
13. *Portrait,* p. 297.

[4]

Stephen Dedalus, Poet or Aesthete?

[1964]

This essay was first sent to the *Sewanee Review,* where it was rejected at about the same time as "Joyce and the Epiphany: The Key to the Labyrinth?" was rejected by *PMLA.* Ironically, each one, then sent to the other journal, was accepted, with the result that the one with footnotes, designed for the more scholarly publication, appeared in the critical journal, and this one, without notes, in the scholarly one.

Reading this essay now, I think that it overstates its case somewhat, in its attempt to answer Wayne Booth's overstated case on the other side. My admiration for Joyce was still very strong in those days, and I would not rule out a certain amount of association of my youthful self with Stephen Dedalus. Such investments, however ludicrous they seem in later years, remain an important part of the reading process. They also help to give academic essays like this one a certain urgency that extends their durability a bit. My project here connects directly to the previous essays on *Portrait,* in that it reads the presentation of Stephen as being less ironical than most people felt it to be. Wayne Booth argued that *Portrait,* like many other modern works, suffered from being too ambiguous in its value judgments. That is, he shared my view that the book was not dominated by an ironical distancing of Stephen. But Booth found this a problem because of his own ethical stance: he would have liked more ironic distancing than he found. I, on the other hand, was too close to both Stephen and Joyce to want any more distance than I encountered. For a time, I took Joyce to be exactly what a modern writer ought to be—the very model of literary perfection.

The problem of Stephen Dedalus is one of the most curious and interesting in modern letters. One aspect of the problem has been brought to our attention recently in a very impressive book by Wayne C. Booth, *The Rhetoric of Fiction* (Chicago, 1961). Booth notes that *A Portrait of the Artist as a Young Man* was not, by its first readers, thought to be an ironic work. It was after the publication of *Ulysses,* with its presentation of Stephen as the fallen Icarus, that the reassessment of Stephen's character began; and it was the publication of the *Stephen Hero* fragment in 1944 which really accelerated the movement toward a view of the novel as mainly ironic, with Stephen seen as a posturing aesthete rather than an actual or even a potential artist. The most extreme version of this ironic view of Stephen has been proposed by Hugh Kenner, in his *Dublin's Joyce* (1955).

Joyce's Flaubertian refusal to provide authoritative commentary on his characters within his works seems to open the way to any possible interpretation, making a definitive or even a consensus interpretation extremely difficult. And, however much our New Critical yearnings make us want to consider *Portrait* as a work-in-itself, we are led by Joyce's own writings in ever-widening circles. If the Stephen in *Ulysses* is the same person as the Stephen in *Portrait*—and there seems to be no question about this—then we must consider *Ulysses* in interpreting *Portrait.* By a similar chain of reasoning we find ourselves led to *Stephen Hero,* with its theory of the epiphany, thence to Joyce's own epiphanies—those little prose pieces which he wrote from his own observation and then often used as fictional incidents or descriptions in *Stephen Hero* and *Portrait*—until finally we reluctantly discover that everything about Joyce is relevant in some way to our interpretation of *Portrait,* and we either devote a large chunk of our lives to the problem of Joyce or give up the problem in despair. How much simpler the problem would be if we had only to consider Stephen as he appears in those works which Joyce meant for publication, in *Portrait* and *Ulysses;* but the publication of *Stephen Hero* is equivalent for us to the opening of Pandora's box. It is too late now to go back. We can never recover our lost innocence.

I mean to suggest that since we cannot go back we must go on. Since we cannot rely on our innocence to preserve us from the dangers of misinterpretation, we must gain the maximum of experience. In a fallen critical world we must commit all the fallacies, including the intentional, in order to work out our own salvation. It is in this spirit that I wish to turn to one specific aspect of the problem of Stephen Dedalus, in the hope that it may illuminate the problem as a whole. The question is raised by Booth in his discussion of "The Problem of Distance in 'A Portrait of the Artist'" (*Rhetoric of Fiction,* pp. 323–36). He focuses our attention on the poem which Stephen writes in the last chapter of the book: "Finally, what of the precious villanelle? Does Joyce intend it to be taken as a serious sign of Stephen's artistry, as a sign of his genuine but amusingly pretentious precocity, or as something else entirely. . . . Hardly anyone has committed himself in public about the quality of this poem. Are we to smile at Stephen or pity him in his tortured longing? Are we to marvel at his artistry, or scoff at his conceit?"

I think we can answer some of those questions now with considerable assurance—at least insofar as Joyce's intentions in the matter are concerned. And I hope to provide a generally satisfactory interpretation of the episode of the poem. We must begin by reviewing the composition of the poem in its narrative context. It follows directly the long episode of the aesthetic discussion with Lynch, which closes with a rain-shower. Stephen and Lynch take refuge from the rain under the library arcade. There, after the shower, Stephen sees the girl who has most interested him in his youth. He has come to feel as alienated from her as from those aspects of Ireland he associates with her—the Gaelic League, the priests, and the comfortable hypocrisy of the Philistine citizens of Dublin, who are preoccupied with piety but are neither spiritual nor religious. As he sees her going off demurely with some other girls after the shower, he wonders if he has judged her too harshly. At this point the episode closes. In the next sentence we are with Stephen as he wakes the following morning, after an enchanting dream in which he has "known the ecstasy of seraphic life" (Viking Compass edition, p. 217).

As he wakes, Stephen finds that he has an idea for a poem, which he begins at once to compose. The composition of the poem is presented to us in detail during the next few pages of narration, along with Stephen's thoughts, which center on the girl, on other women who have called out to him in the street, and on the mysterious country woman who had invited the gentle Davin into her cottage, all of whom merge into a composite symbol of Irish womanhood–batlike souls waking to consciousness in darkness and secrecy. Between them and him lies the shadow of the Irish priesthood. To the priest, the girl (E.C.) "would unveil her soul's shy nakedness, to one who was but schooled in the discharging of a formal rite rather than to him, a priest of the eternal imagination, transmuting the daily bread of experience into the radiant body of everlasting life." Despite his bitterness Stephen comes, through the composition of the poem, to an understanding of her innocence, an equilibrium, a stasis, in which his new understanding and pity balance his old desire and bitterness. He turns, finally, from thoughts of the girl to a vision of the temptress of his villanelle, a personification of a feminine ideal, something like the white goddess-muse of Robert Graves's mythology. Stephen's spiritual copulation with her is a symbolic equivalent for that moment of inspiration when "in the virgin womb of the imagination the word was made flesh" (p. 217):

> A glow of desire kindled again his soul and fired and fulfilled all his body. Conscious of his desire she was waking from odorous sleep, the temptress of his villanelle. Her eyes, dark and with a look of languor, were opening to his eyes. Her nakedness yielded to him, radiant, warm odorous and lavishlimbed, enfolded him like a shining cloud, enfolded him like water with a liquid life: and like a cloud of vapour or like waters circumfluent in space the liquid letters of speech, symbols of the element of mystery, flowed forth over his brain. (p. 223)

The temptress of his dream suggests his service to art, just as at the end of the previous chapter the girl on the beach, the "envoy from the fair courts of life," symbolizes the freedom of life as opposed to the cloistered virtue offered Stephen in the priesthood: "To live, to err, to fall, to triumph, to recreate life out of life!" (p. 172). The creation of life out of life is the privilege of both the lover and the artist. The physical copulation of the human animal and the spiritual copulation of the artist in which the word is made flesh are valid and complementary manifestations of the same human impulse toward creation. There is no hint of mockery in Joyce's reverent attitude toward the creative process.

In order to fulfill the term of Stephen's aesthetic gestation, it was necessary for Joyce to present us with a created thing, with a literary work which was the product of his inspiration. He chose for this purpose the Villanelle of the Temptress. Why? And what, as Booth asks, are we to make of it? Here we must turn to biographical information and manuscript material for help. The poem itself (or a version of it) was actually written by Joyce long before *Portrait.* It dates from one of his early collections of verse, probably the lost "Shine and Dark" of 1900 or 1901 (see Stanislaus Joyce, *My Brother's Keeper* [New York, 1958], pp. 85–86). It is a distinctly better poem than most of the surviving fragments of that collection, as the reader may verify by consulting Richard Ellmann's *James Joyce* (New York, 1959), pp. 84–85, where these fragments have been published. That Joyce thought it superior is attested to by his keeping it for fifteen years though he destroyed nearly every other sample of his pre-*Chamber Music* verse, leaving us only the tattered fragments which his brother saved. But Joyce's overriding reason for using this particular poem must have been its subject. It was the perfect poem, and it had been written by himself when he was only slightly younger than Stephen. The poem thus satisfied both the naturalistic urge and the symbolic urge in Joyce. As fact and symbolic artifact it was indisputably the right thing. (His continuing interest in this subject and the poetic materials of the Villanelle is evidenced by his reuse of them in the poem "Nightpiece" of *Pomes Penyeach,* which is very close to Stephen's poem in theme and imagery, though very different in prosody.)

How perfectly its subject matter suited Joyce's purposes can be seen only when the poem is understood. To this reader it seems obvious that the failure of critics to understand the function of the villanelle stems from their failure to understand what the poem is about. It is ironic that in this one instance, in which Joyce himself has provided a commentary on his own work, such problems in understanding should have arisen; for the poem comes to us, in *Portrait,* embedded not only in the circumstances of its creation but in an elaborate explication as well. But even with Joyce's explicatory narrative the poem is a difficult one. The difficulty stems from its complexity of thought. It is a far richer poem than the ninetyish verses which it appears to resemble. So that my commentary may be specific, here is the full text of the poem:

> Are you not weary of ardent ways,
> Lure of the fallen seraphim?
> Tell no more of enchanted days.

Your eyes have set man's heart ablaze
And you have had your will of him.
Are you not weary of ardent ways?

Above the flame the smoke of praise
Goes up from ocean rim to rim.
Tell no more of enchanted days.

Our broken cries and mournful lays
Rise in one eucharistic hymn.
Are you not weary of ardent ways?

While sacrificing hands upraise
The chalice flowing to the brim.
Tell no more of enchanted days.

And still you hold our longing gaze
With languorous look and lavish limb!
Are you not weary of ardent ways?
Tell no more of enchanted days.

The first question which must be resolved is the nature of the person addressed. She is, as I have suggested above, a composite figure, but I want now to elaborate on her composition, taking my cues from the explication provided. In describing the moment of inspiration as that instant when "In the virgin womb of the imagination the word was made flesh," the narrator has established a parallel between artistic creation and the divine begetting of the Son of God. The next sentences gloss this parallel and provide an interpretation of the first tercet:

> Gabriel the seraph had come to the virgin's chamber. An afterglow deepened within his spirit, whence the white flame had passed, deepening into a rose and ardent light. That rose and ardent light was her strange wilful heart, strange that no man had known or would know, wilful from before the beginning of the world: and lured by that ardent roselike glow the choirs of the seraphim were falling from heaven. (p. 217)

In this violently compressed fusion of myth and theology the ardent heart of the virgin mother of the Redeemer is seen as the cause of the fall of the rebellious angels. This is a variation on the *felix culpa* notion that Adam's fall was fortunate because its result was the birth of the

Redeemer. Joyce's version upsets chronology and causality as well as theology by making one of the results of Satan's fall function as the prime cause of that fall. Mary is the "Lure of the fallen seraphim." The poem is addressed, initially at any rate, to her.

The second tercet is explicated similarly: "The roselike glow sent forth its rays of rhyme: ways, days, blaze, praise, raise. Its rays burned up the world, consumed the hearts of men and angels: the rays from the rose that was her wilful heart" (p. 217). Here the ardent glow is seen to perform two functions. In Stephen's mind it inspires rays of rhyme for his artistic creation. In its more general manifestation it has consumed the hearts of men and angels.

In the third tercet the smoke from the burning heart of man rises as "incense ascending from the altar of the world." At this point Stephen's thoughts turn from the earth as a "ball of incense" to the phrase "an ellipsoidal ball," which is an echo of vulgar student scatology coming into Stephen's mind by association and breaking the spell of inspiration. His thoughts wander through all the various female associations mentioned above until his image of himself as "a priest of the eternal imagination transmuting the daily bread of experience into the radiant body of everlasting life" returns his mind to the altar and incense of the villanelle; and he composes the fourth and fifth tercets around the image of the Eucharist. The "smoke of praise" and the rimmed ocean suggest the thurible and the chalice—images which Stephen handles in the poem, though he will "never swing the thurible before the tabernacle" in actuality. After his mind has wandered back again to E.C. and his youthful romantic feelings for her, his thoughts dissolve in the moment of spiritual copulation quoted above. Here he finds his image for the "languorous look and lavish limb" of the conclusion.

The paradox of the Virgin as Temptress has given the whole poem a peculiar tone, which, if we did not consider carefully, we might be tempted to write off as merely blasphemous. But the poem is not *merely* anything. It is a commonplace of biblical exegesis that Eve, in the Old Testament, is a type of Mary in the New Testament, just as Adam is a type of Jesus. Joyce's awareness of this derives from his reading of St. Augustine and other church fathers, as shown in this passage from the "Oxen of the Sun" section of *Ulysses:*

> Desire's wind blasts the thorntree but after it becomes from a bramblebush to be a rose upon the rood of time. Mark me now. In woman's

womb word is made flesh but in the spirit of the maker all flesh that passes becomes the word that shall not pass away. This is the postcreation. *Omnis caro ad te veniet.* No question but her name is puissant who aventried the dear corse of our Agenbuyer, Healer and Herd, our mighty mother and mother most venerable and Bernardus saith aptly that she hath an *omnipotentiam deiparae supplicem,* that is to wit, an almightiness of petition because she is the second Eve and she won us, saith Augustine too, whereas that other, our grandam, which we are all linked upon with by successive anastomosis of navelcords sold us all, seed, breed and generation, for a penny pippin. (Modern Library, unrevised edition, p. 385)

Beyond the parallel between Eve and Mary, Joyce seems to have in mind a similar and even more paradoxical parallel between Satan and Gabriel. Satan literally fell from heaven, but Gabriel was lured "to the virgin's chamber" so that the word could be made flesh. And Stephen himself has known in the arms of his dream temptress "the ecstasy of *seraphic* life" (my italics). Thus the term *fallen seraphim* of the first tercet applies not only to Satan but to Gabriel as well, and finally, by his own imaginative extension, to Stephen himself and the male principle in general—what may be said to be represented by that rising-fallen phoenix culprit HCE in *Finnegans Wake.* And, by a similar mental process the temptress can be Eve in relation to Satan, Mary to Gabriel, E.C. to Stephen, and the female principle in general—the Anna Livia Plurabelle of *Finnegans Wake.*

The medievalness of Joyce's mind can hardly be overemphasized. Not only is he capable of a medieval kind of religious parody without blasphemy (comparable to the *Second Shepherds' Play* and other biblical romps) but he thinks in types and tropes constantly. The whole "metempsychosis" motif in *Ulysses* is allegorical in its operation, and the various multicharacters of *Finnegans Wake* are conceived in that medieval spirit which could not consider even Hercules without seeing Christ superimposed on him. The kind of mental process which culminates in *Finnegans Wake* seems to be operating in Joyce's handling of the villanelle in *Portrait.* His original conception of the poem may even have been trivial. In *Stephen Hero* we are told that the insipid epiphany of the Young Lady and the Young Gentleman (New York, 1955, p. 211) set Stephen composing "some ardent verses which he entitled 'Vilanelle [*sic*] of the Temptress'." But by the time he rewrote the last part of *Portrait* for publication he had seen larger possibilities in the poem, which he exploited by connecting its inspiration to Stephen's glimpse of E.C. at the library (instead of the Young Lady and Gentleman) and providing the poem with the narrative commentary which we now have. We cannot be sure, of course, that we are dealing with the same poem. Joyce's drastic revision of "Tilly" for *Pomes Penyeach,* in which he completely reversed the mood and meaning of the poem from a sentimental idyll to a bitter cry of anguish, is warning enough to make us proceed with caution here (see Chester Anderson's essay in *PMLA,* 73, June 1958, p. 285). But Joyce certainly reinterpreted the poem, possibly revising it in accordance with his new view, making it unmistakably clear from the context that the "you" addressed in the opening line is, initially at least, the Virgin Mary.

Eve is our first mother and Mary is our second, a "second Eve" as Augustine saith (according to Stephen in the "Oxen of the Sun"). But in the Bible Eve figures as first temptress as well as first mother. And this feminine principle–irrational, sensual, seductive–becomes in Joyce's inversion of traditional typology equally the property of Mary and Eve. The ardent heart of the Virgin lured Gabriel the seraph to her chamber and precipitated, in advance of her own birth, the fall of Satan and his seraphim, who, through Eve, caused the fall of man. Not only are Eve and Mary fused in the image of the Temptress (and that other temptress, Lilith, perhaps) but such other figures as E.C. herself, girls who have laughed at Stephen or called out to him in the street, and the mysterious woman who invited Davin into her cottage. The last woman is of special significance. She brings the Celtic Twilight into Joyce's narrative. Davin rejected her offer partly through his innate goodness and innocence, and partly through a vague fear that she was not all she seemed to be. The Irish fairies, the Shee, hover over Davin's story. And one in particular hovers over Stephen's poem. "The Leanhaun Shee (fairy mistress)," Yeats wrote in his collection of *Fairy and Folk Tales of the Irish Peasantry* (1888),

> seeks the love of mortals. If they refuse, she must be their slave; if they consent, they are hers, and can only escape by finding another to take their place. The fairy lives on their life, and they waste away. Death is no escape from her. She is the Gaelic muse, for she gives inspiration to

> those she persecutes. The Gaelic poets die young, for she is restless and will not let them remain long on earth—this malignant phantom . . .
>
> She is of the dreadful solitary fairies. To her have belonged the greatest of the Irish poets, from Oisin down to the last century. (pp. 80, 146)

Though Oliver Gogarty addressed him as the Wandering Ængus (letters in manuscript at Cornell), Joyce had specifically repudiated the "Gaelic League" approach to literature. Stephen's poem is more Catholic than Celtic. Its literary models are the poems of the nineties: the villanelles of Ernest Dowson and such "mother" poems as Swinburne's "Mater Triumphalis" (especially ll. 33–44 and 93–105), and Francis Thompson's "The After Woman." And its ancestors are such romantic treatments of this theme as Blake's "The Mental Traveller" and Keats's "La Belle Dame Sans Merci." Thus, Stephen's villanelle must be read partly as an effort in this recognizable subgenre, where its compressed coolness compares quite favorably with the feverish looseness of Swinburne and Company. But the Leanhaun Shee, nevertheless, haunts Stephen's poem because it is a muse-poem. Joyce has unerringly selected for Stephen's single poetic effort in *Portrait* a great poetical archetype—what Robert Graves has called the "single poetic theme."

Joyce, steeped in Catholic theology more strongly than in Celtic mythology, nevertheless knew his Yeats as well as anyone and knew most of the nineteenth-century Irish poets as well—as his essays on Mangan indicate. He might even have known a muse-poem such as Thomas Boyd's "To the Leanán Sidhe." In the "Villanelle of the Temptress" Stephen is writing a poem to his muse, who is a traditionally feminine and mythic figure, though the imagery through which she is presented is drawn almost exclusively from Catholic ritual and ceremony. He sees himself a priest of the imagination celebrating a eucharistic ritual of transubstantiation—the daily bread of experience becoming the radiant body of everlasting life—and a ritual of incarnation as well—in the virgin womb of the imagination the word is made flesh. And to render these qualities in his vision artistically he presents them in a rigidly prescribed aesthetic form, the villanelle, in which the temptress-muse is worshiped in a eucharistic ritual. From the heart set ablaze by the langorous look of the temptress rises incense of praise. For the virgin who lured the seraphim from heaven a flowing chalice is raised in celebration.

The strange woman who tempted Davin has been recognized by Stephen, while writing the poem, as a "figure of the womanhood of her country." And so is Stephen's temptress such a figure. Like the Leanhaun Shee herself, Ireland is a female figure who destroys those who serve her. They call her Kathleen ni Houlihan or Dark Rosaleen or the Shan Van Vocht or the old sow that eats her farrow. Stephen's particular problem is to help the batlike soul of this female to awake, to serve her without being destroyed by her; to forge in the smithy of his own soul the uncreated conscience of *her* race. He wants, among other things, to turn her from the enchanted Celtic Twilight to the daylight of his own time. The villanelle is half his self-dedication to a hopeless task and half a prayer for release from the pitiless muse and country whose service is his accepted destiny. The appearance of the milk woman in the opening scene of *Ulysses* starts Stephen's mind working along these same lines (pp. 15–16).

That Joyce intended the poem to be the product of genuine inspiration can be readily demonstrated by an examination of the manuscripts. In Trieste, during the years 1907 to 1914, Joyce kept a notebook in which he jotted down many thoughts and descriptions later used in *Portrait* and *Ulysses.* Whole sentences and large parts of paragraphs on Cranly, Lynch, Buck Mulligan, and Stephen's parents come from his notebook, which Joyce began after he had abandoned the *Stephen Hero* version of *Portrait.* The section of this notebook labeled "Esthetic" is directly relevant to Stephen's composition of the villanelle. Here are several entries from this section of the notebook:

> An enchantment of the heart.
>
> The instant of inspiration is a spark so brief as to be invisible. The reflection of it on many sides at once from a multitude of cloudy circumstances with no one of which it is united save by the bond of merest possibility veils its afterglow in an instant in a first confusion of form. This is the instant in which the word is made flesh.
>
> There is a morning inspiration as there is a morning knowledge about the windless hour when the moth escapes from the chrysalis, and certain plants bloom and the feverfit of madness comes on the insane. (unpublished manuscript, the Cornell Joyce Collection, item 25)

All three of these entries are intended as statements of Joyce's aesthetic theory. The first phrase, "an enchantment of the heart," finds its way into Stephen's discourse to describe the moment when the aesthetic image is first conceived in the imagination (p. 213). The other two aesthetic entries quoted here were employed by Joyce in the episode of the villanelle, and the first phrase was repeated there, making a bridge between aesthetic theory and practice. Stephen woke early:

> It was that windless hour of dawn when madness wakes and strange plants open to the light and the moth flies forth silently.
>
> An enchantment of the heart! The night had been enchanted. In a dream of vision he had known the ecstasy of seraphic life. Was it an instant of enchantment only or long hours and years and ages?
>
> The instant of inspiration seemed now to be reflected from all sides at once from a multitude of cloudy circumstances of what happened or what might have happened. The instant flashed forth like a point of light and now from cloud on cloud of vague circumstance confused form was veiling softly its afterglow. O! In the virgin womb of the imagination the word was made flesh. (p. 217)

The words and images are drawn directly from the aesthetic jottings in the notebook, but they have been transformed from exposition to narration. Joyce has deliberately set out in his description of Stephen's inspiration to fulfill the theoretical requirements he had himself set up for such inspiration. The inspiration and the poem are both intended to be genuine. And the poem, after all, is a poem about inspiration. The emotions and sensations felt by Stephen in his spiritual copulation with the temptress-muse provide him with some of the vocabulary he employs in the poem. In his aesthetic discourse with Lynch, Stephen remarked, "When we come to the phenomena of artistic conception, artistic gestation and artistic reproduction, I require a new terminology and a new personal experience" (p. 209). The episode of the villanelle provides him with both experience and terminology, locked in such a tight embrace that they produce not a theory but a poem. It is at this point that Stephen ceases to be an aesthete and becomes a poet.

[5]

James Joyce, Irish Poet

[1965]

In this essay I wanted to emphasize Joyce's Irishness, a matter that seemed to get lost in the process of turning him into an international grand master of modern literature. Perhaps, I was paying some sort of homage to my father, who had died a few years earlier and whose ethnic heritage was a mixture of English and Irish. In addition, however, I meant in this essay to emphasize Joyce's connection to a specific tradition in European poetry. Of course, my investment in his "greatness" is as plain in this text as can be, especially in its closing lines. But I think the essay still has some use because it approaches Joyce from an unfamiliar angle, thus helping to present him intertextually, as an allegorical poet in a European tradition and as a young man who was continually aware of the work of that elder statesman of Irish poetry, W. B. Yeats. Joyce is such an intertextual writer that he depends upon professors, not only to keep writing about him endlessly, as he predicted, but also to keep alive, through teaching them, those many other works upon which his own depends, from Homer to Yeats.

> –They drove his wits astray, he said, by visions of hell. He will never capture the Attic note. The note of Swinburne, of all poets, the white death and the ruddy birth. That is his tragedy. He can never be a poet. The joy of creation . . . (Mulligan to Haines of Stephen, at "The Ship": *Ulysses,* p. 245)

> ... I am a poor impulsive sinful generous selfish jealous dissatisfied kind-natured poet ...
> ... *one day* you will see that I will be something in my country ...
> ... the Abbey Theatre will be open and they will give plays of Yeats and Synge. You have a right to be there because you are my bride: and I am one of the writers of this generation who are perhaps creating at last a conscience in the soul of this wretched race. ... (Joyce to his wife in letters of 23, 24 Dec. 1909 and 22 Aug. 1912, manuscript at Cornell)

The first of the two quotations prefixed to this essay is not merely an excerpt from a work of fiction. It represents Joyce's view of the attitude present in certain Dublin quarters toward his own artistic ambitions, and specifically toward his pretensions to being a poet. The second, made up of excerpts from three letters to his wife from Dublin, presents Joyce's view of himself and his rightful position in the literary firmament of the Irish capital. Whatever his success in the various literary centers outside Ireland, Joyce's thoughts always turned, on publication of one of his works, to its reception at home. Was it being reviewed in the Dublin papers? And what were they saying of it there and thinking of him there? In these questions he never lost interest. His letters to his London publishers are full of requests for information about the Irish reviews of his books. In a particularly hubristic moment he even wrote his wife that he hoped to "be able to give you the fame of sitting beside me when I have entered into my kingdom" (c. 21 Aug. 1912, manuscript at Cornell). And he meant this kingdom to be a literary one, located specifically in Dublin.

Joyce's desire for a very specific kind of success—in Dublin, as a poet—accounts for some peculiar and interesting facets of his work. I have begun here by asking the reader to consider this rather limited and specialized side of Joyce's literary intention as a prelude to offering for consideration a much more complex aspect of his approach to the creation of literature. I think we can safely say that Joyce began and ended his literary career with a desire to be an Irish poet. From *Chamber Music* to *Finnegans Wake* his concept of the meaning of "Irish poet" no doubt evolved considerably, beginning with a notion of someone who was born in Ireland and wrote elegant verses, but culminating with the idea of squeezing the universe inside the four walls of a Dublin pub. In just this manner we must expand our own concept of what an Irish poet might be, in order that we may encompass and accommodate Joyce's peculiar genius.

We do not usually think of Joyce as a poet. He wrote some verse, but it seems unmistakably minor—both in relation to the work of those poets whom we think of as "major" and in relation to his own work as a whole. Yet we cannot easily think of him as anything else. He is not a dramatist, though he wrote two plays, nor is he really a novelist either. As a novel, *Finnegans Wake* is an absurdity, and even *Ulysses,* though there is a novel in it, is obviously something more than a novel also. Many of us would be ready to abandon the distinction between prose and verse as a criterion for distinguishing the poet from the nonpoet. The dean of the education school at the University of Wisconsin has published a volume of verse—but this does not make him a poet. And, conversely, many would agree that passages of Joyce's prose (the close of "The Dead," or of chap. 4 of *Portrait,* or of *Finnegans Wake,* for examples) might properly be called poetic. But there are other assumptions about the nature of poetry, more subtle and more significant than the mere distinction between prose and verse, which color our usual application of the word *poet* and raise special problems when we think of applying that word to Joyce. Since the Romantics, poetry has generally been considered to be at the emotional border of the domain of literature, far removed, by its very nature, from things learned and things intellectual. We are certain that Dylan Thomas is a poet. But, like Matthew Arnold, we have our doubts about Alexander Pope. We are not likely to think of praising a poet nowadays in such terms as occurred to the fifteenth-century English poet John Metham when he set out to commend one of his contemporaries for both his learning and his "craffty imagynacionys off things fantastyk." The highest praise that Metham could think of was "that hys contynwauns made hym both a poyet and a clerk." In our time, we like to believe, the true poet is to be found only far from academe, in a tavern, or, better still, a coffeehouse. We are suspicious of poetry which is either too ratiocinative or too learned.

As an intellectual gesture typical of the current attitude, we can find a bright and aggressive graduate student of English in one of our respected literary quarterlies attacking *Finnegans Wake* as "over-intellectual" and "cute." Though some would disagree with these criticisms, a large body of serious modern readers would probably agree that it is not good for a literary work to be too intellectual, and especially not for a work which aspires to the condition of poetry, as *Finnegans Wake* and all Joyce's works seem to do. The charge against *Finnegans Wake* in the attack we are considering here is that it is too clever and complicated; that it does not make the direct and moving appeal to the heart, imagination, and intellect that a work like Mann's *Joseph and His Brethren* obviously does; that it is, in a word, a book written for professors to use as a showcase for their ingenuity. If we accept the notion that learning and intellect are separate from and opposed to emotion and imagination through some sort of segregation in the psyche; if we accept the "dissociation of sensibility" as an actuality and not a concept; then perhaps we may be right to dismiss Joyce's greatest effort as a triumph of pedantry and an artistic failure—a colossal nonpoem. But need we accept this view of the psyche and the aesthetic which follows from it? To the individual with no interest in theology, Dante's "Paradiso" is not much fun. Does that mean we must declare it also a nonpoem?

Though Joyce thought of himself at times as a "classicist" rather than a "romantic," he was really neither. By inclination and training his mind approached most closely—more closely than any other modern writer's—the spirit of the later Middle Ages and the emerging Renaissance. His intellectual affinities are with the humanists, allegorizers, and systematizers: with Pico and Bruno, with Dante and Spenser, with Joachim of Flora and Giambattista Vico. And the best defense of the poetry of *Finnegans Wake* is to be found in part twelve of the fourteenth book of Boccaccio's *Genealogia Deorum Gentilium:*

> But I repeat my advice to those who would appreciate poetry, and unwind its difficult involutions. You must read, you must persevere, you must sit up nights, you must inquire, and exert the utmost power of your mind. If one way does not lead to the desired meaning, take another; if obstacles arise, then still another; until, if your strength holds out, you will find that clear which first looked dark. For we are forbidden by divine command to give that which is holy to dogs, or to cast pearls before swine. (trans. by Charles C. Osgood)

To consider Joyce as a poet, we must conceive of poetry not as the Romantics did but as the humanists did. And we must avoid the common absolutistic feeling that we of the mid-twentieth century have in our ultimate wisdom finally arrived at the only true definition of poetry. Boccaccio says (*Genealogia,* 14, 7) that "whatever is composed as under a veil, and thus exquisitely wrought, is poetry and poetry alone." And in dealing with Joyce, Boccaccio will be more helpful to us than Coleridge or Richards or even Whitehead. What Boccaccio means by "composed as under a veil" is that poetry always approaches the condition of allegory. Where most moderns have accepted the notion that literature holds a mirror up to nature, Boccaccio believed that poetry "veils truth in a fair and fitting garment of fiction." And so, for that matter, did Sidney, though he phrased it differently. We have heard of *The Mirror and the Lamp;* now we must think for a moment of the implications of the mirror and the veil. To the Renaissance mind, delighting in the play of intellect over the accumulations of history, literature, and philosophy, a poem which encouraged this kind of mental activity was the ideal kind of poem. When Spenser called the *Faerie Queene* a "dark conceit," he meant that in it truth was veiled, and he certainly intended some of the reader's pleasure to come from the intellectual exercise which the continued allegory would afford. Of course, he required a learned and intelligent reader. To such a reader he was willing to give helpful hints, as in his letter to Ralegh, which is really aimed at a larger audience and was in fact incorporated into the book by an early printer. Joyce's habit, in giving such men as Stuart Gilbert, Frank Budgen, and Samuel Beckett clues to the meaning of *his* dark conceits, is not some modern aberration of eccentric genius but behavior characteristic of all allegorical poets. In this Joyce resembles not only Spenser but Dante as well, whose famous letter to Can Grande della Scala is analogous to Spenser's to Ralegh.

One place where we can see Joyce's allegorical habit of mind in action on a small scale is in his verse. The only critical attempt thus far to see this verse as allegorical has been Tindall's reading of *Chamber Music* as an elaborate dirty joke. If Joyce's allegory is to lead us only into the blind alleys of scatology, perhaps we might do well to abandon any plan of considering him as an allegorist, or a poet in Boccaccio's sense. But there are other avenues of exploration open to us. A more usual approach to Joyce's verse than the scatological is the biographical. For this approach there is not only precedent, but obvious justification as well; and it has clearly had its successes in illuminating Joyce's works. His prose as well as his verse can often be traced back to its sources in the actualities of his own life. But this is not necessarily the best and most fruitful way to approach either his minor or his major works. Joyce is an allusive writer as well as an elusive one. But the great question we must face in dealing with his allusiveness is the nature and the context of his allusions. By emphasizing one context of allusion or another in reading his work, we can place it in a variety of perspectives. The usual practice has been to emphasize the biographical allusions. The argument about to be developed here is that we often (and perhaps always) would do more justice to Joyce as a poet if we would subordinate the biographical approach to a more purely literary one. Let us consider two poems: one clearly a success, and one, just as clearly, an enigma. The first is "Ecce Puer," a dramatic lyric written long after *Chamber Music* and *Pomes Penyeach,* on the occasion of Joyce's becoming a grandfather.

Ecce Puer

Of the dark past
A child is born
With joy and grief
My heart is torn

Calm in his cradle
The living lies.
May love and mercy
Unclose his eyes!

Young life is breathed
On the glass;
The world that was not
Comes to pass.

A child is sleeping:
An old man gone.
O, father forsaken,
Forgive your son!

This does not appear, at first glance, to be an auspicious poem on which to base the argument that the biographical method for penetrating the veil of Joyce's poetry is not the best one. For that reason it is of special importance for us. If it can be established that the effects of this poem depend more on another context of allusion than the biographical, then we shall have come a long way toward accepting the view that the biographical context should not be the dominant one in any reading of Joyce. For this poem is both personal and occasional. In it

Joyce celebrates the birth of his grandson and mourns the recent death of his father. Our knowledge of Joyce's life and of the problems and difficulties he faced both as a son and as a father cannot fail to invest the poem, for the biographically knowledgeable reader, with greater significance and emotion than it might otherwise have. But the question is not whether biographical knowledge can add to our appreciation of poetry. Almost always it can. The question here is whether or not it is the most important context of allusion in this poem.

To answer this question we should first consider what the poem might mean to a reader deprived of this context. Such a reader could be expected to note that the speaker is torn between joy over the birth of a boy-child and grief over the passing of an old man. The inference which jumps most readily to the reader's mind is that the dead man is the speaker's father, the child his son. As the last lines indicate, this poem, like *Ulysses,* is deeply concerned with the relationship between fathers and sons. The poem, then, would be seen as presenting the universal emotions appropriate to a speaker mourning his father's death and celebrating his son's birth. The apparently close juxtaposition of the two events in time enables the poet to heighten both emotions by their proximity and the dramatic conflict this proximity engenders in the heart of the speaker. The old man and the child represent also the past and the future between which the speaker himself is poised. In the last two lines the exclamation of the speaker leads us to believe that he has left his father at some time in the past and now, too late, asks forgiveness. It also must raise the unspoken question of what will be the relationship between the speaker and his son in the future. If the sensitive but unbiographically oriented reader we have postulated here should finally turn to biography for further help, would that help be forthcoming? From the biographical data he would learn much about Joyce's father that might add poignancy to the poem for him. But he would also learn that the child involved was not Joyce's son but his grandson. The neat trinity of the three generations—analogous to that of Laertes, Odysseus, and Telemachus which Joyce remarked in the *Odyssey*—would be spoiled by the biographical facts, if those facts were allowed to dominate the poem. But it may well be that while time and fate chose to juxtapose the death and birth over a span of four generations, the poet in Joyce saw, in this situation which moved him as a man, the possibility for the even more moving and dramatic juxtaposition of the two events spanning only three generations. Thus he did not in the poem specify names, relationship, or generations and he left that reader whom Fielding called sagacious to make the inference which was right for the poem though wrong for the facts.

But the poem does not depend for its effect on the inferable dramatic situation alone. There is a context of allusion here which adds, for the knowledgeable reader, overtones and reverberations which enhance the poem and raise its intensity to a higher pitch. The last two lines allude to the primal Christian archetype of the confrontation between father and son: the "My God, My God, why hast thou forsaken me" of Matthew and Mark, and the "Father, forgive them; for they know not what they do" of Luke. Joyce's lines, "O, father forsaken, Forgive your son!" are a witty conflation and inversion of the biblical expressions, but the wit is poet's wit, designed to control, even while it displays, a deep emotion. Within the reader who pierces the veil of allusion (surely not too difficult a task in this case) an emotion corresponding to that of the speaker is also engendered. Perhaps we can paraphrase Eliot and say that here Joyce has employed an allusive correlative. The cries of Jesus and of the speaker in this poem are cries for atonement—in all the senses of that word—and the human cry may be the more poignant of the two because it is made too late, to ears that cannot hear it.

The alert reader, having seen this much, will also see how the title of the poem alludes to the same context. Pilate's exclamation, "Ecce Homo," which has been used as the title for countless paintings of Christ's passion (including one by Munkacsy on which Joyce wrote a youthful essay) is modified here to apply to the birth of a boy-child rather than to the passion of the Son of Man. In this title there is perhaps more of Christmas than of Easter. But the speaker is a son, also, and it is *his* passion which the poem dramatizes and expresses through an intense combination of situation and allusion.

The other poem to be presented here as an example of Joyce's allusive art is a more difficult one. It was first published in *Pomes Penyeach* under the title "Tilly," which refers primarily to the fact that it is the extra item in this baker's dozen of poems. But it had previously existed for a long time in manuscript under the titles of "Cabra" and "Ruminants." The "Cabra" version was the first, and had been written as early as 1903, when Stanislaus Joyce referred to it in his diary (*The Dublin Diary of Stanislaus Joyce,* ed. G. H. Healey, Cornell, 1962, p. 14).

Cabra

He travels after the wintery sun,
Driving the cattle along the straight red road;
Calling to them in a voice they know,
He drives the cattle above Cabra.

He tells them home is not far.
They low and make soft music with their hoofs.
He drives them without labour before him,
Steam pluming their foreheads.

Herdsman, careful of the herd,
Tonight sleep well by the fire
When the herd too is asleep
And the door made fast. (typescripts at Cornell)

At some later date this version acquired the title "Ruminants," a significant change in the light of the final version of the poem. As "Cabra" the poem is a brief pastoral idyll. The change to "Ruminants" suggests Joyce's shifting attitude toward his subject, and is probably meant–as the final version would indicate–to include the herdsman as well as the herd, emphasizing their common bond of placid animality. When it appeared as "Tilly" in *Pomes Penyeach* the poem read this way:

Tilly

He travels after a winter sun,
Urging the cattle along a cold red road,
Calling to them, a voice they know,
He drives his beasts above Cabra.

The voice tells them home is warm.
They moo and make brute music with their hoofs.
He drives them with a flowering branch before him,
Smoke pluming their foreheads.

Boor, bond of the herd,
Tonight stretch full by the fire!
I bleed by the black stream
For my torn bough!

The differences between the two versions have been dealt with in considerable detail by Chester Anderson (*PMLA,* 73, 3, pp. 285–98) and will not be rehearsed here. The change in attitude is reflected in many changes in diction throughout the poem, but primarily through the introduction of a new image and the dramatic specification of the speaker's situation. The herdsman now drives his herd with a flowering branch, apparently torn from the living bush or tree which is the speaker of the poem.

The only two previous attempts to treat this poem seriously which have come to my attention are those of Chester Anderson and Richard Ellmann. Both relate the poem to the biographical context of allusion. Anderson (in the essay cited above) suggests that the poem is about Joyce's relationship with J. F. Byrne (the "boor" of the poem in this reading); Ellmann suggests that the poem is about the death of Joyce's mother (the "bough" in this reading–see *James Joyce,* New York, 1959, p. 140). For a number of reasons another context than the biographical seems preferable in the case of "Tilly." First of all, Joyce was still making new copies of the "Cabra" version of the poem as late as 1916, which he would certainly not have done if he had supplanted it by the opposed "Tilly" version (see manuscript no. 54 in the Cornell University Joyce Collection), and as late as 1919 the old version, with the title changed to "Ruminants," was the current version (see manuscript no. 4.A in the University of Buffalo Joyce Collection). The drastically revised version of the poem probably dates from shortly before its first publication in 1927. (The only known holograph manuscript [in private hands] is of that date.) This removes the poem in time from the psychological moments of composition appropriate to either J. F. Byrne or Joyce's mother as subject matter, making either subject dubious on biographical grounds alone. Furthermore, a purely literary context exists which will provide us with a reading more satisfactory than the biographical. The bleeding bush or tree is a poetical image used by many of the greatest poets, including some Joyce most admired and knew best. The context to which Joyce is alluding here is a literary one, the knowledge of which will open the poem easily to us and enable us to perceive both its meaning and its excellence.

Vergil used this image in book 3 of the *Aeneid* (24–68). Here Aeneas, himself now a wandering exile, seeks to prepare an altar for a sacrifice to his mother, Venus. On plucking some myrtle boughs he is horrified to see black blood welling from the injured tree. The tree speaks. It is Priam's son Polydorus who had been sent abroad, exiled for safety's sake by his father, only to be betrayed and slaughtered treacherously on the shore of Thrace.

In book 8 of the *Metamorphoses* (which provided Joyce with the epigraph for *Portrait*) Ovid introduced an oak tree which bled when struck with an axe, and spoke to warn that its death would be avenged. But the image of the bleeding tree was employed most powerfully of all by Dante, in canto 13 of "The Inferno." There, beside the boiling river of blood, Dante and Vergil enter the wood of the Christian suicides. At Vergil's bidding Dante plucks a small branch from a thorn tree and is startled to see the tree bleed and to hear words bubbling forth with the dark blood. Vergil reminds Dante that he has recounted such a wonder in the *Aeneid,* and he asks the tree to tell Dante of its history. The tree in life had been Pierre delle Vigne, poet, scholar, and advisor to Frederick II of Sicily. Through envy Frederick was led to accuse his counselor of treason and ultimately to have him blinded, banished, and imprisoned, driving him to suicide.

In book 1, canto 2 of the *Faerie Queene,* Spenser employed the bleeding tree in a similar context. Taking shelter under two "goodly trees" the Redcross Knight plucks a bough to make a garland for the false Duessa, whom he knows as Fidessa. The tree begins to bleed and speak, telling of how as a man he had been seduced by Duessa and betrayed, existing now "enclosed in wooden walls full faste / Banished from living wights." Spenser here was following Ariosto (*Orlando Furioso,* 6, stanzas 26–56), whose French knight Astolfo was seduced by Alcina and then transformed to a myrtle tree on the shore of a magic island far from his home. The exile and betrayal of Polydorus, the betrayal and banishment of the blinded Pierre delle Vigne, the seduction, betrayal, and banishment of Astolfo and Fradubio—these provide us with the context against which "Tilly" must be considered. Joyce's poem is a variation on a traditional theme.

Through the image of the bleeding tree, with its rich heritage in literary history, Joyce has established as a context for "Tilly" an atmosphere of betrayal and banishment. The specific details of the speaker's situation are not developed as in the narrative poems of Vergil, Dante, Ariosto, and Spenser. They must be worked out by the reader inferentially, employing his awareness of the poem's allusiveness. For the reader who does this, what seems originally to be an enigma will be found to yield its meanings once it is seen in its proper and necessary contexts of allusion. In addition to the context suggested by the image of the bleeding tree itself, we may also turn to the context suggested by the themes of betrayal and exile which cluster about the image as an accumulation from its literary past. In *A Portrait of the Artist as a Young Man,* the play *Exiles,* and *Ulysses* these themes are of considerable importance. The reverberations set up between "Tilly" and these larger works add to the poem's richness of meaning and to the satisfaction of that kind of reader whom Boccaccio desired for poetry. The reader alert to the literary history of the image of the bleeding tree, and to the importance of the themes of exile and betrayal in Joyce's work as a whole, will readily perceive in the boor with the flowering branch driving the herd another of Joyce's characterizations of the stay-at-homes of Irish literature, who cater to the rabblement (as Joyce accused Yeats's Irish Literary Theatre of doing in "The Day of the Rabblement"), flourishing the garlands they have usurped from the true poet, who has been banished for trying to create the conscience of his race. With the boor we must associate a gallery of characters, ranging from the sympathetically treated Gabriel Conroy of "The Dead" to Malachi Mulligan, the "usurper" of *Ulysses,* and including Cranly in *Portrait* and Robert Hand in *Exiles.* Richard Rowan, the autobiographical character in *Exiles,* derives his name from the rowan tree, the ash with its bell-like berries, believed to have magical properties and often cut for switches, wands, and walking sticks. In Richard and Robert we can readily see the torn bough and the tearing hand. Joyce's interest in the themes of betrayal and banishment was a continuing preoccupation, which he never kept long out of his writing, from his first literary production, the lost "Et tu, Healey," to *Finnegans Wake.*

His interest in the theme of exile, in particular, may have brought to his attention a poem of Yeats's on this theme, in which we find exile and a torn bough closely juxtaposed. It first appeared as the dedication to a collection of Irish tales edited by Yeats and published in 1891. (Stanislaus Joyce said that his brother had read "all of Yeats," and there is no reason to think there is much exaggeration in the statement, especially as far as the early Yeats is concerned.) In its first appearance the poem was simply called "Dedication:"

> There was a green branch hung with many a bell
> When her own people ruled in wave-worn Eri,
> And from its murmuring greenness, calm of faery
> —A Druid kindness—on all hearers fell.

It charmed away the merchant from his guile,
And turned the farmer's memory from his cattle,
And hushed in sleep the roaring ranks of battle,
For all who heard it dreamed a little while.

Ah, Exiles, wandering over many seas,
Spinning at all times Eri's good tomorrow,
Ah, world-wide Nation, always growing Sorrow,
I also bear a bell branch full of ease.

I tore it from green boughs winds tossed and hurled,
Green boughs of tossing always, weary, weary,
I tore it from the green boughs of old Eri,
The willow of the many-sorrowed world.

Ah, Exiles wandering over many lands,
My bell branch murmurs: the gay bells bring laughter,
Leaping to shake a cobweb from the rafter;
The sad bells bow the forehead on the hands.

A honied ringing! under the new skies
They bring you memories of old village faces,
Cabins gone now, old well-sides, old dear places,
And men who loved the cause that never dies.

In 1892 Yeats included the poem in his volume *The Countess Kathleen and Various Legends and Lyrics.* Joyce may well have come to know the poem in this edition, for one of his favorite Yeats poems, "Who will go drive with Fergus now," was originally a song in the play "The Countess Kathleen" in this volume. If not in this edition he would probably have found it in the *Poems* of 1895 or in one of the many later reprints of this volume. We should not have to be concerned with the various reprintings of the "Dedication" poem, were it not that its history parallels the history of "Tilly" in a very interesting way. In the *Irish Statesman* of 8 November 1924 Yeats published a new version of the poem under the title "An Old Poem Re-written":

There was a green branch hung with many a bell
When her own people ruled this tragic Eire;
And from its murmuring greenness, calm of Faery,
A Druid kindness, on all hearers fell.

It charmed away the merchant from his guile
And turned the farmer's memory from his cattle,

And hushed in sleep the roaring ranks of battle:
And all grew friendly for a little while.

Ah, Exiles wandering over lands and seas,
And planning, plotting always that some morrow
May set a stone upon ancestral Sorrow!
I also bear a bell-branch full of ease.

I tore it from green boughs winds tore and tossed
Until the sap of summer had grown weary!
I tore it from the barren boughs of Eire,
That country where a man can be so crossed;

Can be so battered, badgered and destroyed
That he's a loveless man: gay bells bring laughter
That shakes a mouldring cobweb from the rafter;
And yet the saddest chimes are best enjoyed.

Gay bells or sad, they bring you memories
Of half-forgotten innocent old places:
We and our bitterness have left no traces
On Munster grass and Connemara skies.

This new, more somber version then replaced the old in the section called "The Rose" of the collected *Early Poems and Stories* of 1925. It may be found today in this section of the standard editions of Yeats's verse, not far from "Who Goes with Fergus," which was dropped from the play "The Countess Kathleen" and added to "The Rose" in the *Poems* of 1912. These dates are important, for "Tilly" did not appear in print until Joyce's *Pomes Penyeach* volume of 1927. We know that as late as 1919, Joyce had not rewritten "Tilly," but we do not know exactly when he did rewrite it. The suggestion offered here is that he may well have redone his old poem after encountering Yeats's "An Old Poem Re-written" in the *Irish Statesman* of 1924 or the *Early Poems and Stories* of 1925 (where the new version appeared under the original title). The theme of exile in the two poems, combined with the striking image of the torn branch, links them in fact, whether or not Joyce's poem was intended to be an answer to Yeats. It is tempting, however, to see in "Tilly" a direct answer of sorts—an address to the tearer of boughs and leader of the rabblement by the torn and rejected arch-exile himself. But we ought not to think of merely substituting Yeats for J. F. Byrne or any other individual in our reading of the poem. The function of the contexts of allusion Joyce has invoked in the poem is to establish a frame of reference which is at once general and specific. Once aware of these contexts we are in no doubt that this is a poem about betrayal and exile, about the contrast between the contented ruminants who are located specifically in Cabra, Ireland, and the speaker, bleeding from his torn bough by some nameless dark stream. Unlike "Ecce Puer" this poem does not have any situational level which can be apprehended in realistic terms. Cabra and the black stream are as far apart as "that . . . country" and Byzantium in Yeats's "Sailing to Byzantium." If we seek merely to particularize the poem, to equate Byrne or Yeats or Gogarty or any other individual with the leader of the herd, we succeed only in diminishing the poem's meaning and its importance. It is a song of exile, a bitter echo brought to life, perhaps, by Yeats's "gay bells," but itself awaking reverberations, answering notes from our cultural and literary tradition. In his introduction to the anthology of Irish tales for which he wrote this "Dedication" poem, Yeats observed that "No modern Irish writer has ever had anything of the high culture that makes it possible for an author to do as he will with life, to place the head of a beast upon a man, or the head of a man upon a beast, to give to the most grotesque creation the reality of a spiritual existence." Joyce aspired to the kind of culture Yeats had in mind here and sought in his most ambitious works to invest his own grotesque creations with "the reality of a spiritual existence." And in "Tilly" it is precisely this culture which justifies the grotesque image of the bleeding tree. Joyce did not, of course, merely aspire to high culture. He went a long way toward achieving it. In 1902 George Russell (AE) had written to Yeats, "I want you to meet a young fellow named Joyce whom I wrote to Lady Gregory about half-jestingly. He is an extremely clever boy who belongs to your clan more than to mine and more still to himself. But he has all the intellectual equipment, culture and education which our other clever friends here lack." (This letter, and others of interest from Yeats and Lady Gregory, is included in Richard Ellmann's two volumes of Joyce letters, published by Faber and Faber, London.)

Joyce, in a way, was just the kind of young man Yeats and his friends who cared for Irish literature were hoping would arise—a man with enough culture and education as well as the genius to be a great poet. Though Joyce's independence—apparent to Russell and Yeats from the start—only grew as he matured; though he went into voluntary exile from Ireland, blasting Yeats and Russell and both their "clans" with his broadside verses *The Holy Office;* Yeats in particular must have derived some well-deserved satisfaction in having seen what Irish literature needed in 1891, and having later recognized it in Joyce, who had not been ten years old when Yeats wrote his introduction to the Irish tales. He did more than merely recognize talent in Joyce. He was of considerable practical assistance in getting this difficult young man reviewing work which kept him alive in Paris in 1902 and 1903 and in introducing him to people who could help him, including finally Ezra Pound, who was an enormous help to Joyce when he needed it most. All this assistance, of course, did not prevent Joyce from developing a sense of injured merit, and it did not stop him, in particular, from measuring himself as a poet against Yeats and Russell and their protégés. If Joyce wished, in some way, to see "Tilly" set off by Yeats's "Dedication," he may also have wished to see "Ecce Puer" set off against another of Yeats's poems. No artistic work is produced without connection with past works of similar kinds. The metrical scheme of "Ecce Puer" did not come to Joyce out of nowhere as the appropriate vehicle for the celebration of the birth of his grandson. He undoubtedly used the scheme he did because Yeats had employed almost the identical meter and rhyme scheme for a similar poem. (Again, this poem is to be found in the "Rose" section of the standard collections of Yeats's poems.)

A Cradle Song

The angels are stooping
Above your bed;
They weary of trooping
With the whimpering dead.

God's laughing in Heaven
To see you so good;
The Sailing Seven
Are gay with His mood.

I sigh that kiss you,
For I must own
That I shall miss you
When you have grown.

Joyce rhymed only the second and last lines of each stanza, while Yeats rhymed the first and third as well, but aside from the minor difference the similarity in prosody and situation is striking. Even the juxtaposition of the newborn and the dead in Yeats's first stanza anticipates the contrast between the generations which is the dramatic fulcrum of Joyce's poem.

Joyce consistently measured himself against other Irish artists, and he was always more interested in the reviews of his work in Irish periodicals than in any others. In *Dubliners* he had deliberately set out, with George Moore's collection of Irish stories *The Untilled Field* in hand, to write better stories than Moore or any other Irishman could write. Even in *Finnegans Wake* he was partly motivated, no doubt, by a desire to show that when he wanted to he could do more with Irish mythology than Lady Gregory and Yeats and the rest of the Irish Literary Revival put together. It is also likely that in the two dramatic lyrics we have been considering, "Tilly" and "Ecce Puer," he was driven by the same desire to measure himself against the best in poetry that Ireland could produce–and he had no doubt that Yeats was the best.

In his introduction to that collection of tales dedicated to the Irish exiles, Yeats had remarked, "Most things are changed now–politics are different, life is different. Irish literature is and will be, however, the same in one thing for many a long day–in its nationality, its resolve to celebrate in verse and prose all within the four seas of Ireland. And why should it do otherwise? A man need not go further than his own hill-side or his own village to find every kind of passion and virtue. As Paracelsus wrote: 'If thou tastest a crust of bread, thou tastest of all the stars and all the heavens.' " This prophetic statement by the leader of the Irish Literary Revival certainly suggests for us now Joyce's method as poet–as maker, that is, not only of verses but of huge symbolic edifices which move from the crusts of personal experience toward the stars and all the heavens.

Even in the two little poems we have been investigating here, we have seen Joyce reaching out toward the Western heritage of pagan and Christian literature for the archetypes and images which will make the bridge from the personal and the Irish to the universal. In all his works, from these minor poems to the most ambitious flights of *Finnegans Wake,* the bridge is there. It is not always easy to cross, but it is worth crossing. Boccaccio observed long ago (*Genealogia,* 16, 7) that "this fervor of poesy is sublime in its effects: it impels the soul to a longing for utterance; it brings forth strange and unheard-of creatures of the mind; it arranges these meditations in a fixed order, adorns the whole composition with unusual interweaving of words and thoughts; and thus it veils truth in a fair and fitting garment of fiction." Between the crust of bread and all the heavens lies the veil of poesy. If we do not wish to be left with the crust alone, we must seek to penetrate the veil. We must read, we must presevere, we must sit up nights, we must inquire and exert the utmost powers of our minds, so that works of poetic genius are not to us as pearls cast before swine. If we approach Joyce's works as Boccaccio insisted we must approach the works of a poet, we shall find him to be what he always meant to be–an Irish poet, and one of the greatest.

[6]

Joyce and Symbolism

[1968]

In 1968 I published a little guide to the reading of fiction, designed for introductory courses in literature. In writing it, I found myself drawn to the use of Joyce's early work for illustrations of fictional processes. I reprint here a brief discussion of Joyce's use of the human tongue as a symbol in *Portrait,* followed by a discussion of the story "Clay," from *Dubliners,* which, in the pamphlet *Elements of Fiction,* follows directly after the story itself. I have allowed to stand some references to Maupassant's story "Moonlight" because I think they are clear enough in this context and helpful in my exposition of Joyce's method. The tone of my writing in this text, intended as it is for beginners in literary criticism, is obviously different from the more professional manner of the other essays. I include this material here because I believe that the requisite simplicity of exposition has not prevented me from saying some useful things about the texts in question—indeed, it may even have helped me to do so.

From "Design: Juxtaposition and Repetition in the Structure of Fiction"

At the end of the second chapter of James Joyce's novel *A Portrait of the Artist as a Young Man,* the young man of the title,

Stephen Dedalus, has been led by the urgings of physical desire into the arms of a prostitute. This is the last paragraph of that chapter:

> With a sudden movement she bowed his head and joined her lips to his and he read the meaning of her movements in her frank uplifted eyes. It was too much for him. He closed his eyes, surrendering himself to her, body and mind, conscious of nothing in the world but the dark pressure of her softly parting lips. They pressed upon his brain as upon his lips as though they were the vehicle of vague speech; and between them he felt an unknown and timid pressure, darker than the swoon of sin, softer than sound or odour.

By the end of the third chapter, Joyce has taken Stephen Dedalus through a period of disgust, remorse, and repentance. In the last paragraphs of the chapter we find Stephen receiving Holy Communion:

> He knelt before the altar with his classmates, holding the altar cloth with them over a living rail of hands. His hands were trembling, and his soul trembled as he heard the priest pass with the ciborium from communicant to communicant.
>
> —*Corpus Domini nostri.*
>
> Could it be? He knelt there sinless and timid: and he would hold upon his tongue the host and God would enter his purified body.
>
> —*In vitam eternam. Amen.*
>
> Another life! A life of grace and virtue and happiness! It was true.
>
> —*Corpus Domini nostri.*
>
> The ciborium had come to him.

In the last sentence of the second chapter, Stephen felt the woman's tongue, pressing through her kiss—"an unknown and timid pressure." In the last lines of the third chapter, his tongue receives the body of Our Lord. Could the contrast be made more striking, or more rich in emotional and intellectual implications? Design here is powerfully carrying out Joyce's intention, which is to make us see Stephen poised between sinful and holy extremes, both of which attract him powerfully, but neither of which can hold him finally—as the later chapters demonstrate. The focus on tongues in these two episodes is the crucial repeated element which makes the contrast Joyce wishes. And in the context of the whole story, it reminds us that tongues are not only for kissing or receiving the sacrament. They are also instruments of expression. Stephen ultimately must strive to express himself as an artist of languages, using his gift of tongues. In these two episodes, Stephen has been passive, the receiver. Later he will learn to speak out.

What we have been considering is the way that an object—in this case the tongue—can by its use in a fictional design acquire a metaphorical value that points in the direction of meaning. When this happens, the object becomes a symbol. The process of symbolism will be examined further in the commentary on "Clay."

A Commentary on "Clay"

I can remember vividly my first encounter with "Clay," and this is partly why I have chosen it for inclusion here. I was a freshman in college and my roommate handed me the anthology they were using in his English class and asked me what I made of one story in it which baffled him. The story was "Clay," and I remember that it baffled me too. It was not like the stories I knew and admired—by Poe, O. Henry, Maupassant. It seemed to me to have no plot and to be about nothing in particular. By one of those ironies which operate in life as well as in art, I have since devoted a good deal of my time to working on Joyce. So "Clay" is here both because I know it well and respect it and because I can remember so well what it was like not to understand it.

Like "Moonlight" it is realistic, dealing with ordinary people and situations. It is, in fact, much more concerned to document a kind of reality than to tell a crisp and comic tale. It is more realistic than "Moonlight" and more pathetic than comic in its effect. As the Abbé Marignan's story is amusing, Maria's is sad. And as his story is one of education, hers is one of revelation. He *learns* from his experience; she is revealed to us through her experience, but without any increase in awareness on her part. The Abbé's day, after all, is an extraordinary one in his life. Maria's is merely typical. Nothing of great importance happens in it. This is one reason why "Clay" can be so baffling. It is hard to "see" a story in it, since nothing of any consequence happens. Nevertheless, it is a story, and it will respond to a careful consideration of its elements.

To begin with the matter of plot, it is not easy to find one in "Clay," but one is there all the same. Part of it has to do with the

Halloween game that Maria and the others play. The game is not explained but there are enough clues in the story for us to reconstruct its method. We first hear of the game while Maria is still at the laundry:

> There was a great deal of laughing and joking during the meal. Lizzie Fleming said Maria was sure to get the ring and, though Fleming had said that for so many Hallow Eves, Maria had to laugh and say she didn't want any ring or any man either; and when she laughed her grey-green eyes sparkled with disappointed shyness and the tip of her nose nearly met the tip of her chin.

Later, Maria plays the game at Joe Donnelly's house, so that, taken together, the two scenes make the beginning and end of a line of action in the story. And since the title points directly toward the second of these scenes, we are surely right to consider it important. In this scene we first learn more about the operation of the game, as the children and the next-door girls play it:

> The next-door girls put some saucers on the table and then led the children up to the table, blind-fold. One got the prayer-book and the other three got the water; and when one of the next-door girls got the ring Mrs Donnelly shook her finger at the blushing girl as much as to say: *O, I know all about it!*

And later, after the game has gone "wrong" once and been played over, Maria is gently teased by Mrs Donnelly also: " . . . Mrs Donnelly said Maria would enter a convent before the year was out because she had got the prayer-book."

The game, as we can reconstruct it from the clues in these three passages, is a simple, fortune-telling affair. A blind-folded person chooses among three saucers and the choice indicates the future event. The ring indicates marriage, the prayer-book foretells entering the Church, and the water—we are not told, but I should guess a sea-voyage. In reading this story we must continue to perform exactly this kind of reconstruction. Where Maupassant told us everything he wanted us to know in the most direct way possible, Joyce is *in*direct, making us do a good deal of interpretive labor ourselves. But having figured out the game, we must now arrive at an understanding of its significance in Maria's story.

At the beginning of this line of action, Maria was teased by Lizzie Fleming about being "sure to get the ring"—which would mean marriage. At the end she is teased about having got the prayer-book, which means a life of chaste seclusion from the world. But between these moments, Maria has actually made her real selection:

> They led her up to the table amid laughing and joking and she put out her hand out in the air as she was told to do. She moved her hand about here and there in the air and descended on one of the saucers. She felt a soft wet substance with her fingers and was surprised that nobody spoke or took off her bandage. There was a pause for a few seconds; and then a great deal of scuffling and whispering. Somebody said something about the garden, and at last Mrs Donnelly said something very cross to one of the next-door girls and told her to throw it out at once: that was no play. Maria understood that it was wrong that time and so she had to do it over again: and this time she got the prayer-book.

By calling his story "Clay," Joyce made sure that we would be able to understand this episode and its significance, even though Maria herself, from whose point of view we are perceiving things, never realizes what substance she has encountered. The next-door girls have played a trick on her by putting clay into one of the saucers. We know what the ring, prayer-book, and water signify in this game. But clay is not regularly a part of it. Its significance is a matter for our interpretation. Clearly, we will not be far wrong if we associate it with death, realizing that Maria is not likely to marry or enter a convent, but certainly is destined to die and become clay—as are we all. Clay is the substance out of which the first man was made. It conveys the essence of human frailty. Indeed, "that was no play." The clay intrudes on this Halloween scene like a ghostly presence, reminding us of the reality of death and decomposition. Thus, with some scrutiny, this strand of the action becomes both clear and meaningful. But at least one other must be accounted for. If we are to grasp the entire story we must understand such episodes as Maria admiring her body in the mirror, Maria responding to the "colonel-looking gentlemen," Maria losing her plumcake, and Maria mistaking the verses of her song.

Since the mistake in singing is the very last thing in "Clay," we might well consider it for possible revelations. What mistake does Maria make? "When she came to the second verse she sang again: . . . But no one tried to show her her mistake." She repeats the first verse, which is to say, she leaves out the second. What does she leave out? The omitted second verse goes this way:

I dreamt that suitors sought my hand,
That knights on bended knee,
And with vows no maiden heart could withstand,
They pledged their faith to me.

And I dreamt that one of that noble band,
Came forth my heart to claim,
But I also dreamt, which charmed me most,
That you loved me all the same.

Joyce could have told us what was in this verse that Maria omitted, but he chose simply to leave out what she left out and include the verse she repeated. He made sure we knew she had left something out, but he did not tell us its nature. As with the game, he insists that we do the work of interpretation, which in this case includes research into "I Dreamt That I Dwelt," so that we can supply the missing verse. He continually requires us to share the work of constructing this story in order to understand it. But what does the missing verse tell us? It tells us that Maria unconsciously rebelled at singing "suitors sought my hand"; that a subject such as "vows that no maiden heart could withstand" bothered her enough that she repressed it and "forgot" the second verse. Can we relate this to the other episodes in the story?

When Lizzie Fleming teased her and predicted she would "get the ring," Maria "had to laugh and say she didn't want any ring or man either." But she adorns her "nice tidy little body," and she gets so flustered by an inebriated "colonel-looking gentleman" that she misplaces her plumcake while talking to him. In its very different way from Maupassant's, Joyce story is also about feminine *tendresse,* or "yearning." The missing verse fits into this pattern perfectly. Maria is a reluctant spinster, homely as a Halloween witch, with the tip of her nose nearly meeting the tip of her chin. She feels superior to the "common" women who work in the Dublin by Lamplight laundry (a title intended to suggest that the laundresses have been reclaimed from a distinctly "fallen" status), but she takes several drinks when Joe "makes" her. Her appetites are more like those of the "common" women than she would admit. All in all, she is a pathetic figure—

a "peace-maker" whose "children" have quarreled so bitterly that she is powerless to reconcile them, and whose suspicions about the children eating her missing plumcake turn them temporarily against her and perhaps lead to the trick by the next-door girls. Clay certainly, common clay.

The title of this story points much more insistently toward its meaning than does the title of "Moonlight" (though the French title, "Clair de Lune," is stronger than its English equivalent in suggesting a metaphoric "light" in the sense of mental illumination). Like the title of "Moonlight," the title of "Clay" points toward something that is present in the story, but this clay of Joyce's story is more richly and subtly meaningful than Maupassant's moonlight. The substance, clay, acquires metaphorical suggestions of mortality and common human weakness. The object in the story—that dish of clay in the Halloween game—becomes a symbol for these complicated qualities. And symbolism is the richest and most complicated of metaphorical processes. Metaphorical possibilities range from the simple and straightforward simile to the symbol. The simile indicates precisely the nature of the comparison it makes with words like *as* and *so.* But the symbol opens out from an object or image in the direction of an unspecified meaning. We should add that though the meaning of a symbol is extensive and not precisely limited, this meaning is always directed and controlled in some way. A symbol in a work of fiction, like the clay in this story, cannot be made to "mean" anything we happen to associate with the word *clay.* Only those associations both suggested by the substance clay and actually related to Maria's fictional situation belong in our interpretation of the story. Meanings like "mortality" and "common weakness" are traditionally associated with clay in Western tradition, from the Bible on, and clay is used to symbolize similar things in other cultures as well. But we must demonstrate a connection between these traditional meanings and the story in order to establish their appropriateness. Plot, character, and symbol work together to shape our final understanding of the story.

We should note in passing that "Clay" is a special kind of short story in that it is actually part of a sequence of stories put together by its author for a purpose beyond that realizable in any single short piece. In this case, Joyce called his sequence *Dubliners* and meant it as a representation of life in his native city of Dublin. In its proper setting, the meaning of "Clay" chimes with the meaning of the other stories, as Maria's spinsterhood and common humanity are echoed by and contrasted with the situations and qualities of other Dubliners. But even though it gains in resonance when placed in *Dubliners,* "Clay" is quite sufficient to be of interest by itself.

Joyce is sparing of metaphor in "Clay," aside from its central symbol. But he is very careful about his control of tone. The tone he establishes at the beginning never falters. How should it be described? "The kitchen was spick and span. . . . The fire was nice and bright." What kind of prose is this? Or consider the short fourth paragraph: "And the sub-matron and two of the Board ladies had heard the compliment. And Ginger Mooney was always saying what she wouldn't do to the dummy who had charge of the irons if it wasn't for Maria. Everyone was so fond of Maria."

The syntactical pattern of "And . . . and . . . And" is just one facet of the excessive simplicity of this prose. It is echoed by the quality of cliché that we find in phrases like "spick and span" or "nice and bright." Though Maria herself is not telling this story to us, the narrator is using language closely approaching her own. That is one reason why any striking use of metaphor has been ruled out. Complicated sentences, complex words, and brilliant turns of phrase are all inappropriate here. Joyce said once that he had written *Dubliners* in a style of "scrupulous meanness." That expression is exactly appropriate to the style of "Clay." But Joyce's simplicity is in considerable part devoted to giving us Maria's own view of her situation. Her view is undoubtedly limited. Everyone is not *so* fond of her as she would like to think. But we are not really standing off from her and subjecting her to an ironic scrutiny. We are *with* her to some extent here, as well as detached from her. This paragraph in "Clay" is mainly pathos, with perhaps a slight admixture of satire.

All the way through the story, Joyce keeps very close not only to a style of language appropriate to Maria, but also to Maria's perspective. Only rarely, as when Maria responds to Lizzie's teasing, does he tell us directly something she could not perceive herself. And there, when he tells us her "eyes sparkled with disappointed shyness," he is giving us an important clue to the "disappointed" quality of her spinsterhood. Usually he avoids such direct transcendence of Maria's perspective and makes us do the work of inference ourselves. Even at the end, when he tells us something that Maria does not know—that she has left out a verse of the song—he does not tell us what is in the verse, for to do so would take us too far from her perspective. By holding us so close to the viewpoint of his central character, Joyce makes it necessary for us to infer a good deal in order to achieve a distance from her sufficient to focus on her with the clarity of detachment. In effect, he makes us see Maria with a double vision, engaged and detached, sympathetic and ironic. And not only Maria but the other characters as well must be seen in this way. Joe, at the close of the story, weeping so much he cannot find the corkscrew to open another bottle, could be seen as a caricature only—another drunken, sentimental, stage Irishman. But Joe's booze-induced sentimentality is also genuine warmth—a mixture of the genuine and the spurious which is, for better or worse, very common in life. Joyce leaves the evaluation to us. The comic clarity of Maupassant does, in a sense, make a better story. The delicacy and complexity of Joyce make a more realistic one. Fortunately, we do not have to choose between one and the other. We can have both ways, and many more, whenever we want.

Design in "Clay" is mainly a matter of the organization of parts to bear on the revelation of Maria's common disappointments. The central symbol of the clay itself, which is established in the story's climactic episode, is the pivot around which everything else turns. The story appears to us to be almost a plotless, designless "slice of life," and we have to look carefully to note the care of its construction. Actually, design operates much more powerfully in *Dubliners* as a whole than in any single story. The arrangement of stories was very carefully worked out by Joyce to achieve certain juxtapositions, and the stories are designed so that each contains elements that repeat and echo their counterparts in the others. The larger any work is, the more important plot and design become as elements of coherence. A collection of stories, which has no plot, must depend extensively on design for its structural interconnections. But Joyce preferred design to plot, and his longest narratives, *Ulysses* and *Finnegans Wake,* are scantily plotted and elaborately designed.

[7]

Counterparts

[1969]

This essay on a story from *Dubliners* was written for a collection of essays, edited by Clive Hart, in which each writer discussed one of the stories in Joyce's book. I cannot now remember whether I chose "Counterparts" or simply accepted it as an assignment. At any rate, I found it congenial and was able to use it to make a larger point about the method of *Dubliners* as a whole and Joyce's growth as a writer. My admiration for Joyce's skill in *Dubliners* is still very apparent, and my method of reading is still mainly a blend of new and ethical criticism that was quite common in the fifties and sixties.

"Counterparts" offers us, in its title and in its plan, a major clue to the whole structure of *Dubliners*—to the almost musical fabric of themes and variations on the people of Dublin which Joyce has so carefully arranged for us. The title of this story suggests both the harmonious balance of counterpointed musical parts and the anonymous interchangeability of cogs in a great machine. In the story itself, Mr. Alleyne bullies the shiftless Farrington and Farrington bullies the hapless Tom. The Farringtons—father and son—are counterparts as unlovely victims. But Farrington and Mr. Alleyne are counterparts as abusers of authority. And beyond this story, the brutal Farrington's return to his wifeless home and whining son is the counterpart of Little Chandler's encounter with *his* tiny son in the previous story, "A Little Cloud." Similarly, Gallaher in that story is related to Weathers in "Counterparts," representing an alien London world which challenges and in some sense defeats Dublin (as the Englishman Routh defeats Jimmy Doyle at cards in "After the Race"). From story to story we can trace strand after strand of such linkage. The "Gallant" Corley with his slavey's coin in his palm is connected by a thread of counterpointed irony to Lily, the caretaker's bitter daughter (in "The Dead"), with Gabriel Conroy's clumsily bestowed but well-meant coin clutched in her hands. Gabriel cannot, of course, compensate Lily for a city full of Corleys and Lenehans, and that is part of the irony, but the connection of the coins enriches our perspective on these events and other similar ones with many shades of thought and feeling beyond simple irony. Connections like these, multiplied many times over, are the principal means by which Joyce has blended his separate stories into an imposing portrait of a city and a whole race of people. Not just details, but details alive with echoes and resonances, make these Dubliners vibrate with significance for us.

Farrington himself, waiting for a tram with twopence in his pocket after his evening of frustration, reminds us of the boy in "Araby," with eightpence in *his* pocket and a fourpenny train ride home ahead of him: both are "driven and derided" by similar but separate vanities, even as they are frustrated financially. The finances of "Counterparts"—so carefully accounted for—remind us of the astonishing role petty cash plays in so many of these stories. The pettiness of Dublin life as Joyce presents it here is in part a response to the pressures of financial distress on a pretentious gentility. The "Gallant" Lenehan, "glancing warily up and down the street" lest he should be seen entering a cheap eating house and thereby lose another iota of his remnant of status, is a typical figure in this shabby-genteel society. Even in the upper reaches of Joyce's resolutely middle-class spectrum, Mrs. Kearney ("A Mother") grimly struggles for the extra shilling that makes a pound a guinea; and Gabriel Conroy, casting about for a safe subject to cover his sexual embarrassment, mentions to Gretta the surprising return of a pound he had lent Freddy Malins. The question "And how does he knock it out?" which Mr. O'Connor asks Mr. Henchy in "Ivy Day," referring to the disreputable Father Keon, is a great question for many of these Dubliners. M'Coy's stratagem (in "Grace"), of borrowing (and presumably pawning or selling) valises, echoes the "Gallant" Lenehan's adroit shifts in sponging. And Weathers's trick of ordering costly Irish and Apollinaris at Farrington's expense makes Farrington think of him as a "sponge," soaking up the precious six shillings he has obtained by pawning his watch. In story after story, we find ourselves counting shillings and pence. Farrington, insisting on six shillings for his watch instead of the five offered him ("a crown"), is typical of many of these Dubliners in that he has much more trouble "knocking it out" than modern citizens of affluent societies and welfare states can readily appreciate.

The financial stagnation which contributes to the musty odor Joyce felt he had achieved in *Dubliners* has *its* counterpart in the city's spiritual paralysis. The paralyzed priest of "The Sisters" is a counterpart to the Blessed Margaret Mary Alacoque—the paralytic saint who presides over Eveline Hill's failure of nerve and loss of faith in her beloved at the North Wall. In "Counterparts" Farrington's wife seeks at the chapel a consolation which is the counterpart of that which Farrington seeks in the pub (where a waiter is called a curate); and little Tom Farrington vainly calls on Mary the Intercessor to save him from the wrath of a father who is definitely not in heaven. Maria, the virgin of "Clay," appears on the page following Tom's invocation, but she is a Peacemaker who cannot even reconcile her own "children"; and—though a maiden—she is not blessed but victimized by her celibacy: flustered by an inebriated "colonel-looking gentleman," she loses her plumcake; and, confronted with the marriage verse of "I dreamt that I dwelt," she makes a revealing Freudian slip by omitting it. But nobody tells her about "her mistake." Maria's spinsterhood, the counterpart of Mr. Duffy's purposeful but destructive chastity in the following story ("A Painful Case"), is ironically related to the bad marriage forced upon Bob Doran in "The Boarding House"—partly through economic and religious pressure. (Its badness is confirmed by his reappearing in *Ulysses* as a hopeless drunkard.) It also reminds us of the other marriages we see, including that of the Farringtons. They are a well-matched couple in that she "bullied her husband when he was sober and was bullied by him when he was drunk." A puritanical religion of senseless rigidity insists upon a destructive chastity for these Dubliners, and it often combines neatly with powerful financial pressures to add to their worldly torments. The religious and financial motifs of *Dubliners* blend into a symphony of simony in "Grace," when Father Purdon encourages commerce between Christ and Mammon, in the process reducing the spiritual life to the bland mathematics of bookkeeping.

In a letter to his wife, Joyce once explained that he, like other Irish writers, was trying "to create a conscience" for his race. This phrase, which he also gave to his character Stephen Dedalus at the end of *Portrait,* has much to do with *Dubliners.* Why, we must ask, should a people need to have a conscience created for them—especially a people so conspicuously religious as the Irish? Joyce felt—and his letters support the evidence of the works themselves—that it was precisely their religious orthodoxy, combined with other sorts of "belatedness," that made the Irish so conscienceless. They had turned over the moral responsibility for their lives to their confessors and religious leaders. Thus their ability to react sensitively to moral problems, to make ethical discriminations—to use their consciences—had atrophied. In *Dubliners* he offered his countrymen his own counterpart to St. Ignatius's *Spiritual Exercises.* The evaluation of motive and responsibility in these stories—the histories of "painful" cases for the most part—must inevitably lead the reader beyond any easy orthodoxy. These delicately imagined case histories encourage us to exercise our spirits, develop our consciences. They lead us inevitably toward the view that morality is a matter of individual responses to particular situations rather than an automatic invocation of religious or ethical rules of thumb. And though Joyce's own race—the Irish—was first in his mind, he was certainly addressing all of us. Nothing is easier than to slip into the habit of invoking formulae instead of making judgments. New orthodoxies always arise to replace the old. All rebellious prophets tend to become saints in the end—as the history of Freudian ethical thought so clearly shows. But Joyce's painful cases always bring us back to individuality. In entering the world of *Dubliners* we all acknowledge our Irishness. As Martin Cunningham so complacently puts it, "we're a nice collection of scoundrels, one and all." But what *we* must see—precisely what Mr. Cunningham does not—is that it is our moral complacency that *makes* us scoundrels. Because the spiritual life is an art and not a science, because it is rich and subtle beyond all orthodox formulae, only art can begin to do it justice.

Joyce's art has the necessary delicacy. Not only does Joyce develop a formidable structure of interconnections, making of his separate cases a portrait of a city; he also presents each of these cases with an exquisite control of tone. Inviting us to judge and evaluate, he guides our responses without coercing them; he allows us freedom of response but suggests an order in which some responses are more valuable than others. These stories do justice to the complexity of moral evaluation without denying its possibility. Even Farrington, as crude and simple as any character in the book, is presented with a patient attention to detail that makes him worthy of our interest and prevents us from dismissing his brutality as too banal to require any consideration from us. Joyce's care in such matters is well worth our investigation, for by studying the texture of his work we can begin to appreciate the extent to which his range and power as a writer derive from a delicacy of feeling which manifests itself through his special linguistic gifts. In all his work, Joyce has shown an amazing ability at the fundamental task of poetic or imaginative writing: putting the right words in the right order to do his subject the most justice. And even in a story like "Counterparts"—a simple episode in the life of a crude man—we can, if we look carefully, discover the sources of Joyce's literary strength.

We can, for example, consider such an apparently trivial thing as the way the narrator of this tale refers to the central character. In the office scenes we learn Farrington's name through its use by Mr. Alleyne. But to the narrator—and hence to us—he is just "The man": "The man muttered"—"The man entered"—"The man stared"—"The man recognized"—"The man drank"—"The man went"—"The man glanced"—"The man returned"—"The man listened"—"The man got up"—"The man answered"—"The man glanced." So many simple declarative sentences beginning with "The man." Why? What is their effect? The effect—which is worked for us without our being especially aware of how it is managed—is to give us a keen sense of the dull routine of Farrington's existence: of the extent to which he is in his work merely a replaceable cog in a mechanical operation—that sort of counterpart. Calling him "The man" emphasizes both his dullness and his plain brutal masculinity. And the repetitious sentence pattern drums into our heads the dull round of the man's workaday existence which has certainly helped to brutalize him, just as in the larger pattern of the story the man's bullying of his son shows us the brutalizing process at work upon the coming generation.

After work Farrington becomes more human. He is still sometimes called "The man" but he is mainly "He" (as he occasionally was before). In the pawnshop he is reduced to his contractual status—"the consignor held out for six shillings"—but finally, in the pub, he is given by the narrator for the first time the dignity of being referred to as "Farrington." When Nosey Flynn stands "Farrington a half-one,"

Farrington has achieved–temporarily–a human individuality which persists until O'Halloran's "one little smahan more" concludes the evening's festivities. After that we hear his name no more. He is, when we next see him waiting for his tram, not even "the" but "a" man: "A very sullen-faced man stood. . . . " And in the final scene we have not "Farrington" and "Tom" but "The man" and "The little boy," as father and son are reduced by Joyce's distancing conclusion to the general outlines of bully and victim.

In this small matter we can see how Joyce's selection of words and sentence patterns has conveyed to us the whole rhythm of Farrington's life in the course of presenting a few episodes from it. By such subtle guidance Joyce makes us aware of the quality of Dublin life in all these stories. In the early story "Araby" the boy hears his uncle come home: "I heard him talking to himself and heard the hallstand rocking when it had received the weight of his overcoat. I could interpret these signs." The uncle had been drinking, but we are not told so directly. Like the boy himself we must "interpret these signs." This is Joyce's way in story after story. We must interpret for ourselves, but the signs are meaningful, making some interpretations better than others. In the work of interpretation, sifting and weighing details, listening carefully for the various tones of irony and pathos, we develop and refine our consciences.

That this *is* indeed Joyce's way is borne out by some interesting revisions he made in "Counterparts" between its first completion in July 1905 and the time it appeared in print. Here, for comparison, are the earlier and later versions of a short passage from the pub scene:

> Farrington said he wouldn't mind having the far one and began to smile at her but when Weathers offered to introduce her he said "No," he was only chaffing because he knew he had not money enough. She continued to cast bold glances at him and changed the position of her legs often and when she was going out she brushed against his chair and said "Pardon!" in a Cockney accent. (105–6)

> Farrington's eyes wandered at every moment in the direction of one of the young women. There was something striking in her appearance. An immense scarf of peacock-blue muslin was wound round her hat and knotted in a great bow under her chin; and she wore bright yellow gloves, reaching to the elbow. Farrington gazed admiringly at the plump arm which she moved very often and with much grace; and

> when, after a little time, she answered his gaze he admired still more her large dark brown eyes. The oblique staring expression in them fascinated him. She glanced at him once or twice and, when the party was leaving the room, she brushed against his chair and said *O, pardon!* in a London accent. He watched her leave the room in the hope that she would look back at him, but he was disappointed. (95)

These revisions were undertaken in part because a potential publisher felt that there might be objections to the sexual frankness of the passage (though it seems tame enough now). But in working over the passage Joyce himself must have come to agree that the passage was too outspoken—not that it was too licentious but that it was too heavy-handed and obvious, telling the reader too much and not allowing him to infer enough. The narrator of the first version conveys all too clearly his disdain for the "bold" glances and "Cockney accent" of the woman. In the second version we are closer to Farrington's own perspective on the scene. We register the impression on him of the woman's graceful arms and fascinating eyes, the alien allure of her "London accent." By putting us into closer and more sympathetic touch with Farrington's point of view here, Joyce makes it harder for us to take a merely disdainful attitude toward Farrington. We have enough information to make up our minds about the behavior of all concerned. We can form our own impression of the "striking" blue-and-yellow outfit worn by the woman, and we can make the easy inference from "London" to Cockney. But we must do it ourselves, and we must do it with full awareness of how real and exotic is the appeal of this creature for Farrington. We can see Joyce growing as a writer and as a man in this revision, broadening his range of sympathy and refining his control of irony, moving toward the richness of vision which makes his later work such a rewarding challenge for the thoughtful reader. Joyce invites us to judge Farrington, but he insists that we first understand and feel his situation—that we see the connections between him and his counterparts in all the other stories who feel the appeal of an exotic feminine otherness, including Gabriel Conroy, whose situation is so rooted in Joyce's own biography, and the boy in "Araby," who is so clearly a counterpart of the young Stephen Dedalus.

Joyce's way, then, as illustrated in this story, is to give us much food for interpretation and put the work of interpretation squarely upon us. He gives us the maximum of conscience-creating labor by inviting us to participate with him in the creative process. To become the ideal reader of *Dubliners* each of us must accept this complicity. Between the mind of the reader and the mind of the artist these stories can flower fully and achieve their richest shape. The opportunity–and the challenge–offered us is that of becoming, in our own small way, Joyce's counterparts.

[8]

Ulysses: A Structuralist Perspective

[1972]

This essay was first written to be delivered at a symposium held at the University of Tulsa on the fiftieth anniversary of the publication of *Ulysses.* For me, it was my first real attempt to address the Joycean texts beyond *Portrait,* and it also marked the occasion of my public adoption of structuralism as a literary method. I was working on the book that became *Structuralism in Literature,* and, indeed, a version of this text ultimately found a place in that book. Not having been trained in French literature and culture, however, I was coming to structuralism as a rank outsider, and I see now that I never got it quite right. That is, my structuralism always had in it more of Piaget than most insiders would have accepted, so that I found it easy to include figures like Gregory Bateson within my definition, which was altogether more of an ecological form of structuralism than that current in France. I also never fully accepted a certain exaggeration of the Saussurean theory of language that became central to structural and semiotic thought. In my work a dogged insistence on referentiality combined with ecological attitudes to make me a structuralist and semiotician with a difference. That difference is apparent in the following essay, in which I attempt to use this "new" methodology to throw some light on aspects of *Ulysses.*

"We are still learning to be Joyce's contemporaries." So run the opening words of that extraordinary achievement in biography, Richard

Ellmann's *James Joyce.* I take it that a conference on "*Ulysses:* From the Perspective of Fifty Years" is asking for a progress report on our attempt to become contemporaneous with Joyce. What have we learned in fifty years that enables us to see *Ulysses* more clearly than it could have been seen by those who were contemporary with it in mere chronology? And by this question is implied some progress not only in that narrow domain called "Joyce studies," to which some of us present here may claim a partial title, but in the larger world of humane learning as a whole.

My response to this question is a fairly simple thesis. I believe that the most important thing we have learned in the past fifty years is a way of thinking called "structuralism," which is based on linguistics and cybernetics, and has profoundly altered our ontology and our epistemology. Or rather it *should have* altered our fundamental concepts of being and mind, but it has met with a very understandable resistance—especially in literary studies. We men of letters have been reluctant to give up a view of the human situation that has seemed correct since Copernicus, and which we hold responsible for all individual achievement since the Renaissance. As a part of my thesis, I will maintain that the reluctance of many critics to accept the later Joyce (and by this I mean the last chapters of *Ulysses* as well as *Finnegans Wake*) is an aspect of this larger reluctance to accept the structuralist revolution. In a very real sense, some of us do not *want* to become Joyce's contemporaries, and we find the collapse of individuated characterization in the later Joyce as threatening as the loss of our own identities in some dystopian nightmare of the future. In this perspective the closing words of the first miniversion of *Portrait,* which once seemed merely the posturings of a confused young idealist, appear much more concrete and consequential:

> Perhaps his state would pension off old tyranny—a mercy no longer hopelessly remote—in virtue of that mature civilization to which (let it allow) it had in some way contributed. Already the messages of citizens were flashed along the wires of the world, already the generous idea had emerged from a thirty years' war in Germany and was directing the councils of the Latins. To those multitudes, not as yet in the wombs of humanity but surely engenderable there, he would give the word: Man and woman, out of you comes the nation that is to come, the lightning of your masses in travail; the competitive order is employed against itself, the aristocracies are supplanted; and

amid the general paralysis of an insane society, the confederate will issues in action.[1]

This passage could be dissected at length, for it is a strange and wonderful combination of Marx, Nietzsche, and d'Annunzio. Certainly that brand of national socialism which came to be called nazism might seem to have been rooted in this kind of thought. But it should be clearly noted that the worst crimes of nazism had to do with its nationalistic character (nationalism leading naturally to racism, genocide, and even ecocide) rather than with its socialism. Joyce's "nation that is to come" is not a nation-state but a kind of global village: individuals cybernetically related through "the wires of the world." As I say, it is tempting to dwell on this passage and explore its implications, but more pertinent matters lie ahead. Let it serve notice here that what I am going to call the revolutionary aspects of the later Joyce are not revolutionary merely from my own perspective, as a critic writing in 1972. Over seventy years ago, Joyce saw himself as one who "would give the word" to those not as yet in the wombs of humanity. Though we have been learning to read him, he may speak more clearly and more powerfully to our children. And the word he brings, in his final work, is the good news of a structuralist revolution.

Of course, both of these terms are currently so abused that it takes some temerity to introduce them in a serious discussion such as this one. If it is possible to have a "bell-bottom revolution," or a "hot-pants revolution," and so on, what mild shift in the breezes of fashion can not be proclaimed revolutionary? "Structuralism," too, has suffered from linguistic inflation, acquiring meanings not only in the sciences but, as Jean Piaget has ruefully noted, "at cocktail parties." Both of these terms are disturbingly modish, and I can only partially take the curse off them by trying to give the phrase "structuralist revolution" a clearly delimited meaning for the rest of this discussion. Once that is accomplished, we may turn more directly to *Ulysses.*

First of all, let it be clear that by revolution I mean a turning over of our ways of thinking. Of course, such turnings over have political implications. The medieval worldview and the feudal political system stood and fell together. But revolution in the sense of a single action confined to the political sphere is not what I am thinking about here. I mean revolution in the larger sense—as we might say that the American Revolution and the French revolution were instances of some larger metarevolution called "liberalism" or "democracy" or some such thing. The revolution I am calling structuralist begins, then, with a turning over of our ways of thinking. This turning over is summed up neatly and vigorously in a recent collection of essays by Gregory Bateson called *Steps to an Ecology of Mind:*

> In the period of the Industrial Revolution, perhaps the most important disaster was the enormous increase of scientific arrogance. We had discovered how to make trains and other machines. . . . Occidental man saw himself as an autocrat with complete power over a universe which was made of physics and chemistry. And the biological phenomena were in the end to be controlled like processes in a test tube. Evolution was the history of how organisms learned more tricks for controlling the environment; and man had better tricks than any other creature.
>
> But that arrogant scientific philosophy is now obsolete, and in its place there is the discovery that man is only a part of larger systems and that the part can never control the whole.[2]

In short, this revolution has put something like God back in the universe—but not a God made in man's image, bursting with individualism and subject to temper tantrums when His will is thwarted. But a God who truly "is not mocked" because It *is* the plan of the universe, the master system which sets the pattern for all others. This God cannot intercede for His chosen favorites and suspend the natural law. Nor can He promise comforts in some afterworld for pain endured here. Here is where It is. God is immanent. It offers us only the opportunity to learn Its ways and take pleasure in conforming to them. For certainly there is only frustration in trying to thwart them. If in some ways this resembles the theology of Dante, then so be it. It would be a strange comment on the ecology of ideas if Catholicism could persist for two millennia without a grain of truth in its theology. It is not Catholic theology which has made the Church obsolescent, but Catholic fundamentalism. Freed from the latter, the spirit of Catholic theology is quite capable of accommodating all the truths of science. But lest I sound too much like an Apologist for the Church I left some twenty years ago, let me hasten back to Joyce.

The point of this particularly "commodius vicus of recirculation" is that Dublin's Dante could work himself into a structuralist position more easily by taking medieval theology as a point of departure than could someone handicapped by conversion to a more "reasonable" worldview. Thus, I submit that Joyce, taking a few ideas well learned from Catholic theology, and adding notions from Vico and others, worked himself into an intellectual position which has much in common with that of Lévi-Strauss or Piaget or Bateson. Let us listen to Bateson again, with Joyce's later work specifically in mind:

> Ecology currently has two faces to it: the face which is called bioenergetics—the economics of energy and materials within a coral reef, a redwood forest, or a city—and, second, an economics of information, of entropy, negentropy, etc. These two do not fit together very well precisely because the units are differently bounded in the two sorts of ecology. In bioenergetics it is natural and appropriate to think of units bounded at the cell membrane, or at the skin; or of units composed of conspecific individuals. These boundaries are then the frontiers at which measurements can be made to determine the additive-subtractive budget of energy for a given unit. In contrast, informational or entropic ecology deals with the budgeting of pathways and probability. The resulting budgets are fractionating (not subtractive). The boundaries must enclose, not cut, the relevant pathways.
>
> Moreover, the very meaning of "survival" becomes different when we stop talking of something bounded by the skin and start to think of the survival of the system of ideas in the circuit. The contents of the skin are randomized at death and the pathways within the skin are randomized. But the ideas, under further transformation, may go on out in the world in books or works of art. Socrates as a bioenergetic individual is dead. But much of him still lives as a component in the ecology of ideas.[3]

It is clear to me that Joyce is one of the few writers of his time, perhaps the only one, who arrived at a concept of fiction which is cybernetic rather than bioenergetic. As his career developed, he accepted less and less willingly the notion of characters bounded by their own skins, and of actions which take place at one location in space-time, and then are lost forever. Unlike Lawrence, for instance, who reacted against "the old stable ego of the character" simply by giving us characters with unstable egos, Joyce attacked the ego itself, beginning with his own. But not initially. The cybernetic serenity of his later work was long coming and hard won. For he had a good deal of ego to disperse. Nothing could be sharper than the division between self and others as we find it in his early epiphanies, with their focus upon the verbal or gestural "vulgarity" of others and the "memorable" phases of his own mental life. This same bioenergetic separation persists through *Stephen Hero, Dubliners,* and *Portrait.* Though there are hints of it in this latter work, it is only in *Ulysses* that we really find the ego breaking down. I think it is reasonable to say that Stephen Dedalus is Joyce's bioenergetic self-portrait, while Leopold Bloom is his cybernetic self-portrait.

Since Ellmann's biography of Joyce, we have complacently referred to Bloom as well as Stephen as "autobiographical"—but surely we need to distinguish between these two kinds of autobiography. And it is not enough to say that Stephen is a young Joyce and Bloom is a mature Joyce. For Stephen "is" Joyce in a different way from the way Bloom "is" Joyce. Stephen is Joyce in his skin, with all the significant features that would make him recognizable. And with no features that Joyce himself did not possess. Insofar as Joyce could create a "true" self-portrait, Stephen is that portrait (somewhat retouched from book to book). But Bloom contains large elements of Joyce's neural circuitry without being recognizable as Joyce; and at some important levels of experience he is a "truer" representation of Joyce than Stephen. But that cellular integrity which marks Stephen as Joyce himself and not any other person is lacking in Bloom. He is a Joyce interpenetrated with others: with the far-wandering Odysseus and with a pathetic Dubliner that the Joyce family actually knew. (And with other figures from life and art as well.) This characterization of the peripathetic Bloom is remarkable not because it shows Joyce creating a great character who is unautobiographical, but because it shows us an autobiographical characterization without egocentricity.

If Flaubert truly thought of Emma Bovary on occasions as himself (*"C'est moi!"*), he must have donned her skin with a naturalistic *frisson,* prompted by his sense of how different it was from his own. But for Joyce in *Ulysses* there is no hint of such *nostalgie de la boue.* He lived *là-bas,* and thus his works lack the delight in slumming which is often one aspect of naturalism. And by *Finnegans Wake* he had come to accept the Homais in himself as Flaubert never could. It might also be well to recall at this point how in the *Wake* Joyce's ego is not only diffused among the whole range of major figures and minor; it has also spread out to include the "inanimate" rivers, rocks, and trees of Dublin and the world. Which ought to remind us that if Beckett is Joyce's heir, he is a model of filial rebellion. For the nausea and alienation which he has chronicled so articulately are the very antitheses of the acceptance of the ecosystem that animates *Finnegans Wake.*

It should be clear by now that from my perspective on *Ulysses* "fifty years after," it is a transitional work par excellence. It is transitional in Joyce's treatment of his own ego and in many other respects as well. This very transitional nature of the book has led one school of critics (call it the Goldberg variation) to see the book as a failed novel, which goes off the novelistic track in the later chapters due to Joyce's self-indulgence in various linguistic capers. It would be just as reasonable to invert this critique and see the early chapters as a false start of somewhat too traditional flavor, corrected by the brilliant new devices of the last part. These views I reject as equally wrong. *Ulysses* is a transitional work for us as well as for Joyce. In reading it we learn how to read it; our comprehension is exercised and stretched. We are led gradually to a method of narration and to a view of man (the two inseparable) different from those found in previous fiction. This method and this view I am calling structuralist, asserting that Joyce's later work can not only be seen more clearly from a structuralist perspective but that it is structuralist in its outlook and methodology.

In testing this thesis against the mass of *Ulysses* in such short space, much will have to be taken for granted. But I will try to look at certain representative aspects of *Ulysses* in the light of a few structuralist notions derived from Saussurean linguistics and the genetic epistemology of Jean Piaget, beginning with Piaget's definition of structure: "In short, the notion of structure is comprised of three key ideas: the idea of wholeness, the idea of transformation, and the idea of self-regulation."[4] This triad leads to a more satisfying aesthetic than the one Joyce called "applied Aquinas," and in fact it is more applicable to Joyce's later work. But before applying it we must elaborate on it a little bit. By *wholeness* Piaget indicates elements arranged according to laws of combination rather than merely lumped together as an aggregate. Such wholeness is a quality of all recognizable literary works. It is, in fact, one way we recognize them. They have the wholeness of all linguistic utterances and the more intense wholeness of discourse specifically literary. Since this is a characteristic of all fiction, it need not be especially remarked in *Ulysses.* By *transformation* Piaget means the ability of parts of a structure to be interchanged or modified according to certain rules, and he specifically cites transformational linguistics as an illustration of such processes. In *Ulysses* the metempsychotic way in which Bloom and Odysseus are related is one notable principle of transformation, and there are other transformational aspects of the book to which we will return. By *self-regulation* Piaget refers to the "interplay of anticipation and correction (feedback)" in cybernetic systems and to "the rhythmic mechanisms such as pervade biology and human life at every level." Self-regulating structures are both "self-maintaining" and "closed." I would like to suggest that in *Ulysses* the Homeric parallels function as a kind of feedback loop, operating to correct imbalance and brake any tendency of the work to run away in the direction of merely random recitations from Bloom's day. And there are many other such loops. Each chapter, in fact, is designed to run down when certain schematic systems are complete and when a certain temporal segment of the Dublin day has been covered. Whereupon the next Homeric parallel is activitated to provide a diachronic scheme for the following chapter.

This system can be illustrated by a brief consideration of the much maligned "Oxen of the Sun" chapter. It exhibits all of the structural properties I have been discussing, and can thus serve to illustrate their working in some detail. This chapter is basically a simple narrative segment of the day: Stephen and Bloom happen to come to the same place, a lying-in hospital where Mrs. Purefoy is engaged in a long and difficult accouchement. After young Mortimer Edward is born, Stephen and some medical students, accompanied or followed by Bloom, go off to a pub for some superfluous drinking. This base narrative is transformed according to a complex set of rules. Rule 1: the events must be narrated by a sequence of voices that illustrate the chronological movement of English prose from the Middle Ages to contemporary times. Rule 2: each voice must narrate an appropriate segment of the events taking place. That is, a Pepysian voice must deal with Pepysian details and a Carlylean voice with a Carlylean celebration. Which assumes rule 3: the voices must be pastiches or parodies of clearly recognizable stylists or stylistic schools.

The purpose of these rules is not merely to show off Joyce's skill as a parodist and pasticher, which is considerable, but to enrich our experience of the characters presented and events narrated. And it is their interaction which gives shape to events that in themselves are only minimally shapely. In this chapter Joyce operates with roughly six sets of narrative materials, to be arranged according to these rules. He has Bloom's present words and deeds, plus his thoughts of the past, and the same two sets of present and past for Stephen. He also has the simultaneous actions of the medical students, Haines, and so on, along with a sixth item, the birth itself. The selection of what comes when, in the necessarily linear sequence of prose narrative, is thus the result of a complex interaction among these rules and sets of possibilities. (The Homeric parallel, in this chapter, offered the initial idea, but had less influence on structure than in some other chapters.) In this chapter, the selection of the moment of birth, for instance, is saved from arbitrariness by the appropriateness of the voices of Dickens and Carlyle to celebrate the new arrival. And if *they* are to celebrate him, young Mortimer must appear in the middle of the nineteenth century, the era of phyloprogenitiveness. Similarly, the drunken conversation that closes the chapter functions in a structural way because it is a linguistic transformation of the antistructural randomization of an afterbirth: a melange of entropic noise. It is what structure prevents *Ulysses* from becoming, though for those who cannot perceive the structure it is precisely what the book seems to be.

This kind of structure, of course, is a function of Joyce's massive unwillingness to get on with it and tell a simple linear tale. And thereby hangs a good deal of critical hostility. In discussing this aspect of *Ulysses* some terminology from linguistics will be helpful. Saussurean structuralism is founded on a distinction between synchronic and diachronic views of language. From this initial position a further distinction between the syntagmatic and paradigmatic aspects of any particular utterance has been derived. In a given sentence, for example, the meaning of a single word is determined partly by its position in the sentence and its relation to the other words and grammatical units of that sentence. This is the word's syntagmatic aspect, often conceptualized as a horizontal axis along which the sentence is spread out in its necessary order. The meaning of a single word in a sentence is also determined by its relation to some groups of words *not* in the actual sentence but present in a paradigmatic (or "vertical") relationship to the actual word. A word is thus defined partly by all the words which might have filled its place but have been displaced by it. These displaced words may be conceived as belonging to several paradigmatic sets: other words with the same grammatical function, other words with related meanings (synonyms and antonyms), other words with similar sound patterns—these are three obvious paradigmatic sets. Our actual selection of a word in a sentence involves something like a rapid scanning of paradigmatic possibilities until we find one that will play the appropriate role in the syntax we are constructing. In structuralist literary theory, it is customary to see narrative literature as a transformation by enlargement of our basic sentence structure. Characters are nouns; their situations or attributes are adjectives; and their actions are verbs. And fiction is defined by its emphasis of the syntagmatic or linear (horizontal) dimension of linguistic possibilities, whereas poetry is less concerned with syntagmatic progression and more inclined to play with paradigmatic possibilities.

Joyce, in *Ulysses,* is often very reluctant to speed along the syntagmatic trail like an Agatha Christie. Often, it is as if he cannot bear to part with many of the paradigmatic possibilities that have occurred to him. He will stop and climb up the paradigmatic chain on all sorts of occasions, such as the various lists in "Cyclops" (I shall resist the temptation to pause and make a meta-list at this point), in which displaced possibilities are allowed to sport themselves and form syntagmatic chains of their own. These lists *do become* syntagmatic in themselves, and they further relate to other lists and other parts of the whole narrative in a syntagmatic way. A book as long as *Ulysses* which was really paradigmatic in its emphasis would be virtually impossible to read—as *Ulysses* is for those who do not see its structure. But even the lists in *Ulysses* if examined closely will prove to have both an internal syntagmatic dimension and an external one.

The lists in "Cyclops," for instance, tend to follow some basic comic laws which depend on syntagmatic expectation. For instance, they may establish an innocent pattern, apparently a simple process of repetition, and then violate it while appearing to continue in the same manner—as in this sequence from the opening of the list of ladies attending the "wedding of the grand high chief ranger of the Irish National Foresters with Miss Fir Conifer of Pine Valley. Lady Sylvester Elmshade, Mrs Barbara Lovebirch . . . " and so on.[5] We quickly pick up the basic principle of these names—or we think we do. There is to be an appropriateness between the first and last names of these arboreal damsels which makes it amusing to consider them. Such names further down the list as "Miss Timidity Aspenall" or "Miss Grace Poplar" are constructed by animating an attribute of the tree names in the last name and deriving a first name from this attribute. Poplars are graceful and aspens may easily be thought of as timid. (And by extension, Miss rather than Mrs. is appropriate for them too.) In this list, the opening "Fir Conifer" and "Sylvester Elmshade" establish this pattern without being as clever as some of the later combinations—thus allowing for some syntagmatic progression. But this pattern is enriched by some others, which add a different kind of comedy to the list and complicate its syntagmatic relationships. That third name, "Barbara Lovebirch," introduces into this green world the whole motif of sadomasochistic perversion which will culminate in the "Circe" chapter. The name "Lovebirch" not only includes the masochistic idea but refers to the author of the pornographic novel *Fair Tyrants* (James Lovebirch), which Bloom has inspected in "Wandering Rocks" and rejected ("Had it? Yes") as not so much in Molly's line as *Sweets of Sin.* And of course in "Circe" Mrs. Yelverton Barry accuses Bloom of making "improper overtures" to her under the nom de plume of James Lovebirch. Among the list of innocent trees the barbaric lovebirch is comically sinister. And once directed this way the reader may well see sexual connotations lurking beneath every bush. Is "Mrs Kitty Dewey-Mosse" innocent? Thus even what appears to be a purely paradigmatic excursion in *Ulysses* proves to have a system of its own and beyond that to exhibit connections of the syntagmatic sort with other events and episodes.

The process illustrated here in little is related to the larger processes of the book. The "Oxen of the Sun" is written as it is not merely to vary our perspective on Stephen and Bloom, showing aspects of them that could only be shown through the styles employed. The chapter also represents an acknowledgment of all the narrative voices that have been displaced by Joyce in uttering *Ulysses.* The whole chapter is a climb up a particular paradigmatic ladder on the level of style. And it serves not only to throw new light on Bloom and Stephen. It also takes Bloom and Stephen and the whole world of *Ulysses* back through the system of English literature and allows this work of 1922 to intermingle with the past. If Carlyle's voice can celebrate Theodore Purefoy in 1922, then Carlyle's cybernetic self still lives through Joyce's agency. And if the "Oxen of the Sun" chapter serves partly to install Bloom and Stephen among the literature of the past, the "Ithaca" chapter serves a similar purpose with respect to science.

The technological and scientific perspectives of "Ithaca" extend Bloom and Stephen to new dimensions without aggrandizing them. (And without dwarfing them as is sometimes contended.) Space-time does not permit me to trace this process in detail, but I want to close by focusing on what I take to be the final lesson of "Ithaca" and one of the most deeply embedded meanings in the entire book. At the end of this chapter, after a day of anxiety, Bloom rearrives at an equilibrium which is not merely that of a body at rest but that of a self-regulated system operating in harmony with other systems larger than itself. He views his wife's adulterous episode "with more abnegation than jealousy, less envy than equanimity" for a very important reason: because it is "not more abnormal than all other altered processes of adaptation to altered conditions of existence, resulting in a reciprocal equilibrium between the bodily organism and its attendant circumstances."[6] Blazes Boylan is Molly's adjustment to Bloom's sexual retreat. As she might say herself, "It's only natural." Bloom is homeostatic man, centripetal, his equilibrium achieved. And Stephen is young, therefore centrifugal, and therefore to be forgiven. In time he too will return, like Shakespeare reading the book of himself, and writing it too. Stephen and Bloom and Molly have other roles to play in *Finnegans Wake,* permutations and combinations hardly dreamed of in 1922. And for this total achievement, we may say of Joyce what Bateson said of Socrates. As a bioenergetic individual he is indeed dead. "But much of him still lives in the ecology of ideas."

Notes

1. "A Portrait of the Artist," in *The Workshop of Daedalus: James Joyce and the Materials for "A Portrait of the Artist as a Young Man,"* ed. Robert Scholes and Richard M. Kain (Evanston: Northwestern University Press, 1965), pp. 67–68.
2. *Steps to an Ecology of Mind* (New York: Ballantine Books, 1972), p. 437.
3. Ibid., p. 461.
4. *Structuralism,* trans. Chaninah Maschler (New York: Basic Books, 1970), p. 5.
5. *Ulysses* (Modern Library, 1961), p. 327.
6. Ibid., p. 733.

[9]

In Search of James Joyce

[1973]

This essay, devoted mainly to Joyce's earliest writing, was intended as a draft of the first chapter of my book on Joyce that never got written. It goes over some of the ground covered earlier in my essay on the epiphanies of Joyce, but it does a fuller job of situating him among his Romantic and aesthetic predecessors. Though I do not mention him, it seems to me now that I also must have written this essay with a constant awareness of Georg Lukàcs's definitions of aestheticism and naturalism—and his strictures against both of them. This great critic's hostility toward Joyce has always seemed to me an error, though I did not get around to addressing it until a later essay, and even then only obliquely. Both Lukàcs and Erich Auerbach, two of the theoreticians of narrative from whom I have learned the most, were wrong about Joyce, I believe, because they were wedded to a formal realism that could no longer serve for the representation of certain modern realities. This is not the place to develop that argument, but I mention it here because my own move toward cultural studies was greatly influenced by my reading of these two powerful critics and theoreticians of narrative.

In searching, we tend to discover what we set out to find. Stumbling upon a new continent, we may not recognize it. We are likely, in fact, to give it the name of an old one—the one we were looking for in the first place. In mental search, where we are not likely to be confronted by anything so solid and hard to explain away as a new continent, it is even more difficult to discover anything but the original object of our search. Which is why we must be very careful in designating that object.

The object of my search for James Joyce, it should be said at once, is not the Sunny Jim whose youthful gaiety brightened a peripatetic Dublin household. Nor is it the young man whose air of seedy hauteur annoyed and intimidated the literati of his native city; nor the bitter bank clerk of the Eternal City, the casual but pedantic teacher of languages, the sadomasochistic voyeur, the epistolary coprophiliac, the self-centered sponge, or the tender parent. In short, the biographical Joyce (Ellmann's Joyce, if you will) is not the one who interests me here. I acknowledge his relevance and his reality, but I am looking for another, without whom the biographical Joyce would merely be an eccentric and pathetic Irishman, like his father and some of his other relatives. I am looking for Joyce the artist and Joyce the thinker—a kind of super-Joyce, who took his sustenance from the biographical figure but cannot be accounted for or understood by biography alone. The super-self of many a weak and venal artist has given strength and comfort to others which the man's life may seem almost to mock. Art is one of the places where we transcend ourselves and become better than we are.

How Joyce's mind worked when he turned it to artistic questions—this is my true subject. My aim is to understand the workings of this mind so as to read Joyce's works with the fullest possible comprehension of meaning and attitude, tone and nuance. My method is not simply to give my own readings of the major works for others to admire and emulate—far from it. Rather I shall look for the roots of Joyce's way of writing in his early literary and critical productions, only partially tracing them through his later works. I shall be concerned to set his early works against their proper intellectual background, to formulate the problems they raise, to consider the solutions they offer. Ultimately, I hope to generate a view of Joyce's mind and art which will prove useful to all those who, like myself, feel that his work deserves the fullest possible comprehension.

The essay that follows is intended to be the first chapter of a work in progress that will take some time to complete. It initiates the program outlined in the above paragraph, through a consideration of some of Joyce's earliest writings and their background.

Portraits and Epiphanies

Clearly, James Joyce himself was always in search of the artist James Joyce. An early document attesting to this search is a brief narrative essay called "A Portrait of the Artist" that he wrote in 1904. In the first paragraph of this essay he formulated the problem of portraiture in a fashion that should prove useful in the present inquiry. It will prove useful, however, only after it has been deciphered, for it is couched in the tortured phraseology he frequently adopted in his youth, designed to impress and baffle the auditor while revealing its meaning only to those patient and dedicated enough to study each sentence and each word with care. And this, too, is significant for the present investigation. But here is the opening paragraph of that early Joycean portrait:

> The features of infancy are not commonly reproduced in the adolescent portrait for, so capricious are we, that we cannot or will not conceive the past in any other than its iron memorial aspect. Yet the past assuredly implies a fluid succession of presents, the development of an entity of which our actual present is a phase only. Our world, again, recognises its acquaintance chiefly by the characters of beard and inches and is, for the most part, estranged from those of its members who seek through some art, by some process of the mind as yet untabulated, to liberate from the personalised lumps of matter that which is their individuating rhythm, the first or formal relation of their parts. But for such as these a portrait is not an identificative paper but rather the curve of an emotion.[1]

In this paragraph Joyce seems to be discussing both the way to make portraits and the way to look at them. He is announcing his method as a portraitist and telling us how to look at the portrait he is making. But what exactly does he tell us? Because life is a "fluid succession of presents" there is always the danger that a portraitist will capture the image of a single moment and mistake that for his subject. If he does this he acts "capriciously," trying to freeze the past in "its iron memorial aspect." Whereas a true portrait must be visionary, capturing in its image of the moment something which is not momentary but transcends time, suggesting the future and illuminating the past. The portraitist, Joyce asserts, must locate "an entity of which our actual present is a phase only." This entity which is outside of time, persisting throughout all the surface changes in a person's existence—

what is it? Much of the difficulty of the passage stems from Joyce's avoiding the word *soul* in this context. The entity in question is in fact a soullike thing, and in earlier contexts Joyce did not hesitate to call it by this name; it is Aristotle's first entelechy, the "form of forms" which, as Stephen recalls in *Ulysses,* persists "under everchanging forms" (*U* 189). A "Universal language," Stephen reflects, would render "visible not the lay sense but the first entelechy, the structural rhythm" (*U* 432).

The problem of self-portraiture thus becomes a test of the artist's ability to find a "universal language" which can capture the "individuating rhythm" that animates and organizes his own being. By discovering that the entity which distinguishes him from other "personalised lumps of matter" is his very ability to distinguish this entity in himself, the young man proves that he is an artist. His self-portrait doubly demonstrates his artistic nature. Joyce's continual return to self-portraiture throughout his career, from the essay we have been examining to Shem the Penman in *Finnegans Wake,* reveals him continually rediscovering the same entelechy, laying it bare more deeply and thoroughly with each treatment. As a man and an artist he had the great satisfaction of becoming more and more himself as he aged.

The problem of self-portraiture was not the only artistic problem Joyce faced in his work, but it was the central problem. And self-portraiture was closely connected in his thinking and his work with the portraiture of others and with the whole mimetic problem of representing life in art. Looking at Joyce's work as a whole it appears as if he needed an image of himself in every work as a way of verifying its reality, as a measuring gauge for the validity of his other portraits, real and imaginary. And surely the whole of Joyce's work testifies that for him the great aesthetic questions were *not* the purely formal ones elucidated by Stephen in his famous disquisition on aesthetics. They were not the sort of problems that could be dispatched by "dagger definitions." They had to be solved finally in concrete ways—by performance. We can best appreciate the way these problems presented themselves to Joyce, and the difficulty he had in solving them, by looking at his early critical essays and at his first serious attempt at a solution.

Joyce's youthful essays in criticism seem to have been designed mainly to impress his teachers and his peers with an exotic blend of knowing allusiveness and shocking iconoclasm. But beneath this indurated surface lurked the real problems and confusions of a young man trying to work his way out of a heritage of muddled aesthetic thought bequeathed him by his nineteenth-century masters—for, despite his occasional reliance on Plato, Aristotle, and Aquinas, Joyce was more deeply influenced by the English Romantics and their squabbling progeny: the aesthetes and naturalists. The depth of his concern—and his confusion—is apparent in his early manifesto "Drama and Life," a talk delivered to the baffled and astonished members of the University College Literary and Historical Society on 20 January 1900.

The essay, as its title suggests, is an attempt to spell out the relationship between a kind of art—"drama"—and something else called "life." A secondary purpose is the glorification of Ibsen at the expense of Shakespeare and the Greeks, and at times this secondary purpose takes over and entangles Joyce in some highly sophistic special pleading; but I propose to ignore all that and concentrate on the larger issue. Joyce begins his serious discussion by making a distinction between "drama" and "literature." The distinction is not a formal one. In a later essay, in fact, he repeats the same distinction but as between "poetry"—not drama—and "literature." This is the formulation as he presented it in "Drama and Life":

> Human society is the embodiment of changeless laws which the whimsicalities and circumstances of men and women involve and overwrap. The realm of literature is the realm of these accidental manners and humors—a spacious realm; and the true literary artist concerns himself mainly with them. Drama has to do with the underlying laws first, in all their nakedness and divine severity, and only secondarily with the motley agents who bear them out. (*CW* 40)

> By drama I understand the interplay of passions to portray truth. . . . if a play or a work of music or a picture presents the everlasting hopes, desires, and hates of us, or deals with a symbolic presentment of our widely related nature, then it is drama. (*CW* 41)

"Drama" (or poetry) is a higher kind of literature. The lower kind would seem to include most realistic fiction—which seeks to represent the surface of life in all its "accidental" aspects. The relationship of Joyce's mere "literature" to fiction becomes clearer if we look at the source of his distinction. Consider this statement:

> There is this difference between a story and a poem, that a story is a catalogue of detached facts, which have no other connection than time, place, circumstance, cause and effect; the other is the creation of actions according to the unchangeable forms of human nature as existing in the mind of the creator, which is itself the image of all other minds. The one is partial and applies only to a definite period of time and a certain combination of events which can never again recur; the other is universal and contains within itself the germ of a relation to whatever motives or actions have place in the possible varieties of human nature.[2]

This is Shelley, in his *Defense of Poetry*—a work Joyce knew well—and the closeness of his words to Joyce's shows us just how much of a Platonic poet could be swallowed by a supposedly Aristotelian writer of fiction. Of course, Joyce did not know in 1900 when he wrote this essay that his gifts were fictional rather than dramatic or poetic (or aesthetic either for that matter). Perhaps if he had known he might have found a different terminology, but he would not have repudiated the idea. It is essentially this same idea that he was reworking in that first paragraph of the 1904 "Portrait"—only in terms that owed more to Blake and Aristotle than they did to Shelley—an idea that conceives of representational possibilities in terms of an opposition between surface and symbol, matter and spirit, temporal and eternal. In "Drama and Life," however, this distinction is only a part of a larger aesthetic position Joyce tried to enunciate. After separating "drama" from "literature" he went on to suggest more fully what drama should and should not be. It should reject any insistence that it be ethically instructive, Joyce maintained—unsurprisingly. And it should reject also any insistence that it be formally beautiful—a somewhat more surprising remark for a budding aesthetician. Rejecting the Good and the Beautiful as necessary constituents of "drama," Joyce insisted finally that "truth has a more ascertainable and more real dominion." And truth in drama for Joyce included fidelity to the material surface of existence: "Shall we put life—real life—on the stage?" he asked (*CW* 44). And he answered,

> Still I think out of the dreary sameness of existence, a measure of dramatic life may be drawn. Even the most commonplace, the deadest among the living, may play a part in a great drama. . . . Life we must accept as we see it before our eyes, men and women as we meet them in the real world, not as we apprehend them in the world of faery. The

great human comedy in which each has share, gives limitless scope to the true artist, to-day as yesterday and as in years gone. (*CW* 45)

Well said! we are tempted to cry out, especially for an eighteen-year-old who was to write *Ulysses* in about twenty years. And yet; and yet. Just *how* does one put "real life" into words without the result being mere literature rather than drama. "Drama and Life," like the rest of Joyce's critical writing, is silent on this crucial subject. In certain respects Joyce's essays in criticism and aesthetic theory led him into a dark wood of confused terminology from which he could not aestheticize his way out. But he was well nicknamed Dublin's Dante. Such problems as he could not reason his way through he solved ultimately by artistic intuition—inspiration, if you will. It is the critic's job to rationalize and render intelligible this magical process. In the pages that follow we shall be investigating the history of Joyce's responses to the problem revealed in this early essay: the problem of writing realistically without producing what Shelley called a "catalogue of detached facts, which have no other connection than time, place, circumstance, cause and effect," and what Joyce called "whimsicalities and circumstances . . . accidental manners and humours." In a sense this is the problem of portraiture writ large, with Life itself, in all its fearful asymmetry, defying the artist's hand and eye.

Joyce's first important response to the problem fell short of being a satisfactory solution. It was a failure, though a very interesting one, which he took seriously for several years, and which is still very revealing for us. This imperfect solution is to be found in the theory and practice of epiphanization. We know that Joyce kept a book of epiphanies, written between 1900 and 1904, numbering over seventy. We have forty of them—enough to appraise their intent and achievement. And we have a theory of epiphany, presented as an invention of Stephen Daedalus in *Stephen Hero.* In chapter 3 we have already considered the epiphanies in some detail. But here it is necessary to return and relocate the theory of epiphany, in relation to the concerns already revealed in "Drama and Life," and as this theory clarifies the background and the thrust of Joyce's critical thought. We must begin with a fresh look at the perhaps over-familiar passage from *Stephen Hero,* wherein Stephen conceives the idea of epiphany:

He was passing through Eccles' St one evening, one misty evening, with all these thoughts dancing the dance of unrest in his brain when a

> trivial incident set him composing some ardent verses which he entitled a "Vilanelle of the Temptress." A young lady was standing on the steps of one of those brown brick houses which seem the very incarnation of Irish paralysis. A young gentleman was leaning on the rusty railings of the area. Stephen as he passed on his quest heard the following fragment of colloquy out of which he received an impression keen enough to afflict his sensitiveness very severely.
>
> The Young Lady—(drawling discreetly) . . . O, yes . . . I was . . . at the . . . cha . . . pel . . .
>
> The Young Gentleman—(inaudibly) . . . I . . . (again inaudibly) . . . I . . .
>
> The Young Lady—(softly) . . . O . . . but you're . . . ve . . . ry . . . wick . . . ed . . .
>
> This triviality made him think of collecting many such moments together in a book of epiphanies. By an epiphany he meant a sudden spiritual manifestation, whether in the vulgarity of speech or of gesture or in a memorable phase of the mind itself. He believed that it was for the man of letters to record these epiphanies with extreme care, seeing that they themselves are the most delicate and evanescent of moments. (*SH* 210–11)

The crucial terms here are *triviality* and *spiritual manifestation.* Together, they unite the two apparently unreconcilable aspects of aesthetic truth that Joyce had emphasized in "Drama and Life." When Joyce insisted in "Drama and Life" that "out of the dreary sameness of existence a measure of dramatic life may be drawn" he was expressing a hope rather than outlining a program or suggesting a method. But method and program had not long to wait. They must have suggested themselves to Joyce in much the way that he presented their occurrence to Stephen Daedalus in the passage under consideration.

An epiphany was real, it was actual, because it was a verbatim record of experience. But it possessed also the higher truth of dramatic universality because it was a *spiritual manifestation.* What Joyce and Stephen meant by this expression is clarified a few pages later in *Stephen Hero,* where we find Stephen explaining to Cranly the concept of epiphany, relating it to the three stages in aesthetic apprehension which he has derived from Aquinas. The epiphany is associated with the third and final phase of aesthetic apprehension. After the wholeness and symmetry of the object are apprehended, its radiance becomes manifest:

> —Now for the third quality. For a long time I couldn't make out

> what Aquinas meant. He uses a figurative word (a very unusual thing for him) but I have solved it. *Claritas* is *quidditas.* After the analysis which discovers the second quality the mind makes the only logically possible synthesis and discovers the third quality. This is the moment which I call epiphany. First we recognise that the object is *one* integral thing, then we recognise that it is an organised composite structure, a *thing* in fact: finally, when the relation of the parts is exquisite, when the parts are adjusted to the special point, we recognise that it is *that* thing which it is. Its soul, its whatness, leaps to us from the vestment of its appearance. The soul of the commonest object, the structure of which is so adjusted, seems to us radiant. The object achieves its epiphany. (*SH* 213)

From this explanation we can see that by *spiritual manifestation* Joyce meant the revelation of the soul through the vestment of the body.

That trivial episode which first caused Stephen to conceive the idea of epiphany should now be examined more closely. It has two dimensions: setting and characters. The setting is described as the steps of "one of those brown houses which seem the very incarnation of Irish paralysis." The word *incarnation* is not used loosely here. The house is a material representation of a spiritual reality—both actual and symbolic at the same time. It gives substantial form to the soul of Irish paralysis. Similarly, the nameless young man and young lady are also incarnations which proclaim a spiritual reality: the hollow emptiness of Irish romance, in which the banal piety of every-Irish-woman ("at the . . . cha . . . pel") flirts with the flabby gallantry ("you're . . . ve. . . ry . . . wick . . . ed") of every Irishman, against a backdrop of Irish paralysis. No wonder the scene made an impression on Stephen "keen enough to afflict his sensitiveness very severely."

Joyce's idea of epiphany can be further clarified by comparison with a closely related concept presented in a work which he (like every literary young man of the time) knew well. In *The Renaissance,* Walter Pater discussed the way that certain painters seemed to select ideal moments for representation:

> Now it is part of the ideality of the highest sort of dramatic poetry, that it presents us with a kind of profoundly significant and animated instants, a mere gesture, a look, a smile, perhaps—some brief and wholly concrete moment—into which, however, all the motives, all the interests and effects of a long history, have condensed themselves, and which seem to absorb past and future in an intense consciousness of

> the present. Such ideal instants the school of Giorgione selects, with its admirable tact, from that feverish, tumultuously coloured world of the old citizens of Venice—exquisite pauses in time, in which, arrested thus, we seem to be spectators of all the fullness of existence, and which are like some consummate extract or quintessence of life.[3]

Pater is developing here an idea drawn from the Romantic aesthetic as enunciated in England by Wordsworth and Coleridge among others. Wordsworth's version of this notion lurks everywhere in his writing but is presented most explicitly in book 12 of *The Prelude* in the passage that begins (line 208):

> There are in our existence spots of time,
> That with distinct pre-eminence retain
> A renovating virtue. . . .

Wordsworth emphasized the "renovating virtue" of his "spots of time." They had a distinctly moral and spiritual effect on the sensitive being in whose memory they lived. And for Wordsworth, of course, these moments had a kind of religious quality because in them Nature, and the power behind Nature, spoke to the soul of the poet. They were, in Joyce's phrase, "spiritual manifestations" in a way that Joyce's own epiphanies were not, because in them a Supreme Being revealed a part of himself. A part of Joyce's problem, both in "Drama and Life" and in the theory of the epiphany, then, stems from taking over Romantic concepts from Shelley and Wordsworth without taking over their transcendental metaphysic. He wants, so to speak, his spiritual manifestations without accepting the notion of Spirit. For this reason Pater's rationalization of the romantic aesthetic must have appealed to Joyce.

Pater's "ideal instants" differ from Wordsworth's "spots of time" in a number of important respects, despite the obvious similarities. In his chapter on Leonardo, for instance, Pater writes of the special moment of well-being (*bien-être*) "which to imaginative men is a moment of invention." Here he is close to a Romantic theory of inspiration, but he alters the Romantic view by insisting that the artist's vision in these moments is simply clearer, not deeper. Pater actually speaks of a "cloudy mysticism" being "refined to a subdued and graceful mystery" in such moments. Art makes life *less* not more mystical for Pater. In the passage on the school of Giorgione (quoted above) he also makes it clear that what the artist captures in these "ideal instants" is not a spiritual manifestation or revelation of the supernatural, but a "consummate extract or quintessence of life." In Pater's Epicurean aesthetic the consciousness of the supernatural in Nature is replaced by a heightened consciousness of the natural. In these moments the artist is inspired only to the extent that he discerns in his subject (with "admirable *tact*"), and "selects" to represent, some "gesture" in which "all the interests and effects of a long history have condensed themselves."

Pater has not only rationalized the Romantic moment of revelation, he has also humanized, urbanized, and historicized it. Giorgione and his school depict men not nature, the world of Venice rather than the Lake Country, and the condensation of "a long history" rather than a glimpse into the eternal. All of these modifications take him in Joyce's direction. But one aspect of Pater's Epicurean aesthetic never satisfied Joyce. Pater praised Giorgione and the genre painters in general for rejecting the iconographical tradition, and Joyce must have accepted this praise as appropriate. What he could not accept was the value that Pater found in the work of these painters to replace the ones they rejected. Their pictures, Pater says, "serve neither for uses of devotion, nor of allegorical or historic teaching–[they represent] little groups of real men and women, amid congruous furniture or landscape–morsels of actual life, conversation or music or play, but refined upon or idealised, till they come to seem like glimpses of life from afar."[4] Like Pater's Giorgione, Joyce wanted to represent an urban actuality: "real men and women" or "morsels of actual life." And he felt, like Pater, that this actuality was best caught in certain fleeting moments. Throughout his whole career, in fact, Joyce showed a preference for significant moments–scenes and portraits–over the linear arrangements which dominate most fiction. What Joyce could not accept from Pater was the notion that art "refined" and "idealised" the things that it represented. In "Drama and Life" Joyce had specifically rejected the claims upon dramatic art of both the Good and the Beautiful–singling out the latter as the more insidious of the two. Joyce's answer to "art for art's sake" was "Art is true to itself when it deals with truth" (*CW* 43-44). And he added, "Art is marred by . . . mistaken insistence on its religious, its moral, its beautiful, its idealizing tendencies" (*CW* 44).

Joyce's resistance to the idealizing aspect of Pater's aesthetic is a function of his adherence to the anti-aesthetic aesthetic of the naturalists. Unlike Henry James, for instance, who shared many of Joyce's aesthetic attitudes, Joyce accepted from the naturalists the view that man is most himself when he is most ordinary, especially in the performance of his excremental and sexual acts, and in his abuses of the gift of language. Joyce's early acquaintance with theology helped to preserve him from the extreme naturalistic concept of a malevolent deity supervising the affairs of men with mischievous intent, and from the other aspects of simplistic determinism which informed much naturalistic fiction. But Joyce never abandoned the naturalistic concern to document accurately the actual life around us in all its trivial vulgarity. In the theory of the epiphany he made his first attempt at an artistic solution to the aesthetic problem that his various concerns posed for him. In the moment of epiphany, the eternal verities would shine through the carefully documented naturalistic surface. Actual life would be recorded just as it was, but the deeper realities would manifest themselves, too, spiritually. That the spiritual values would actually be there, without any effort on the artist's part to do more than record them, Joyce seems to have taken on faith. They would be there because he *wanted* them to be there, because they *were* there. With this gaping hole in its aesthetic armor, it is no wonder that the theory of epiphany did not satisfy Joyce for long. But we have not yet exhausted the resources of the theory as a revelation of Joyce's early aesthetic ideas. We must return to consider further that first epiphanic moment in *Stephen Hero.*

When he first thinks of collecting such moments in a "book of epiphanies," Stephen thinks of them as being of two kinds. They are spiritual manifestations, (a) in the vulgarity of speech or of gesture, and (b) in a memorable phase of the mind itself. Stephen's own soul will reveal itself in *"memorable"* phases of his mind. The souls of others will be revealed through the *"vulgarity"* of their speech and gestures. This young man sees himself with the eye of Wordsworth and the others with the eye of Flaubert. He seems ready to write *The Prelude* and *Bouvard et Pécuchet* simultaneously.

Joyce's own "book of epiphanies" was collected largely between the delivery of his talk on "Drama and Life" and the composition of *Stephen Hero* itself, in which the theory of epiphany was set forth. The forty surviving items from the original collection (which extended to over seventy) reveal that Joyce himself had proceeded according to the method outlined in Stephen's thoughts. He collected two kinds of epiphany, which are quite distinct for the most part: they emphasize either the sensitive mind of the young artist or the vulgarity of those around him. And of course all the records of vulgarity imply the sensitivity of the recording instrument. The sensitive romantic artist in vulgar naturalistic surroundings—how much of Joyce's early subject matter is there! But just as Joyce himself had to outgrow that posture in order to become the author of his best work, the concept of epiphany had to give way to other artistic formulations in order for Joyce's best work to come into being. And just as he found it necessary to accept the sensitivity of vulgar Leopold Bloom, and the vulgarity of sensitive Stephen Dedalus, he found it necessary to reject the notion of an easy and automatic spiritual revelation which involved no more effort than jotting down his own dreams or the stupid sayings of those around him.

After 1904 Joyce kept notebooks but no book of epiphanies. And when the Stephen Dedalus of *Portrait* presented *his* aesthetic theory, the notion of epiphany was not merely absent, it was specifically rejected. In the discussion with Lynch which replaced the discussion with Cranly as the vehicle for the presentation of aesthetic theory in *Portrait,* we arrive ultimately at a moment analogous to the moment in *Stephen Hero* when *claritas,* or radiance, was explained as the achievement of epiphany:

> —The connotation of the word, Stephen said, is rather vague. Aquinas uses a term which seems to be inexact. It baffled me for a long time. It would lead you to believe that he had in mind symbolism or idealism, the supreme quality of beauty being a light from some other world, the idea of which the matter is but the shadow, the reality of which it is but the symbol. I thought he might mean that *claritas* is the artistic discovery and representation of the divine purpose in anything or a force of generalisation which would make the esthetic image a universal one, make it outshine its proper conditions. But that is literary talk. I understand it so. When you have apprehended that basket as one thing and have then analysed it according to its form and apprehended it as a thing you make the only synthesis which is logically and esthetically permissible. You see that it is the thing it is and no other thing. The radiance of which he speaks is the scholastic *quidditas,* the *whatness* of a thing (*Portrait* 212–13).

This second formulation quite specifically repudiates all the Shelleyan idealism which animated the notion of epiphany in *Stephen Hero.* The "symbolism" or "idealism" which Stephen and Joyce once thought of as showing through the vestments of the commonest object is here dismissed as mere "literary talk." This is a tougher-minded Stephen and a tougher-minded Joyce. Any "force of generalisation" in Joyce's work after *Stephen Hero* was to be earned by artistic effort rather than assumed as the divine right of aesthetic sensitivity.

By the time of *Ulysses* both Joyce and Stephen had attained a distance from the epiphanies sufficient for mockery. In Stephen's interior monologue on Sandymount Strand they appear like an ironic spot of time, annoying rather than refreshing, and are subject themselves to a renovating scrutiny: "Remember your epiphanies on green oval leaves, deeply deep, copies to be sent if you died to all the great libraries of the world, including Alexandria? Someone was to read them there after a few thousand years, a mahamanvantara. Pico della Mirandola like. Ay, very like a whale. When one reads these strange pages of one long gone one feels that one is at one with one who once . . . " (*U* 40).

Thus the epiphany was tried and ultimately rejected as the solution to the problems first posed in "Drama and Life." But the problems did not disappear along with the rejection of this first solution. They remained because they were the problems of the age, which is to say the age's version of the perennial problems of the artist. How to tell the truth, the deep truths about the human condition, without writing mere documentary realism—this was the problem Joyce and his contemporaries faced, and Joyce himself made the problem especially difficult and interesting by insisting that his deep truth do no violence to that shabby surface realism, that vulgarity of speech and of gesture, which he loved and hated, and learned to present with his own kind of radiance in his finest work.

Notes

The following works are cited in the text in abbreviated form: *Critical Writings* (New York: Viking, 1959); *A Portrait of the Artist as a Young Man* (New York: Viking, 1968); *Stephen Hero* (New York: New Directions, 1963); *Ulysses* (New York: Modern Library, 1961).

1. *The Workshop of Daedalus: James Joyce and the Materials for "A Portrait of the Artist as a Young Man,"* ed. Robert Scholes and Richard M. Kain (Evanston: Northwestern University Press, 1965), p. 60.
2. Percy Bysshe Shelley, "A Defense of Poetry," in *Shelley's Prose or the Trumpet*

of a Prophecy, ed. David Lee Clark (Albuquerque: University of New Mexico Press, 1954), p. 281.

3. *The Renaissance* (1873; New York: Modern Library, n.d.), pp. 123–24.

4. Ibid., p. 116.

[10]

Semiotic Approaches to a Fictional Text: Joyce's "Eveline"

[1979]

This essay, which belongs to my phase as a hard-core semiotician, appeared first in a "Structuralist/Reader Response" issue of the *James Joyce Quarterly* and later in my own book *Semiotics and Interpretation.* It constitutes more evidence, if more were needed, that for me literary theory and the text of James Joyce were made for each other. The formal procedures of this kind of narratology are out of fashion now, but I am convinced they still have their pedagogical and hermeneutic uses. Certainly, what I learned from Barthes, Genette, and Todorov about narrative structures and ways of reading has remained with me as a reader of texts of all kinds. Once again I return to the early work of Joyce, where I believe my best work has been done. This essay, for all its semiotic flourishes, still seems to me a strong and useful reading of the story and of Joyce's method in *Dubliners.*

The purpose of this discourse is a simple one. I wish to argue, and to demonstrate as well as possible, that certain semiotic approaches to fictional texts, each incomplete in itself, can be combined in a manner that facilitates the practical criticism of fiction. The three approaches I wish to combine into a single methodology are the following:

1. That of Tzvetan Todorov, as illustrated in his *Grammaire du Décameron.*

2. That of Gérard Genette in *"Discours du récit"* from *Figures III.*
3. That of Roland Barthes in *S/Z.*

In each of these cases the critic has attempted to generate a method of analysis appropriate to the specific material under immediate consideration and to test the method on the material. But in every case the method, it is suggested, may have wider application as well. My thesis in this discourse is that all three of these methods do indeed have wider applications, that they complement one another in addressing the fictional text from different angles, and further, that they even suggest a sequence of use, each of them presenting itself as a segment in a metamethod in which they function as units of a syntagmatic process, units whose order should always be the same. The metamethod I wish to illustrate consists of approaching the text via Todorov, Genette, and Barthes in that order. The illustration will be based upon Joyce's "Eveline."

The three critics actually examine different levels or features of the text, though their work naturally overlaps at certain points. Todorov, who based his method on the hundred tales of Boccaccio's *Decameron,* calls his study a "grammar." Genette, who illustrates his system on Proust's *Recherche,* is interested in "figures" that operate at the "rhetorical" level of the text. Barthes, working with a novella of Balzac, is more completely semiotic, as he seeks to codify all the ways in which a fictional text generates its significations. These three writers, then, offer us a grammar, a rhetoric, and finally a semiotic of fiction. This is true—with certain qualifications, which will emerge from the following discussion.

Todorov's grammar has two main features. He reduces fictions to plot structures that can be represented by a simple symbolic logic, and he codes the semantic features of his symbolic notations so that they reveal the principal thematic concerns of the action in any story. Todorov's method calls for a summary of the story's action to be made first, and then for the reduction of the summary to symbolic form. But this procedure has two large faults. First, the summary must be intuitive, governed by no explicit system, and second, the resulting notation has a spurious exactitude, based upon its resemblance to the summary rather than to the fiction itself. Working with stories as simple and sharply delineated as Boccaccio's, the problem is not so great, but when we seek to move to modern fiction it becomes acute.

The critic of modern fictional texts must employ Todorov's approach as an heuristic tool, a way of focusing interpretation upon features of all fictional texts. Our perception of fictions depends in part upon our understanding of what Barthes calls the code of actions. We recognize a story as a story because we perceive in it a causal/chronological system that has, as Aristotle pointed out, a beginning, middle, and end. Todorov offers us a way of isolating the major action in any work of fiction so as to bring it to the foreground of our attention. Using his system of notation, we seek the story within any work of fiction. Obviously, most fictions are more than stories, especially modern fictions; and some fictions are antistories, pseudostories, in which the idea of story itself is parodied or denied for some ideological or thematic purpose. Todorov offers us a way to seek the story in any fiction and to record the results of that search. If we find no story, or a partial story, that, too, is a significant result.

But what *is* a story? Todorov will help us be precise in answering that question. A story is a certain kind of sequence of propositions. Fictional propositions are of two kinds: attribution and actions. The most fundamental fictional sequence is attribution, action, attribution—beginning, middle, end. Let me illustrate. If characters are nouns, attributes are adjectives, and actions are verbs, we can present a simple story in the following way:

$X - A \; + \; (XA)\text{opt}X \rightarrow Xa \rightarrow XA$

Where

X = Boy

A = love, to be loved by someone

a = to seek love, to woo

opt$X$ = Boy (X) wishes (opt)

$-$ = negation of attribute: $-A$ is to lack love, to be unloved

Thus the sequence reads Boy lacks love plus Boy wants to be loved. which yields Boy seeks love which yields Boy is loved. We know this is a story because it is a sequence of propositions involving the same subject, in which the last proposition is a transformation of the first. An unhappy ending might be a simple repetition of the first proposition: $X - A$. A very unhappy ending might be $X - A!$, Boy lacks love with vengeance.

But happy or unhappy, what makes the sequence a story is the return to the opening proposition at the end. Stories are about the successful or unsuccessful transformation of attributes.

In applying Todorov's method to modern stories, the first problem is often to isolate the major sequences of actions, to find the master story. "Eveline" is rather simple in this respect, but other stories in *Dubliners* are much more difficult. To find a story in "Ivy Day" is not so easy. But even "Eveline" presents problems of another sort. The chain of symbols representing the syntax of a story is just one aspect of its "grammar." The other aspect is lexical or semantic. We must reduce the complex of qualities associated with the characters (what Barthes calls connotative code) to a few summary features which are activated by the story itself. This semantic summarizing is the most crucial aspect of the interpretive process at this level of analysis. In actual practice, the interpreter must simply try out attributions until they seem incapable of further refinement. The method here requires the skill of the interpreter, and it will display any lack of such skill mercilessly—but the method cannot provide it.

Here is a version of the story "Eveline":

$$XA + XB \rightarrow X{-}C + \Upsilon aX + (X{-}A + X{-}B \rightarrow XC)\,\mathrm{pred}X \rightarrow (Xb\Upsilon)\,\mathrm{pred}X + XA! \rightarrow X\mathrm{not}b\Upsilon \rightarrow (XB + X{-}C)!\ \mathrm{imp}$$

Where

X	=	Eveline
Υ	=	Frank
A	=	a Dubliner
B	=	celibate
C	=	happy—respected, secure
a	=	to offer elopement
b	=	to accept elopement
–	=	negative of attribute
not	=	negative of verb
pred	=	predicts or expects
imp	=	is implied by discourse

The annotation may be read as follows: Eveline is a Dubliner—literally a resident of Dublin, but figuratively much more. This attribute, built up over the whole sequence of stories, is in fact what the stories are about, as the title of the book indicates. This story, like most of the others, marks most heavily such features as isolation, deprivation, and repression, combined with an inability to act so as to change this condition of life. Eveline is also celibate. Dubliners tend to be either celibate or unhappily married, and celibacy is usually marked in the stories as a negative attribute, connotating incompletion, frustration, isolation. The third proposition indicates that Eveline is unhappy with her life. This is less than explicit, but can be inferred from her reaction to Frank's proposal and other descriptions of her home life. The action of the story starts with Frank's proposal of elopement, which leads Eveline to imagine that her situation will change for the better, signified by the reversal of sign on the attributes in the fifth proposition. Her prediction of the elopement itself in the sixth proposition is, in fact, bound up with the changes she predicts in the fifth. All this is quite explicit in the text. But Eveline *is* a Dubliner! She finally refuses the elopement, and the story closes with the strong implication that her original condition resumes, only intensified by her having missed this chance to leave Dublin and change her life. This is a simple story, which could easily be coded as the negation of the one of Vladimir Propp's Russian fairy tales. The prince comes to rescue the princess from the villain's dungeon, but she decides finally that the dungeon is less frightening than the thought of leaving it, and sends the hero home empty-handed. Naturalism sometimes generates its "authenticity" by the inversion of romance. But let us return to the process of notation and what it reveals.

Looking simply at the syntactic configuration here we see that the three attributive propositions which constitute the "situation" of "Eveline" are repeated with emphasis at or near the close of the narration. And though this repetition is more a matter of implication than of statement, the implications are quite clear. We can see also that the attributes remain unchanged; an essentially unhappy situation finally persists, even intensifies. This, in fact, is the rule of *Dubliners.* The grammar of these stories tends toward the persistence of unpleasant conditions–from bad to worse. A few stories show a change from better to worse. Only one shows any improvement of an opening situation, and that is "Two Gallants" in which the impecunious Lenehan is finally likely to benefit by sponging off his friend Corley, who has just received a gold coin from a servant girl in exchange for his sexual favors. But behind this "happy" ending the portrait of Lenehan as an aging sponger who is trapped in his Dublinesque existence becomes clearer and clearer. His real condition improves no more than Eveline's.

The point of this discussion is that Todorovian notation forces us to focus on questions of attribution, forces us to thematize the work. When applied to a body of works by a single author, such as the *Dubliners* stories, it brings to our attention recurrent features of syntactic and semantic coding, raising questions about such matters as why so many of these stories turn on celibacy and its various alternatives, and finally about the ultimate attribution, the state of being a Dubliner. This method is relatively crude, examining only two gross features of the text–action and attribution–but its usefulness for the analyst and the teacher is very real indeed.

The most elaborate and systematic apparatus yet developed for the study of fictional texts is that proposed by Gérard Genette in his *"Discours du Récit"* from *Figures III.* In the course of an extended discussion of Proust's *Recherche,* Genette presents a method for analyzing a fictional text according to its tense, mood, and voice–thus borrowing his terminology from the traditional grammar of the verb, on the grounds that all fiction can be seen as "the expansion of a verb." Genette begins by distinguishing three aspects of fictional texts which enable us to recognize them as fictional, and also provide us with points of departure for their study. Every fictional text comes to us in the form of a *récit* or narrative discourse–a text in fact. And this discourse informs us of a set of fictional events which can be distinguished from the text itself. Every fictional discourse conveys to us a story, which exists in a different spatiotemporal situation from the discourse itself, and from its own production or our reading of it. In addition to this, every narrative text also conveys explicitly or implicitly some circumstances of narration, some explanation for its own existence as a text, both in relation to the events narrated and to some *narrataire* or audience. When the narrative situation of a text is examined closely, the narrator and *narrataire* virtually never correspond exactly with author and reader, nor do the circumstances of narration agree with those of a book's actual writing and reading.

Keeping in mind these three elements of all fictional texts (the discourse, the story, and the narration), Genette begins his study of narrative by examining aspects of what he calls fictional "tense." In the temporal arrangements of fiction he discerns three major areas for investigation: order, duration, and frequency. *Order* is the arrangement of events expressed as a relationship between story and *récit,* the chronology of the story as opposed to the way the text arranges this chronology and presents it to us. (This is close to the Russian formalist distinction between story and plot.) *Duration* is a relationship between the temporal extension of events in the story and the attention devoted to them by the *discourse.* This is a matter of speed or velocity, which may be expressed as a ratio between the hours, days, and years of story time and the words and pages of the printed text. The third temporal aspect of a fictional text, *frequency,* involves the ways in which events may be repeated either in the story itself (the same thing happening more than once) or in the *discourse* (the same event described more than one time).

Within these three main aspects of tense Genette makes many further discriminations, only some of which we will attend to here, as not all are significant for a study of "Eveline." The order of presentation of the events in "Eveline" is both simple and complex. The base time of the narrative is the evening of Eveline's projected departure from Dublin. Joyce presents these events in two scenes: the first begins with darkness falling as Eveline sits by her window, and ends with her standing up. The second scene begins after the elipses. The time is that same night (though we must infer this) and the scene continues until the end of the story. Within this simple, chronological scheme, however, this story moves through an extraordinary complexity of temporal arrangement. Confining ourselves for the moment to fairly large and readily distinguishable blocks of time, we can discern a temporal movement in the story something like this:

A = base time (beginning, into second paragraph)
B = childhood (mid-second paragraph)
C = base time (end second paragraph and beginning of third)
D = (a complex section to be scrutinized more closely later on)
E = recent past (Miss Gavan and the Stores)
F = future ("She would not cry many tears . . . ")
G = recent past (Saturday night, etc.)
H = future ("She was about to explore another life . . . ")
I = recent past (Eveline's relationship with Frank)
J = earlier past (Frank's history)
K = base time (—the "evening deepened")
L = earlier past (Eveline's mother's illness and death)
M = base time mixed with future (end of first section)
N = ellipsis in base time
O = base time (whole second scene, with only a hint of future)

Even ignoring many minor temporal shifts we can discern, then, fifteen distinct sections ranging over at least six separate periods of time in the life of Eveline, extending from her childhood to her possible future with Frank. But because of the way that Joyce has handled the perspective of this story, all these times are contained within the base time of the two scenes. They are all presented to us as aspects of Eveline's thought in a base time which is very close to "present" tense, even though narrated in a conventional past. Even the ellipsis indicates a present and dramatic passage of time. Since Genette discusses perspective as an aspect of "mood," we shall return to it after examining more closely certain aspects of tense that we have thus far set aside.

The fourth temporal unit that we noted above is so complicated temporally that I refrained from specifying its location in time. Now let us look at it more closely. The third section has brought us back to base time, with "now" and "home," as Eveline looks around her darkening room. Let us watch closely the temporal movement within a couple of sentences here:

> She looked [base time] around the room, reviewing [base time] all its familiar objects, which she had dusted [past, iterative] once a week for so many years, wondering [past, iterative] where on earth all the dust came from. Perhaps she would never see again [future, conditional, negative] those familiar objects from which she had never dreamed [past, negative, subordinated within future] of being divided [future, within past negative, within future]. (*D* 37)

What we have here is a rapid oscillation between the past seen as iterative, a familiar round of repeated events, dull but comforting, and a future dimly perceived as the absence of these familiar surroundings. The future as absence ("never see again") is a frightening prospect. Because she is trying to "weigh each side of the question," Eveline's thoughts continually move from the past to the future. But for her the future is at worst negative (never) and at best conditional: "she *would* be married. . . . People *would* treat her with respect then. She *would* not be treated as her mother had been . . . " (italics added). And the future inevitably leads her back to the past. She can see it only dimly, negatively, conditionally. It has no reality for her, no more than Buenos Aires as a place has more reality than the Melbourne of her father's "casual" expression. When she begins to think of herself as wife, she fatally concludes by thinking of her mother. We should note in this respect that her future, if she should remain home, is a subject that eludes her even more completely than her future in Buenos Aires, while she is weighing "each side of the question." We know that she has "palpatations" and we know that "latterly" her father has begun to threaten her with physical violence. And we can infer that her mother had been physically abused in the past. Eveline almost admits this thought to consciousness when she reflects that she would not be "treated as her mother had been" and then moves in the next sentence to thoughts of her father's violence. There is much in both the past and the future that is unexpressed in Eveline's revery.

In developing these considerations I have been led from thoughts of tense into questions of voice and perspective. As Genette points out, this kind of thing is inevitable in analysis, since we are arbitrarily dividing for discussion a thing which is indivisible, because we cannot hope to say everything about a text at once. But this analysis will take us even further into the concerns of the story if we let it. Time, as we are seeing, is not simply a feature of the structure of this narrative, it is a major element of Eveline's situation. "Her time was running out" the narrator tells us, and she knows it. She is facing a moment of terrible choice between a future she cannot conceive and one that she will not admit. Human beings are distinguished from other animals by their ability to project, to reach, through language and vision, into the future. But Eveline is so trapped in the past—in her promise to her dead mother, in the ritual of her church—that she not only fears the future but finally retreats from present awareness altogether: "Moving her lips in silent fervent prayer" she has finally lost the gift of speech and all ability to perceive and communicate. She becomes "passive, like a helpless animal."

Turning from the temporal order of a text to its duration, Genette distinguishes four basic speeds of narration:

1. the ellipsis—infinitely rapid;
2. the summary—relatively rapid;
3. the scene—relatively slow;
4. the descriptive pause—zero degree of progress.

The basic novelistic rhythm, he indicates, is an alteration between undramatic summaries which provide connective delays and dramatic scenes in which the decisive action takes place. In "Eveline" we have all four varieties of duration: an ellipsis between the two sections of the narrative; a summary of Eveline's and Frank's past lives; the dramatic scene at the quay; and even some description, though so little as to make virtually no pause in the story. But we need to notice some peculiar aspects of Joyce's employment of these techniques. First of all, he manages things so that all description and summarizing are presented as aspects of Eveline's thought, and hence function as drama or scene. The narrative segments set in base time do in fact constitute a scene of extended duration, in which a relatively short time in the story occupies a long part of the text. And the first scene, with all its temporal oscillation, gives us a sense of base time passing very slowly. Then the second scene, after the ellipsis, by stretching time out even more, emphasizes the passing of seconds, as the inexorable process of the ship's departure (time and tide wait for no man) brings the future and present to a point of congruity, whereupon Eveline, no longer able to weigh past against future, is driven out of human time altogether into the frozen present of animal existence.

Genette's treatment of fictional mood also provides a useful way into Joyce's story. Genette divides mood into two aspects: distance and perspective. Narrative distance is a function of the amount and precision of detail provided in any discourse. The more detail given, the closer we come to scenic description. Some details may be present gratuitously, as it were, to give "the effect of the real," of something named only because it is "really there." In "Eveline" such items as the "odour of dusty cretonne," or the "coloured print of the promises made to the Blessed Margaret Mary Alacoque" seem to function in this "gratuitous" way, as mere bits of "life," but in the hands of Joyce in particular, these informational bits are likely to carry meanings in more than one code. In this respect Genette's approach needs to be supplemented by that of Roland Barthes, as I shall suggest more extensively below.

In his discussion of distance and perspective Genette considers the critical debate on "showing" versus "telling" in fiction and the modernist emphasis on "showing," which he defines as a preference for scene over summary, with an attendant effacement of the narrator. Joyce, it is clear, is a perfect example of this tendency, at least in "Eveline," where scene reaches out to include all summary and where we have to exercise considerable ingenuity to detect a narrative persona manipulating Eveline's voice and perspective. Genette also insists on the analyst's observing a distinction between perspective and voice in critical study. The eyes we see through and the voice we hear are not necessarily the same in narrative, though in "Eveline" there seems to be little significant difference.

The various perspectives adoptable in fiction are matters of focus. Certain aspects of the events in any story may be clarified by the narrative focus, while others may be hidden or obscured, temporarily or permanently. Focus determines how far into the life of a character we may be allowed to penetrate, and how many characters will be open to interior scrutiny. "The type of focus is not fixed for a whole work, necessarily," Genette observes, "but for a determined segment of narrative which may be very brief." He develops a terminology for a number of varieties of perspective—internal, external, fixed, variable, multiple, and unfocused—but like their counterparts in American discussions of fictional point-of-view these terms may not have sufficient analytic value to justify their taxonomic complexity. The shifts in narrative focus that really count may function at a level where linguistic sensitivity and intuition count for more than apparatus. Even here, however, Genette gives us some interesting leads. He points to the tendency of fictions to employ strategies he calls "paralipse" and "paralepse": that is, the withholding from the reader of information which he "ought"—according to the prevailing focus—to receive; and the presenting to the reader of information which the prevailing level of focalization "ought" to render inaccessible. Joyce, it seems to me, is a highly paraleptic writer, in "Eveline" and in other works as well. In this story he chooses what Genette calls a fixed internal focus, all thoughts being filtered through the mind of Eveline herself, and presented in language much like her own in both syntax and diction (though this is technically a matter of voice rather than perspective—or rather *her* language is a matter of perspective, *his,* the narrator's, is a matter of voice). In choosing Eveline as a focus, Joyce—as in many other stories—has selected a central intelligence who is not very intelligent. Here is where he differs most from both Proust and Henry James, who preferred an intelligence much like their own at the center of their work. (There are some exceptions to this, as in *What Maisie Knew,* but it can be argued that even Maisie is potentially a Jamesian intelligence, and she is certainly enveloped in a rich, Jamesian voice.) But Joyce favored, in the *Dubliners* stories, an internal perspective fixed in a mind which is not only deprived of certain knowledge about the events of the story but which is absolutely limited in education and intelligence. These limited minds trying to cope with painful situations, more than anything else, give the stories their ironic and naturalistic flavor. And this method posed for Joyce an aesthetic problem that he delighted in solving—the problem of paralepse, of conveying to the reader more information than the code required by his perspective "ought" to convey.

Rhetorically speaking, whenever we encounter paralipse or paralepse we are in the presence of irony. In the case of "Eveline" we have already noted how Eveline suppresses certain thoughts about her future in Dublin, and the way in which she links associatively the ideas of her father's brutality and her mother's insanity and death without acknowledging the logical connection between them. In these instances Joyce is leading us to make inferences that result in our helping to "construct" the story we are reading. We, by an act of inference, piece together some of Eveline's situation, and at the same time are enabled to make the further inference that she is suppressing precisely the matter that we have inferred. This takes Joyce in the direction of what Roland Barthes calls the "scriptible" text, a modernist fiction which forces the reader to participate in the creation of its events and meanings. But I would argue that he stops well short of giving us liberty to construct what meanings we please. Our inferences are guided, unobtrusively but firmly, in ways that we have been investigating and will continue to investigate.

This discussion is taking us beyond the range of Genette's system of fictional analysis, but for a very good reason. His treatment of fictional voice, which is illuminating with respect to Proust, is simply not very helpful when we turn to Joyce, though Joyce is one of the most vocalic of writers. This is because Genette considers under voice only matters involving the relationship between distinguishable narrators and the tales they relate. Joyce's kind of ventriloquial effect, in which he narrates in the voice of a character while seeing the character as a third person, limiting himself to saying what the character might perceive but using this saying to convey the views of an invisible narrator—this possibility is just not sufficiently regarded by Genette, perhaps because it involves an interacting between perspective and voice, which he has been at such pains to separate. It is actually Roland Barthes who comes closest to offering us what we need to complete the analysis of a text like "Eveline."

In *S/Z,* his book-length analysis of Balzac's story "Sarrasine," Barthes works his way through the text, a few phrases or sentences at a time, interpreting these "lexias," as he calls them, according to the ways they generate meanings in five signifying systems or codes. His five codes are as follows:

1. The proairetic code or code of actions, which he calls "the main armature of the readerly text"—by which he means, among other things, all texts which are in fact narrative. Where most traditional critics, such as Aristotle and Todorov, would look only for major actions or plots, Barthes (in theory) sees all actions as codable, from the most trivial opening of a door to a romantic adventure. In practice, he applies some principles of selectivity. We recognize actions because we are able to name them. In most fiction (Barthes's readerly texts) we expect actions begun to be completed, thus the principle action becomes the main armature of such a text. (Todorovian notation seeks to isolate this main armature for study.)

2. The hermeneutic code or code of puzzles plays on the reader's desire for "truth," for the answers to questions raised by the text. In examining "Sarrasine," Barthes names ten phases of hermeneutic coding, from the initial posing of a question or thematization of a subject that will become enigmatic, to the ultimate disclosure and decipherment of what has been withheld. Like the code of action, the code of enigmas is a principal structuring agent of traditional narrative. Between the posing of a riddle and its solution in narrative, Barthes locates eight different ways of keeping the riddle alive without revealing its solution, including equivocations, snares, partial answers, etc. In certain kinds of fiction, such as detective stories, the hermeneutic code dominates the entire discourse. Together with the code of actions it is responsible for narrative suspense, for the reader's desire to complete, to finish the text.

3. The cultural codes. There are many of these. They constitute the text's references to things already "known" and codified by a culture. Barthes sees traditional realism as defined by its reference to what is already known. Flaubert's "Dictionary of Accepted Ideas" is a realist's Bible. The axioms and proverbs of a culture or a subculture constitute already coded bits upon which novelists may rely. Balzac's work is heavily coded in this way.

4. The connotative codes. Under this rubric we find not one code but many. In reading, the reader "thematizes" the text. He notes that certain connotations of words and phrases in the text may be grouped with similar connotations of other words and phrases. As we recognize a "common nucleus" of connotations we locate a theme in the text. As clusters of connotation cling to a particular proper name we recognize a character with certain attributes. (It is worth noting that Barthes considers denotation as simply the "last" and strongest of connotations.)

5. The symbolic field. This is the aspect of fictional coding which is most specifically "structuralist" in Barthes's presentation. It is based on the notion that meaning comes from some initial binary opposition or differentiation, whether at the level of sounds becoming phonemes in the production of speech; or at the level of psychosexual opposition, through which a child learns that mother and father are different from one another and that this difference also makes the child the same as one of them and different from the other; or at the level of primitive cultural separation of the world into opposing forces or values which may be coded mythologically. In a verbal text this kind of symbolic opposition may be encoded in rhetorical figures such as antithesis, which is a privileged figure in Barthes's symbolic system.

Since the space and time for a Barthesian amble through the lexias of "Eveline" are not available, I shall invert his procedure and simply locate some elements of each code as found in Joyce's text.

1. Code of Actions (proairetic). In "Eveline" these range from the relatively trivial "She sat," completed four pages later by "She stood up," to the more consequential action of her leaving Dublin for good, which of course never occurs. This is a story of paralysis, which is a major connotative code in all the *Dubliners* stories. Significantly, we never see Eveline move a single step. Even in the last climactic scene her actions are described as "She stood . . . She gripped . . . She set her face." This increasing rigidity thematizes the connotative code of paralysis.

2. Code of Enigmas (hermeneutic). Joyce does not rely heavily on this code. Above all, he does not feel a need to complete it. We

begin with some questions about who Eveline is, why she is tired, and the like, but there is no mystery about this. Frank is an enigma, of course. The discourse tells us something about him, but only gives us Eveline's thoughts about Frank's version of his life. There is also some mystery attached to Eveline's mother, the cause of her death, and the mysterious phrase she uttered which no one can decipher. But the discourse does not complete or "solve" these mysteries. Like the priest who went to Melbourne, they suggest a world not completely fathomable, beyond the comfortable realism of Balzacian discourse. The final enigma, the reason for Eveline's refusal, forces us back into the text, and out to the other *Dubliners* stories to find solutions that will never have the assurance of discursive "truth."

3. Cultural Codes. Cultural coding in this tale is not so much the property of any narrative voice, or of the discourse itself, as it is something in the minds of the characters. Eveline's father sees Frank under a code of cynical parental wisdom: "I know these sailor chaps." Eveline sees him as codified by romantic fiction: "Frank was very kind, manly, openhearted." The discourse ratifies neither view. It avoids the cultural codes of Dublin, which so dominate the characters' lives. Of these, the most powerful is the code of Irish Catholicism, which would classify Eveline's action as a sin.

4. Connotative Codes. The dominant code is the code of paralysis, which is a major element in Eveline's character as well as in the world around her. It is connoted by Eveline's motionlessness throughout the story. It is even conveyed by the dreary, monotonous sentence structure–subject, verb, predicate, over and over again. And it is signified by such details as the promises made to the Blessed Margaret Mary Alacoque, who was paralyzed until she vowed to dedicate herself to a religious life. The way in which this saintly lady's life comments on Eveline's own, introduces another level of connotation, the ironic. Through its ironic combination of signs, the discourse paraleptically leads us to a view of Eveline's situation beyond her own perception of it. She sees herself as weighing evidence and deciding. But the discourse ironically indicates that she has no choice. She is already inscribed as a Dubliner in Joyce's code, and a Dubliner never decides, never escapes. As Diderot's *Jacques le fataliste* would have it, *il est ecrit en haut* (it is written above)–in Joyce's text.

5. The Symbolic Code. For Joyce in *Dubliners* the primal opposition is not male versus female but sexed versus unsexed, usually presented as celibate versus profligate, an opposition that is almost unmediated by any linking term. Only the dead are fruitful or potent in Joyce's wasteland. In "Eveline," the sailor Frank is set in opposition to the father as rival for Eveline, who is filling her mother's role in the household. In this symbolic opposition Frank is associated with water, freedom, the unknown, the future, and potency. The father's house is dusty, Eveline is a slavey in it, but it is known, rooted in the past, and fruitless. As her father's slave/wife, Eveline will be sterile, impotent, celibate, a kind of nun, a Dubliner. This symbolic opposition emerges most powerfully from the clash of connotations in a single sentence in the final scene, when Eveline sees "the black mass of the boat lying in beside the quay." This "black mass" is an innocent descriptive phrase which also connotes the sacrilegious power of the act Eveline is contemplating here. To board that boat, leave the land and enter upon the sea, would be to leave what is known, safe, already coded. It would be above all to flout the teachings of the church, to sin. The virgin, the nun, a celibate safely within the cultural codification of ritual is opposed to the defiled woman upon whose belly the black mass is blasphemously consummated. But look more closely. In that other harmless descriptive phrase, "lying in," another terror is connoted. To "lie in" is to be delivered of child, to be fruitful, to be uncelibate, not to play the mother's role for the father, but to displace her and the father both, sending them into the past. It is to accept life—and the danger of death. These connotations activate the symbolic level of the text by their juxtaposition of its antitheses. And in that extraordinary figure, "All the seas of the world tumbled about her heart," the discourse connotes both the heart surrounded by amniotic fluid ready to burst with life, and also the fear of drowning in life itself, lured beyond her depth by a person she can no longer allow herself to recognize. Our final vision of Eveline is of a creature in a state of symbolic deprivation. If the symbolic code is rooted in the fundamental processes of cognition and articulation, what is signified in that code at the end of "Eveline" is a creature who has lost those fundamental processes, not only at the level of speech and language but even the more fundamental semiotic functions of gesture and facial signals: "She set her white face to him, passive,

like a helpless animal. Her eyes gave him no sign of love or farewell or recognition." However we interpret the story, we are surely intended to regard with pity and fear the situation of this young woman absolutely incommunicado, capable of giving "no sign."

Works Cited

Barthes, Roland. *S/Z.* New York: Hill and Wang, 1974.
Genette, Gérard. *Figures III.* Paris: Seuil, 1972.
Joyce, James. *Dubliners.* New York: Viking, 1969.
Todorov, Tzvetan. *Grammaire du Décameron.* The Hague: Mouton, 1969.

[11]

x/y Joyce and Modernist Ideology

[1987]

This essay was written to be delivered as a lecture at the International Joyce Symposium at Copenhagen in 1986. It appeared later in the proceedings of that meeting (*Coping with Joyce*) and, somewhat modified, in the first chapter of my *Protocols of Reading.* Though it represents a move on my part away from formal semiotic studies to a more cultural form of criticism, it also represents the continuation of my long search for James Joyce, especially as we find him in his early texts. On this occasion, I work mainly with his letters and some of his crucial early reading, but my search for what Europeans call the "formation" of the writer is clearly the driving force of the essay. Joyce's intentions in *Dubliners* and *Portrait,* insofar as they are political or social, are the main objects of my search, though these questions are inevitably connected to issues of realism and naturalism as well as socialism and fascism. I am also beginning to turn here to the issue of modernism as an ideological structure—a matter that will dominate the final essay in this volume.

I wish I could go to Denmark. Ferrero says that
Abo, Stockholm and Copenhagen are the finest cities in Europe.
[*Letters* 2, 201]

Following Joyce's wish, we have at last rearrived in Denmark, but I have chosen to begin a discussion of the ideology of modernism with these words from Joyce's Roman period, not to direct attention to this fine city, but to notice the authority Joyce gives for his desire. The mediator of this desire is Guglielmo Ferrero, whose book *L'Europa giovane* (Young Europe) Joyce was reading in 1906. (He lists it as next to Mercredy's map of Ireland on shelf J, back, among his books in Trieste.) Joyce was much taken with Ferrero, whose study of European culture, published in 1897, is subtitled "Studies and Voyages in the Countries of the North." In September 1906, Joyce found a picture postcard of Ferrero in Rome and wrote to his brother about it: "By the way, talking of faces I will send you a picture postcard of Guglielmo Ferrero and you will admit there is some hope for me. You would think he was a terrified Y.M.C.A. man with an inaudible voice. He wears spectacles, is delicate-looking and, altogether, is the type you would expect to find in some quiet nook in the Coffee-Palace nibbling a bun hastily and apologetically between the hours of half-past twelve and one" (*Letters* 2, 159). Among other things, these remarks suggest that Joyce saw some parallels between Ferrero and himself.

One day in November 1906 Joyce wrote to Stanislaus that he was thinking of beginning his story *Ulysses* but felt too oppressed with cares. In the next sentence he turned to a discussion of Ferrero's views of Jews and anti-Semitism, noting that "the most arrogant statement made by Israel so far, he says, not excluding the gospel of Jesus, is Marx's proclamation that socialism is the fulfillment of a natural law" (*Letters* 2, 190). In the reference to this letter in the index to Richard Ellmann's edition of the letters, what should be "Ferrero on Marx" unaccountably appears as "Ferrero on Mary." This tiny change, the Freudian slip of a pious compositor, no doubt, is effected by simply cutting off a bit of Marx's "x" (a bit off the bottom, so to speak), turning Marx into Mary with a minimum of fuss. How Joyce would have loved this error! I have borrowed my title from it (x/y) in silent homage to the late Roland Barthes who would no doubt have found this emblematic castration of Marx both amusing and significant.

For me it also symbolizes the tension between Christianity and socialism that constitutes one of the structuring polarities of modernist ideology. The movement of W. H. Auden, for instance, from one end of this polarity to the other over the decade 1929–39 is emblematic of this dimension of modernism. One can also find the two opposites dangerously conflated in a typical thirties poem like C. Day Lewis's *Magnetic Mountain,* as in the following lines from the well-known section that begins "You that love England . . . ":

> You who go out alone, on tandem or on pillion,
> Down arterial roads riding in April,
> Or sad beside lakes where hill-slopes are reflected
> Making fires of leaves, your high hopes fallen:
> Cyclists and hikers in company, day excursionists,
> Refugees from cursed towns and devastated areas:
> Know you seek a new world, a saviour to establish
> Long-lost kinship and restore the blood's fulfilment.
> . . . We can tell you a secret, offer a tonic; only
> Submit to the visiting angel, the strange new healer.
>
> . . . You shall be leaders when zero hour is signalled,
> Wielders of power and welders of a new world.
> (*Magnetic Mountain,* poem 32)

This poem, which first appeared in the tendentious collection *New Country* in 1933, is a communist manifesto, written by a committed party member, but the rhetoric of saviour and angel is thoroughly imbued with Christian connotations, as if Day Lewis could express his hopes convincingly only through discursive features that he should have repudiated. The poem is also full of a deeply felt sense of place that is just a step from nationalism: "You that love England, who have an ear for her music." Similarly, "the visiting angel, the strange new healer" may refer to your local Communist party recruiter, but it exudes disturbing connotations of the *Führer Prinzip.* One of the other structuring polarities of modernism is defined by the opposition between equality and hierarchy or, in more purely political terms, between democratic and authoritarian notions of government. This is a polarity that existed *within* the socialist movement, for instance, and not simply as a difference between socialism and conservative or reactionary parties.

Let x/y, then, symbolize the whole set of polarities that shape the ideology of modernism as it emerged in the late nineteenth and early twentieth centuries. To describe these polarities fully is both theoretically and practically impossible, since each description would itself enter the play of ideological discourse. On an occasion such as this, one can only begin to sketch certain dimensions of this field. I propose, then, to examine some interactions between literature and politics, as we can trace them in the lives of a few young men of Joyce's generation, including, of course, Joyce himself. We can begin with a brief summary of a paradigmatic life story of such a young man.

He was born in the early 1880s into a family with little money which managed nonetheless to send him away to religious boarding schools. A biographer describes his father as one who "like his son after him nurtured a mixture of contradictory ideals" (Smith, 2). The father's carelessness about money made life a struggle for the family. At school the young man was troubled by illness and was punished by the authorities. He preferred reading to playing with the other children. At one point he led a revolt against the quality of the food. He refused to go to Mass and once had to be dragged to church by force. In his second school his interest in music flourished, and he was asked to give a speech at a local theater in honor of Giuseppe Verdi. At the age of seventeen he was known as a hermit and misanthrope, but he made regular visits to a local brothel. He received his diploma shortly after the turn of the century, at which time his biographer describes him in this way: "there was already much of the intellectual bohemian about him. He was writing poems and trying, if unsuccessfully, to get them published. He knew long passages of Dante by heart and was a voracious reader of novels and political tracts" (Smith, 5).

After a brief job as a substitute teacher, borrowing money from a number of people, he went into self-imposed exile, leaving behind debts and unpaid rent. In his adopted country he drifted from one job to another. He was a socialist, but he had "little patience with sentimental reformist socialism or with democratic and parliamentary methods; instead he preached revolution to expropriate a ruling class that would never voluntarily renounce power and possessions" (Smith, 7). He spent some time in Paris in 1904 but did not settle there. He worked on foreign languages and practiced translating books from both French and German. He taught school briefly but had trouble keeping order. His biographer tells us that "his mother's death at the age of forty-six caused him great grief and perhaps some feelings of guilt for having been so inattentive a son" (Smith, 9). He spent hours in a university library "on a somewhat rambling and random course of reading that later stood him in good stead" (Smith, 8). He set up housekeeping and started a family in a one-room apartment in the Italian part of Austria with a woman he later married, who is described as taking no interest in his writing or in politics and having "no intellectual pursuits of her own" (Smith, 16). A knowledgeable observer has described his political views while in his early self-imposed exile as follows: "more the reflection of his early environment than the product of understanding and conviction; his hatred of oppression was not that impersonal hatred of a system shared by all revolutionaries; it sprang rather from his own sense of indignity and frustration, from a passion to assert his own ego" (Angelica Balabanoff, qtd. in Smith, 11). He tried his hand at both journalism and fiction but had trouble finding a publisher for his fiction.

Whose early life is described in this brief sketch? It is much like that of James Augustine Aloysius Joyce, is it not, this early life of the man christened Benito Andrea Amilcare Mussolini? Joyce, of course, was named after three saints and Mussolini after three left-wing revolutionaries, but the patterns of their early lives are strikingly similar. In describing Mussolini's youth I have carefully followed Denis Mack Smith's biography, only I have suppressed the repeated incidents of physical violence and brutality that distinguished the personality of the young Mussolini from that of the young Joyce. Mussolini was quick to rape a reluctant female or stab an antagonistic male, actions that situate him at an enormous distance from the essentially gentle and monogamous Joyce. This violence led to a number of imprisonments that also distinguish the youth of Mussolini from that of Joyce. There are other differences as well, in class background for instance, but these very differences emphasize the strikingly similar patterns in the lives of these two young men who were born a year apart in two troubled countries.

Joyce seems to have abandoned socialism—and all political commitment—some time before war broke out in 1914, though I believe his socialist views were entirely serious in the days when he was reading *Avanti!* and describing himself as a socialist artist. Mussolini, of course, was fervent enough as a socialist to become the editor of *Avanti!* in 1912, at which time he also tried to establish another journal, named *Utopia*, in honor of St. Thomas More, whom he admired as the first socialist. For two years at *Avanti!* Mussolini upheld the international socialist line, but as the war approached he became more nationalistic, to the point where he was expelled from his editorship in November 1914 and by December had founded the first *fascio d'azione rivoluzionaria.* In November 1906, at the height of his interest in socialism, Joyce had expressed his admiration for Arthur Griffith and said in a letter to his brother, "If the Irish programme did not insist on the Irish language I suppose I could call myself a nationalist" (*Letters*

2, 187). Both Joyce and Mussolini were responding to similar nationalistic feelings. One of the polarities that shape the modernist dialectic for several decades is this tension between nationalism and internationalism, which in extreme forms turns into a struggle between socialism and fascism. The Stalinist move to "socialism in one country," preserving the Russian revolution by sacrificing a number of others, is a response to the same nationalistic surge in the ideology of modern Europe felt by Joyce and Mussolini a decade or so earlier. For Mussolini, fascism was the answer to his disillusionment with international socialism. As his Fascist party developed after the war, gaining more and more power, he gradually discarded the socialist elements of his program, abandoning both his anticlericalism and his sympathy for the proletariat. What he kept was his attitude toward parliamentary forms of government, an attitude highly visible in the *Avanti!* of 1906, for instance, which Joyce read and discussed regularly.

The view of parliamentary government that Joyce found most appropriate in the latter part of 1906 was that expressed by the syndicalist Arturo Labriola. Joyce explained this in a letter to Stanislaus which is worth quoting at some length:

> I am following with interest the struggle between the various socialist parties here at the Congress. Labriola spoke yesterday, the paper says, with extraordinarily rapid eloquence for two hours and a half. He reminds me somewhat of Griffith. He attacked the intellectuals and the parliamentary socialists. He belongs or is leader of the sindicalists. . . . They assert that they are the true socialists because they wish the future social order to proceed equally from the overthrow of the entire present social organization and from the automatic emergence of the proletariat in trades-unions and guilds and the like. Their objection to parliamentarianism seems to me well-founded. . . . Of course the sindicalists are anti-militarists but I don't see how that saves them from the conclusion of revolution in a conscriptive country like this. (*Letters* 2, 173–74)

We should notice a number of things in Joyce's analysis, including his lack of faith in parliamentary government (which Americans usually refer to as democracy), a position which he also takes in other letters of this period. The evidence suggests that he accepted the socialist critique of parliaments as tools of the bourgeois oligarchy for maintaining their own power and wealth. Certainly his hatred for what he called "the stupid, dishonest, tyrannical, and cowardly burgher class" (*Letters* 2, 158) and "these insolent whores of the bureaucracy" (*Letters* 2, 164) is well documented.

Joyce's connection of Arturo Labriola to Arthur Griffith is also interesting, but the truly devastating point of his commentary on the syndicalists is his dismissal of any possibility of obtaining power for the proletariat other than revolution. He is quick to reject (in another part of the passage from which I have already quoted at length) the syndicalist dream of a general strike. The most damning thing he says against the syndicalists is that they have come to resemble the English socialists. They repress the necessity for revolution because they ignore the fact that "the Italian army is not directed against the Austrian army so much as against the Italian people." In the years when Joyce gave his serious attention to politics, he favored a revolution that would suppress parliamentary government, expropriate the vast wealth of the Catholic church (*Letters* 2, 165–66), punish the bourgeoisie, and emancipate the proletariat (*Letters* 2, 198). This became, in fact, the program of Mussolini's fascists, until he abandoned the genuinely socialist elements of it in 1921, retaining only its antiparliamentarity.

I do not wish to suggest that Joyce was a protofascist in 1906 but to point out that he had attended carefully enough to the dialogue of the Italian socialists for several years to see the overwhelming problems facing the socialist enterprise in Italy, which boiled down to the question, How do pacificist internationalists make a national revolution in a country with a standing army? It took a world war to answer that question, and even in Russia after 1917 it finally took the authoritarian nationalism of Stalin to sustain that revolution. Joyce's turn away from politics, which took place around the time we have been examining, was no doubt determined by many things, among them the impossible contradictions he could see in the political position he found most congenial. But there is more to the story of Joyce's socialism than this, and we must examine certain features of it more thoroughly to discover some of what he learned during his political years.

For the space of about a year, in 1906 and 1907, when he was finishing *Dubliners* and planning *Portrait* and his "story" *Ulysses,* Joyce thought of himself—frequently and earnestly—as a socialist. After that period he certainly took less interest in politics, but he neither repudiated his earlier views nor adopted any of the alternatives that were so visible and insistent around him. We are generally less aware than we should be of Joyce's socialism, mainly because Ellmann, who has been in most respects an exemplary steward of the Joycean oeuvre, adopted a view of Joyce that did not admit of a serious commitment of this sort, at one point in the biography observing, "At heart Joyce can scarcely have been a Nietzschean any more than he was a socialist" (147), and at another arguing that any interest Joyce took in socialism was motivated by a petty hope for personal gain, believing that "the triumph of socialism might make for some sort of state subsidy of artists like himself" (204).

It is a wise biographer who knows the heart of his subject, but Ellmann is not seeing into a heart, of course; he is constructing a portrait of a writer as a young man. His young man frequently returned to the theme of socialism in letters to his brother. Ellmann's way of acknowledging this is to say that Joyce "labored to make socialism an integral part of his personality" (205), the implication clearly being that such labor was in vain; but producing an integrated personality is more the biographer's problem than the subject's. Consider, for a moment, the passage Ellmann introduced in the biography as an example of Joyce's vain labor:

> It is a mistake for you to imagine that my political opinions are those of a universal lover: but they are those of a socialistic artist. I cannot tell you how strange I feel sometimes in my attempt to lead a more civilized life than my contemporaries. But why should I have brought Nora to a priest or a lawyer to make her swear away her life to me? And why should I superimpose on my child the very troublesome burden of belief which my father and mother superimposed on me. Some people would answer that while professing to be a socialist I am trying to make money: but this is not quite true at least as they mean it. (205)

The passage goes on for some distance. What it reveals, among other things, is that for Joyce his rejections of church and state in his own life—as represented by rejection of formal marriage and baptism or religious instruction for children—are aspects of what he calls his socialism. Ellmann's comment on all this is a laconic put-down: "socialism has rarely been defended so tortuously" (205). Unfortunately, however, socialism has been rarely defended in any way other than tortuously, as a little reading in Marx, Adorno, or Lukács would quickly demonstrate—and there are overwhelming reasons why this must be so. One cannot argue for a new way of thinking from within an old way of thinking except with the kind of self-conscious complexity that is all too easily dismissed as "tortuous." My purpose here, however, is not to defend socialistic discourse but to explore the ways in which socialism and other ideological currents merge and diverge during the period we call modernist. In particular I am interested in the ways in which European culture shaped the minds of those individuals who later helped to change the literary and political map of Europe.

In the case of Joyce, we have never, for instance, properly appreciated the contribution of Guglielmo Ferrero to his thinking. The only serious attempt I know of to accomplish this is Dominic Manganiello's, in his useful book *Joyce's Politics,* but the book has not received much attention, and even Manganiello, who treats Joyce's debt to Ferrero at some length, ignores some small but extremely interesting matters.

One of these is the fact that the source of Joyce's often-repeated characterization of the style in which he had written the stories of *Dubliners* is certainly to be found in Ferrero's *L'Europa giovane.* Joyce alluded to Ferrero in a letter to Grant Richards defending his stories "Counterparts" and "Two Gallants," in which he went on to say that he had written *Dubliners* "for the most part in a style of scrupulous meanness" (*Letters* 2, 133–34). This expression is Joyce's translation of a phrase Ferrero applies to the treatment of sensual love in French novels: "Che cosa si trova in Balzac, in Zola, in Flaubert, in De Goncourt? Descrizione dell'amore sensuale, fatte bene o fatte male, fatte con scrupolosa esatezza di analista" (175). Ferrero goes on to condemn the lack of attention to the mental and moral dimensions of sexual psychology in the French novelists. These are commonplaces of the period. One can find them, for instance, in Henry James's criticisms of Flaubert; but for our purpose that striking phrase *"scrupolosa esatezza di analista"* is more important. In Italian, *esatezza* is a cognate of *esatore,* which means tax collector, one who exacts payment. Joyce's "scrupulous meanness" is simply his astonishingly appropriate translation of *"scrupolosa esatezza di analista."*

Ellmann's note on Ferrero in his edition of the letters describes him as "an Italian historian and antifascist social critic," which is true enough but doesn't really locate him politically; moreover, Ellmann's description of what Joyce learned from Ferrero is bizarre: "Ferrero finds a secret alliance between Puritanism, sexual abberation, and military destructiveness, using Bismarck as his example" (133). In the passage Ellmann cites, Ferrero speaks of Bismarck's hatred for France and his desire to destroy Paris by cannon fire as the action of a puritan, not an ascetic, describing Bismarck as *"un rude monogamo"* who detested the city of "aesthetic vice." If Ellmann is right, we must add "rude monogamy" to the list of sexual abberations, but I doubt if Ferrero would approve.

Ferrero was in fact a classic liberal humanist, a true child of the Enlightenment. It is also the case that he was infected by nineteenth-century racism to some extent. His explanations according to racial characteristics appear ludicrous now, but there is much in *L'Europa giovane* that is still interesting. Joyce's "tortuous" defense of his socialism no doubt owes something to passages like this one:

> A man can become a socialist through class interest; that is, because he sees in the Socialist party the best defense of his own interest. But a man can also become a socialist against the interest of his class, for moral reasons, because the numerous defects and the many vices of modern society have disgusted him; and that is the case of many bourgeois socialists, independent professionals, scientists, rich people, who in many countries of Europe, and especially in Italy, participate in one way or another in the socialist movement. (361, my translation)

That is not so bad for 1897. Ferrero was friendly to socialism and accepted much of Marx's criticism of bourgeois society as justified, but he thought that when it came to the crucial matter of the future, Marx had substituted Semitic religiosity for the science he claimed to profess. Joyce told Stanislaus in a letter of November 1906 that he had just finished reading Ferrero's *Young Europe:*

> He has a fine chapter on Antisemitism. By the way Brandes is a Jew. He [Ferrero] says that Karl Marx has the apocalyptic imagination and makes Armageddon a war between capital and labour. The most arrogant statement made by Israel so far, he says, not excluding the gospel of Jesus is Marx's proclamation that socialism is the fulfilment of a natural law. In considering Jews he slips in Jesus between Lassalle and Lombroso: the latter too (Ferrero's father in law) is a Jew. (*Letters* 2, 190)

This passage is Joyce's own conflation of many pages in Ferrero's book. (Ellmann's note on the passage cites many sections, but they are simply taken from the "Indice" and are not accurate.) Joyce learned about Brandes's Jewishness, for instance, from Ferrero's report on an interview with Brandes in Copenhagen. In Ferrero's book Joyce's interest in Jews and his interest in socialism were both fed. Here are excerpts from a crucial passage:

> The great men of the Hebrews have almost all had a transcendent consciousness of their own missions . . . ; they have all felt themselves, more or less lucidly, to be Messiahs. The old popular legend has become a living sentiment, a reality, in the consciousness of the great representatives of the race. Every great Hebraic man is persuaded, even if he does not say so, of having a mandate to inaugurate a new era for the world; to make, in the abyss of darkness in which humanity lives, the opening through which will enter for the first time, and forever, the light of truth. Of course this consciousness may be more or less clear, take one form or another, have a greater or lesser amplitude according to the times and the individuals, but it is there in all of them; it is in the ancient prophets who were precursors of the Messiah, it is in Jesus come to announce the heavenly kingdom; it is in Marx come to announce the proletarian revolution; it is in Lombroso, come to deliver the true scales of justice, after so many ages in which men through ignorance and malice have adopted the false. (366, my translation)

This passage obviously made an impact on Joyce, providing much of what he reported to his brother in the letter already cited, but it also provided something else: a verbal formula that came in handy when he sought a ringing phrase for the conclusion of his first novel. Look at it again, this time in the Italian: *"La vecchia leggenda del popolo é diventata sentimento vivo e realtà nella coscienza dei grandi rappresentanti della razza."* For years we have wondered where that curious phrase "conscience of my race" came from. Now we know: *"nella coscienza . . . della razza."* Ferrero contributed something to the creation of both Stephen Dedalus and Leopold Bloom (as Dominic Manganiello notes in *Joyce's Politics*). It is supremely ironic, then, that when Joyce and Ferrero met it was at a PEN meeting in Paris in 1937, where a virtually blind Joyce listened to the exiled Ferrero lecture passionately on the burning of books by the fascists, thinking all the time only of the infringement of his copyrights and afterward complaining bitterly that politics had spoiled the meeting (see Potts, 155–56). Ferrero died the year after Joyce, also in Switzerland, where he was teaching at the University of Geneva.

We do not know exactly when the apolitical Joyce whom Ferrero encountered in 1937 displaced the political Joyce of 1906, with his syndicalism and revolutionary fervor, but it may be that Ferrero, by directing Joyce's attention to a religious element in Marxism, helped to disillusion him. We can no longer ignore the fact, however, that certainly in *Dubliners* and probably in much of his other work, Joyce felt himself to be engaged in bringing to consciousness the social problems that beset his nation, or in his own language, in a style of scrupulous meanness creating a conscience for his race. We know enough about his thinking in those years to attempt a summary of his literary and political attitudes.

Joyce was antibourgeois, anticlerical, antiparliamentary, antimilitaristic, antibureaucratic, an Irish nationalist, and definitely not an anti-Semite, though extremely interested in Jews. In literature he admired Ibsen, Hauptmann, Tolstoy, Maupassant. In particular he liked the *"scrupolosa esatezza di analista"* that he found in these writers. What he did not like is well expressed in his comments on George Gissing in a letter of November 1906: "I have read Gissing's *Demos: A Story of English Socialism.* Why are English novels so terribly boring? I think G has little merit. The socialist in this is first a worker and then inherits a fortune, jilts his first girl, marries a lydy, becomes a big employer and takes to drink. You know the kind of story. There is a clergyman in it with searching eyes and a deep voice who makes all the socialists wince under his firm gaze" (*Letters* 2, 186). In this critique Joyce's socialism and anticlericalism are inextricably bound up with his sense of realities and his aesthetic judgment. He is judging by a standard in which realism and aestheticism are allied rather than antagonistic.

Certainly one of the polarities that structure modernist ideology is that between naturalism and aestheticism. That particular division of what had been in the nineteenth century a unified realism is one of the decisive breaks that constitutes modernism as a cultural hegemony. Joyce in 1906 was poised right on that break, seeking a way of extending realism without it fragmenting into aesthetic and naturalistic poles. Certainly, the stories of *Dubliners* can be usefully seen in exactly that light. It will be helpful in appreciating his position to look carefully at his thoughts on a writer whom most critics would see as tending toward the naturalistic pole to a greater extent than Tolstoy,

Maupassant, or Ibsen may be said to do. I refer to Gerhard Hauptmann, whose *Rosa Bernd* Joyce acquired, though he could scarcely afford it, at a time in the autumn of 1906 when he was also taking Danish lessons to read Ibsen more easily in the original. Joyce had admired Hauptman for some years but his appraisal of Hauptmann's drama was this side idolatry:

> I finished Hauptmann's *Rosa Bernd* on Sunday. I wonder if he acts well. His plays, when read, leave an unsatisfying impression on the reader. Yet he must have the sense of the stage well developed in him by now. He never, in his later plays at least, tries for a curtain so that the ends of his acts seem ruptures of a scene. His characters appear to be more highly vivified by their creator than Ibsen's but also they are less under control. He has a difficulty in subordinating them to the action of his drama. He deals with life quite differently, more frankly in certain points . . . but also so broadly that my personal conscience is seldom touched. His way of treating such types as Arnold Kramer and Rosa Bernd is, however, altogether to my taste. His temperament has a little of Rimbaud in it. Like him, too, I suppose somebody else will be his future. But, after all, he has written two or three masterpieces—"a little immortal thing" like *The Weavers,* for example. I have found nothing of the charlatan in him yet. (*Letters* 2, 173)

Joyce's praise of Hauptmann's vividness of characterization, his frankness, and his freedom from charlatanry is balanced by a dissatisfaction that is partly aesthetic (a disparity between characters and actions) and partly ethical: he deals with life "so broadly that my personal conscience is not touched." The immediate contrast, only partly explicit here, is with Ibsen, whose control and balance bring him near the top of Joyce's aesthetic scale. The young Joyce's reactions to Gissing and Hauptmann can help us to locate his own position with respect to naturalism. He rejects the sentimentalized naturalism of Gissing and prefers the harsher, franker naturalism of Hauptman. But he is troubled by two features of Hauptmann's work, a certain lack of aesthetic "control" (which Ibsen so obviously had) and a crudity or broadness that left his "personal conscience" untouched—a criticism similar to Ferrero's critique of the French novelists. The need to reconcile the naturalistic presentation of life with an aesthetic control that would affect the personal conscience emerges from these critiques as the central problem for Joyce as a writer. It is the paradigmatic problem for the modernist writer of plays or stories, a problem that other modernists, such as Hemingway and Lawrence, would also have to solve.

This problem became central in the work of another young man of Joyce's generation, whose experience will serve to close this little excursion into modernist ideology. He was born in the 1880s in a city on the edge of Europe. Though raised in a bourgeois family he rebelled against bourgeois manners and values. He was a bright student in school: outwardly conforming but inwardly rebellious. One of the earliest literary works to impress him was Lamb's *Tales from Shakespeare*. At a later age he discovered "Baudelaire, Verlaine, Swinburne, Zola, Ibsen, and Tolstoy as leaders and guides" (*Record of a Life,* 147; hereafter *RL*). As he matured, he continued to admire the radicalism of Scandinavian and Russian literature. Years later he recalled his relationship with his family in this way: "I was completely estranged from my family, or at least from a part of it. I did not have any relationship with the family at all. . . . My mother was a shrewd woman who soon saw what was happening. She fell seriously ill and died of cancer of the breast. Under pressure from other members of the family, I wrote her a letter. When she received it she said, 'I must be very ill for [my son] to write me a letter' " (*RL,* 35).

Rejecting marriage as a bourgeois convention he went into self-imposed exile. Looking back on his twenty-third year, he wrote, "In my case . . . absolute independence in order to produce, and for that reason silent rejection" (*RL,* 151). This was his version of the Joycean "silence, exile, and cunning." He came to admire the work of a poet who expressed his own values, seeing in this poet in 1906, as he later recalled, "a revolutionary who regarded the revolution as indispensable for his own self-realization" (*RL,* 39). He had ambitions to write a treatise on aesthetics and to be a dramatist. "I started to write plays in the manner of Hauptmann and Ibsen" (*RL,* 31), he later recalled, and he translated *The Wild Duck* into his native language (*RL,* 34). Writing about Hauptmann some time after his youthful enthusiasm, he praised in particular the dramatist's "great and beautiful honesty" (*Reviews and Articles,* 27–28). Living in Italy in his twenty-sixth year he began a major work on aesthetic theory but set it aside the following year. When he was about twenty-five he discovered French syndicalism, which, he says, "at the time I regarded as the only oppositional socialist movement that could be taken seriously" (*RL,* 41). He condemned conditions in his own country, which he seriously hoped to change through his own work, but, as he has said, "this did not mean that I was prepared to accept English Parliamentarianism as an alternative ideal" (*RL,* 44).

The young man I have been describing, as you have no doubt realized, is Georg Lukács, the Hungarian Jew who became Europe's leading Marxist literary critic and theoretician. Considering the fact that he came to be a major opponent of the kind of modernism he felt to be manifested in Joyce's work, it is useful to see how much the two writers shared in the cultural matrix from which modernism emerged. But at the point where Joyce turned from politics to art, Lukács turned in the opposite direction. Toward the end of his life an interviewer asked him about shift of interest:

> INT: You said you gave up aesthetics because you had begun to be interested in ethical problems. What works resulted from this interest?
>
> G.L.: At that time it did not result in any written works. My interest in ethics led me to the revolution. (*RL,* 53)

Both of these young men reached a similar point of decision and made their choices, living the lives that followed from them. They had also made other choices, Joyce abandoning criticism as Lukács abandoned drama, but these were more personal, matters of talent primarily. Perhaps the ideological choices stem as much from personality as anything else, but there is a lot we do not know about these things. In the case of Joyce, for instance, what may have been a crucial year of intellectual decision, 1908, is simply a blank on the biographical record. For the first eleven months of that year we have five lines of correspondence and precious little else. We know a lot about what Joyce was in 1906 and what he later became. About the transition itself, we are ignorant.

We know, however, that Georg Lukács became the most articulate critical opponent of modernism in literature (with the possible exception of Wyndham Lewis). Lukács's critique of modernism has a philosophical basis that allows him to set modernism against realism, in fact to see modernism as a perverse negation of realism. For Lukács realism is based on the view of man as a *zoon politikon,* a political animal. Modernism, on the other hand, is based on a view of human existence as, in Heidegger's expression, a *Geworfenheit ins Dasein,* a "thrownness into being." Realism, says Lukács, depends upon perspective and norms of human behavior, whereas modernism destroys perspective and glorifies in the abnormal. Realism assumes the objectivity of time and modernism assumes time's subjectivity. For Lukács, Joyce acquired the proportions of the archmodernist, whose works displayed an exaggerated concern with form, style, and technique in general, along with an excessive attention to sense-data, combined with a comparative neglect of ideas and emotions.

Lukács's unfavorable comparison of Joyce to Thomas Mann, however, has affinities with Joyce's comparison of Hauptmann to Ibsen. It should also be noted that Lukács does not trivialize Joyce's enterprise. He is perfectly ready to call *Ulysses* a masterpiece, as he does in the following passage: "A gifted writer, however extreme his theoretical modernism, will in practice have to compromise with the demands of historicity and of social environment. Joyce uses Dublin, Kafka and Musil the Hapsburg Monarchy, as the locus of their masterpieces. But the locus they lovingly depict is little more than a backcloth; it is not basic to their artistic intention" (*Realism in Our Time,* 21). Lukács particularly criticized Joyce's use of the stream of consciousness, in which, as he argued, "the perpetually oscillating patterns of sense and memory-data, their powerfully charged—but aimless and directionless—fields of force, give rise to an epic structure which is static, reflecting a belief in the basically static character of events" (18). This is by no means a trivial or inaccurate description of Joyce's major enterprise, though I think the Joycean stream of consciousness is more directed and purposeful than Lukács gives it credit for being. Lukács is surely right, however, when he borrows Walter Benjamin's description of Romantic and Baroque art to characterize the allegorical tendencies of modernism: "Every person, every object, every relationship can stand for something else" (42). It is surely this, and the Joycean sense that history is an endless repetition of such transformations, that makes Joyce a fearful object to Lukács, whose faith in progressive possibilities could only abhor what he called the "religious atheism" that animated Joyce's modernism.

For all their differences, however, they were products of very similar cultural interests and pressures. To emphasize that, I shall close by presenting some excerpts from one of the last things Lukács wrote, his *Gelebtes Denken,* or preliminary notes for an autobiography that he did not live to finish. To my ears they connect him across time, across politics, across experiences, across Europe with the writer who most symbolized for him the mistaken ways of modernist prose.

> Objectivity: the correct historicity. Memory: tendency to relocate in time. Check against the facts. Youth. . . .
>
> No poet. Only a philosopher. Abstractions. Memory, too, organized to that end. Danger: premature generalization of spontaneous experience. But poets: able to recall concrete feelings. . . . That already means at the right place at the right time. Especially: childhood. . . .
>
> Live here: over 80—subjective interest in reality maintained—at a time when the contact with early youth often lost. Long and even now, an undeniably industrious life—my right to attempt to justify this posture. . . .

Thus an old Hungarian Jew, back from exile, planning to justify his life, lapses into a prose somewhere between an outline and a stream of consciousness. He wants to fight the tendency of memory to relocate in subjective time, seeks the objective, the facts, but also says, "No poet. Only a philosopher. Abstractions." He fought to the end the tendency of his own discourse toward modernism and the power of his own subjectivity, which had been formed in the same European crucible as that of those he criticized. Sometimes, at some levels, x = y.

Works Cited

Ellmann, Richard. *James Joyce.* London: Oxford University Press, 1959.

Ferrero, Guglielmo. *L'Europa giovane: Studi e viaggi nei paesi del nord.* Garzanti, 1946.

Joyce, James. *Letters,* vol. 2, ed. Richard Ellmann. New York: Viking, 1966.

Lewis, C. Day. *Magnetic Mountain,* in *Collected Poems, 1929–1933.* New York: Random House, 1935.

Lukács, Georg. *Realism in Our Time.* New York: Harper, 1971.

——. *Record of a Life.* New York: Verso, 1983.

——. *Reviews and Articles.* New York: Merlin, 1983.

Potts, Willard. *Portraits of the Artist in Exile.* Seattle: University of Washington Press, 1979.

Smith, Denis Mack. *Mussolini.* New York: Random House, 1983.

[12]

In the Brothel of Modernism: Picasso and Joyce

[1991]

This essay introduces itself. For that reason, and because it is too recent for me to have much perspective on it, this note will be brief. Obviously, this essay continues my move toward cultural criticism and my critique of modernism. It also represents my swan song as a Joyce scholar, the end—though not the completion—of my thirty-year search for James Joyce.

> Hey what! You here, dear fellow! You, in a house of ill fame? You, the drinker of quintessences! You, the ambrosia eater? Really, this takes me by surprise.
>
> [Charles Baudelaire, "Loss of Halo," *Petits Poèmes en prose*][1]

> But it is precisely modernity that is always quoting primeval history. This happens through the ambiguity attending the social relationships and products of this epoch. Ambiguity is the pictorial image of dialectics, the law of dialectics seen at a standstill. This standstill is utopia and the dialectical image therefore a dream image. Such an image is presented by the pure commodity: as fetish. Such an image are the arcades, which are both house and stars. Such an image is the prostitute, who is saleswoman and wares in one.
>
> [Walter Benjamin, *Reflections,* 157]

This essay has existed in a number of forms: as a series of slides with an accompanying oral patter; as a written text with no visual illustrations;

and as a lecture with slides. In the course of its existence as a lecture, the view of modernism offered here has met with some serious criticism. The present version has been modified to respond to that criticism, and it also includes some material dropped from earlier versions because it seemed likely that only those with a special interest in Joyce might find that material interesting. The criticism to which I shall respond was made by Gayatri Chakravorty Spivak, both publicly, in a lecture following my own, and privately, in a letter to me after the public presentation of this material. I have taken her objections with the utmost seriousness, not simply because we are old friends, nor because I have enormous respect for her learning and her critical intelligence, but especially because her objections focus on the role of women in modernism, which has been a major concern of mine for some years, in the courses I have taught and in my thinking about cultural history. It was precisely by thinking of modernism in terms of gender that I was led to this subject, and was led to see that Joyce and Picasso were connected, at some important level, by their interest in the brothel as an aesthetic space.

Let me begin, then, by quoting from Professor Spivak's letter (31 January 1991) what I take to be the heart of her objections to my talk: "there was a qualitative absence of assuming woman as agent of modernism in your paper laced with masculist humor and what, in that qualitative absence, seemed like a voyeurism painful to many of us. I spoke because many women lamented this after your talk." A serious objection, powerfully stated. My response is that modernism, especially around its Parisian center of activity, was indeed a masculist activity that positioned women voyeuristically and, to an astonishing extent, turned would-be agents into patients. The careers of Djuna Barnes and Jean Rhys, for instance, show how difficult it was—and what a price had to be paid—for a woman to function as a modernist writer in Paris. My argument, then, is that modernism was never a level playing field but a gendered movement, driven by the anxieties and ambivalences of male artists and writers—anxieties and ambivalences that worked to bring the figure of the prostitute to the center of the modernist stage.

Any such argument will be heavily dependent upon definitions. I shall try to define and locate modernism as I understand it, and to explain why Joyce and Picasso are so central to it. In terms of the history of art and literature, modernism follows impressionism (or postimpressionism). All of these new movements in art and literature emerge from a crisis of confidence in aesthetic realism—a crisis shaped by the development of new means of representation, more mechanical or more scientific than the arts had been, and by a growing fragmentation in social life itself. This crisis was marked in painting by the rise of photography and a turning away from the linear perspectivism first generated by the *camera obscura* in the Renaissance—and marked in literature by the rise of social science and a questioning of the power of a single omniscient viewpoint to capture social realities for art. In both visual and verbal art this move away from realism emphasizes the unique perspectives of individual artists, so that it may be said to complete a Romantic swerve away from an aesthetic of imitation toward one based on the creator's own struggle for expression. In the writing of English fiction, impressionism emerges from the work of Walter Pater and Henry James to flourish in the hands of Dorothy Richardson, Virginia Woolf, and the early James Joyce, among others. It is characterized, to an important extent, by an emphasis on the interior monologue as a form, in which various impressions (directly from the senses and from memory and imagination as well) are presented as a stream of prose textuality. Woolf (who seems to me a writer at least as interesting as Joyce) remained an impressionist or postimpressionist throughout her career. In this she was like the painters to whom she was close—her sister, Vanessa, and Duncan Grant, for instance. She never quite became a modernist, in my view, though I see this as a purely descriptive matter rather than an evaluative one. It is only if one accepts the modernist position on art and literature that becoming a modernist assumes a crucial evaluative role. And I do not accept that position.

The modernist position on art is one most of us have internalized to such a degree that we take it to be natural. To free ourselves from it we need to situate it and examine its workings with a more critical eye. I now see modernism as a late—perhaps the last?—phase of the Romantic movement in art and letters. From Romanticism modernism gets its emphasis on originality, on the need to make things "new"—to be perpetually innovative at the level of form and content. It is their perpetual restlessness and formal innovation, among other things, that have put Joyce and Picasso at the center of modernist art and literature. From Romanticism modernism also gets its sense of the artist as a kind of secular priest or prophet whose role it is to purify the language of the tribe or free vision from the shackles of older perspectives, and whose struggle to accomplish this is held to be interesting in itself. And finally, from Romanticism modernism gets its special form of classicism, an emphasis on myths and archetypes that buttresses the modernist claims to timely originality with equally powerful claims to the representation of eternal archetypes or recurring aspects of reality. In modernist literature such archetypal gestures produce what T. S. Eliot called "the mythic method" of writing.

By the standards of this classical modernism, Woolf's refusal to be sufficiently avant-gardist in form and subject matter relegated her to what Hugh Kenner has called "provincial" status with respect to modernism; and, in the case of Gertrude Stein, who was as avant-gardist as one could wish, her refusal to be mythic and archetypal kept her on the margins of modernist writing. Let me hasten to say again that I am not making value judgments here. Woolf and Stein are two of the writers of this period to whom I find myself continually returning, both for the pleasure of reading them and because of their importance in the history of modern culture. In the case of Stein, it is fair to say that she moved directly toward postmodernism in her "portrait" style, without lingering in modernism. In the case of Woolf, she found room for further development of impressionism in ways that suited her chosen subject matter extremely well. Her work has lasted because she solved the problems of impressionism much more successfully than Dorothy Richardson, for example, who never found the best way to focus her obvious talent as an impressionist so as to give narrative as well as descriptive power to her enormous text. By way of contrast, we might think of Proust, also a late or postimpressionist, who brilliantly solved the narrative problem.

Other women writing fiction in English during the modern period found other viable solutions to the breakdown of realism without feeling it necessary to attain the level of flamboyant experimentalism so characteristic of modernism and so obvious in Joyce. I think of May Sinclair, E. H. Young, E. M. Delafield, Rebecca West, Elizabeth Von Arnim, Rose Macaulay, Rosamund Lehmann, Storm Jameson, Ivy Compton-Burnett, and Winifred Holtby—a list that could be extended. Nor do I mean to exclude those international figures whose relationships to modernism are problematic in various ways, such as Djuna Barnes, Jean Rhys, Katherine Mansfield, Hilda Doolittle, and Kay Boyle. One could produce durable fiction during the heyday of modernism without being entirely, or even mainly, a modernist. That is part of my point. But another part of it is that the modernists were adept at claiming the central aesthetic ground. They made artistic life difficult for many writers who lacked patrons, who needed to be published and read regularly for financial reasons, or who simply did not share the modernist aesthetic.

My claim here is that modernism as a literary and artistic movement seems to have been structured in such a way as to exclude, marginalize, and devalue the work of women—or to extract a price from them that hampered their development. This can be traced in specific historical incidents: the attacks on her intellectual integrity that damaged the reputation of Edith Sitwell during her career as a modernist poet; or the rejections by publishers of Stevie Smith's poetry, along with instructions to her to go and write a novel; or the seduction of Jean Rhys by Ford Madox Ford as a way of assisting her with her career; or the impregnation of Rebecca West by H. G. Wells, which hindered West's progress in getting established as a writer; or the misogynistic and anti-Semitic attack of Wyndham Lewis on Gertrude Stein's prose; or Ezra Pound's expulsion of Amy Lowell from the imagists; and so on. Modernism's exclusion or marginalization of women can also be shown in the extraordinary role that prostitution played in the development as modernists of those two giants of the movement, Joyce and Picasso—and that is the burden of the following discussion.

We begin with a myth. The Roman poet Ovid tells us how Pasiphae, the wife of King Minos of Crete, desired sexual contact with a bull and hid herself inside a wooden cow to achieve this. This offspring of this unnatural love was a creature half man and half bull, called the Minotaur. Embarrassed by the existence of this creature who partly bore his name and made his wife's shame visible to all, Minos hired an architect named Daedalus to construct a labyrinth in which the Minotaur could be hidden away. The monster lived in the midst of this maze and was given girls and boys from Athens to feast upon at regular intervals, until the hero Theseus killed him. Daedalus, desiring to leave the island of Crete, set his mind to unknown arts and designed wings for flight. He and his son Icarus flew off the island, but Icarus, ignoring his father's prudent flight plan, flew too high, so that the sun melted the wax holding his wings together, and he fell into the sea, where he drowned. This familiar story has a strange connection with modern art, which I shall make plain in a moment, but first I must tell, very briefly, the stories of two lives.

In late October 1881 a child was born in Málaga, Spain, just across the sea from Africa, who was destined to become the richest and most famous of modern artists. His name was Pablo Ruiz Picasso, and it is said that he could draw before he could speak. His father was an artist, and legend has it that the young Picasso painted so well that his father gave the boy his own palette and brushes and vowed never to paint again, since his son had surpassed him. Picasso grew up in Barcelona and attended art school there, but moved to Paris early in the twentieth century. There he soon attracted attention as a painter, but he was never satisfied with any one mode of art and kept innovating relentlessly, developing the cubist mode of painting but then abandoning his followers, ever moving onward toward new methods, new media, and new ways of recycling found objects and old artifacts. Whenever modernism in the arts is mentioned, Picasso's name holds a central place.

A few months after Picasso was born, in February 1882, a boy was born in Dublin, Ireland, who was destined to share with Picasso a central position in modernism. Christened James Augustine Joyce, he was exceptionally gifted as a writer, as precocious with words as Picasso was with visual forms. He, too, was drawn to Paris, arriving there first in the same year as Picasso but not settling there until after World War I. He did not become rich, but he did become a figure as dominant in modern letters as Picasso was in visual art, whose relentless formal innovations kept the rest of the literary world panting helplessly behind him. It is a curious fact that these two men, born in Catholic countries far from the centers of culture and power in modern Europe, came to live in Paris, the city that Walter Benjamin called "The Capital of the Nineteenth Century," and helped to make it the capital of modernism as well (*Reflections,* 146–62).

These two are linked by other curious facts, so many that their tale becomes, as Alice said, curiouser and curiouser, the more we look into it. Such looking is just what I propose we do on this occasion. We can begin this enterprise by noting how Picasso and Joyce come together most strikingly of all through the mythic structure I have cited from Ovid. Picasso regularly thought of himself and painted himself in the figure of the Minotaur, as a brutal creature with a man's body and a bull's head, the devourer of youths and maidens, ruthless but fascinating in his Nietzschean exultation, in which creation and destruction were merged. Joyce, on the other hand, regularly thought of himself and represented himself in the figure of Daedalus, setting his mind to unknown arts, escaping from his island prison, and building labyrinths of textuality. As the Minotaur, raging against his imprisonment in the labyrinths of tradition, Picasso shares the same myth of self-definition as Joyce, as the indefatigable builder of new labyrinths in which to capture in a web of words the monstrosity of modern life.

I am not suggesting that these two encountered one another meaningfully in life, for they did not, Picasso once even refusing to paint Joyce's portrait when asked. But they belong together nonetheless, not only because they chose different aspects of the same myth in which to figure themselves, but because they shared a preoccupation with bestiality that was intimately connected with the formal innovations that gave each of them a dominant position in modern art. Moreover, at a crucial moment each of them chose to embody his most striking formal innovations, aesthetic breakthroughs that changed the face of modern art and literature altogether, in scenes that share an astonishing number of formal and thematic features. These breakthroughs came as each labored furiously to present a scene set in a house of prostitution, located in the city in which he had spent his youth. This fact, I want to argue, is a coincidence of such monstrous proportions that it requires our most serious consideration if we are to understand what modernism itself was all about. Any such consideration will reveal that modernism and the representation of prostitution are linked in ways that extend well beyond the two texts on which we shall be focusing our attention here.

The idea that there is a special relationship between prostitution and modernism is not new. T. J. Clark, Charles Bernheimer, and others have drawn our attention to this powerfully in recent years. But for me the connection of Joyce and Picasso to this theme—and to one another—did not become clear until I taught a course at Brown University on their work. And even then, I did not quite grasp the situation until I happened, while trapped in a motel in Indianapolis, to see on television a film by Louis Malle called *Pretty Baby.* Let me tell you about that film. The action takes place in New Orleans during World War I—in a brothel, for the most part. As it begins we are with a girl (played by a very young Brooke Shields) who is watching something out of our range of vision. Watching her watching, we are aware of sounds: grunts, groans, heavy breathing. Knowing where we are, we quickly jump to the conclusion that the little girl is watching a scene of sexual intercourse. Not exactly, as it turns out. She is watching her mother give birth to her baby brother, whose arrival she is soon announcing to everyone in the house. *Pretty Baby* is the story of a child prostitute and a photographer, set, appropriately enough, in Storyville, New Orleans, from 1917 to 1920. For reasons that I hope to explain adequately, I want to read this film as an allegory or parable of modernism itself.

The story *Pretty Baby* presents to us is a familiar one in certain respects, in that it is about a male artist and his female model—a text with deep roots and long ramifications in the history of Western culture. What is special about this version is that the model is a child prostitute and the artist is a photographer—a photographer who finds the ideal motifs for his art in the prostitutes who pose for him in their off-duty moments, in natural sunlight, as if he were an impressionist painter. This situation links him to such precursors of modernism as Delacroix, Manet, Degas, and Toulouse-Lautrec. Delacroix, in his later years, posed nude models to be photographed by his friend Eugène Durieu and then sketched from the photographs, regretting that "this wonderful invention," as he called it, had arrived so late in his life (Newhall, 82). Manet, of course, shocked Paris with his paintings of Victorine Meurent in the *Déjeuner sur l'herbe* and *Olympia.* Degas—in addition to painting horses, dancers, milliners, and laundresses—produced over a hundred of his stark brothel monotypes. And Toulouse-Lautrec, who in 1893 and 1894 lived a good deal of the time in two high-class brothels (Bernheimer, 195), produced some paintings and drawings of prostitutes in their habitat that are extraordinary in their freedom from both condemnation and condescension. His work leads directly to the early Parisian paintings of Picasso—and to the photographs of the real E. J. Bellocq, who looked more like Toulouse-Lautrec than like Keith Carradine (who played him in *Pretty Baby*). What distinguished Bellocq from these painters, of course, in life and in Malle's film, is that he was a photographer rather than a painter. But in this film he is specifically inscribed as an artist rather than a mechanical hack; he is a photographer of the old school, an anachronism even in 1917, working under a black hood with glass plates, developing his pictures with dangerous chemicals. In this film the brothel is a refuge, a sanctuary for photography as a form of art. Bellocq is presented as a licensed voyeur in the brothel, of which he neither approves nor disapproves but accepts as providing the best material for his art. After a time he comes to belong in the brothel, on much the same footing as the elegant black man who plays an equally elegant jazz piano—and is called "Professor," of course. Neither of these two "goes upstairs" with the prostitutes. They are themselves prostitutes of a sort, making their livings off the comodification of their arts rather than with the sweat of their bodies. This situation, in which musician and photographer manage to exist both in and on prostitution, practicing their arts in an accommodation with commodity culture, offers us a fruitful image for the situation of the artist under the cultural and economic regime we know as modernism.

It is not a new image, of course, nor is it merely an image. As early as 1843, the arch bohemian Alexandre Privat had proposed (in a letter asking the help of Eugène Sue) to write two novels (which, being a true bohemian, he never wrote): one about "the lives of girls who started out working in various Paris manufactures, and who then became *grisettes* of the Latin Quarter before going on to lives as prostitutes"; and the other about "young men who have had their arms broken by secondary education and have no occupation"—these young men, as Jerrold Siegel has reminded us, "lived by selling their intelligence.... Like the *grisettes,* therefore, they were prostitutes, putting their minds up for sale just as the young women put up their bodies" (137–38). Charles Baudelaire was the first major literary figure to realize fully the cultural importance of prostitution and its resemblance to artistic production in modern, capitalistic Europe. As Susan Buck-Morss has pointed out (following Walter Benjamin), "Baudelaire makes modern, metropolitan prostitution 'one of the main objects of his poetry.' Not only is the whore the subject matter of his lyrical expression; she is the model for his own activity. The 'prostitution of the poet,' Baudelaire believed, was 'an unavoidable necessity' " (185). As Benjamin himself put it, "Baudelaire knew how things really stood for the literary man: As flâneur, he goes to the literary marketplace, supposedly to take a look at it, but already in reality to find a buyer" (qtd. in Buck-Morss, 185).

Benjamin also observed that the prostitute held a special fascination for the modern artist because she was subject and object in one, the seller of flesh and the fleshly commodity that was sold (*Reflections,* 157). This parallel between the situations of artist and prostitute was both fascinating and troubling for male writers and artists. For painters in particular it was complicated by the relationship between artist and model, which recapulates in certain respects the situation of client and prostitute; indeed, many models were also the sexual objects of their painters. We should pause, however, and consider how much more complicated this relationship was for female painters and sculptors in particular. Many of them were both models and artists, objects and subjects with a vengeance. The case of Camille Claudel, one of the sculptor Rodin's models and mistresses, yet a talented sculptor herself, is now, thanks to film, well known. Less well known is the case of Gwen John, one of the finest of English painters, who was also a mistress of Rodin, posing for his sculpture called *The Muse,* whose work is only beginning to be properly known and respected today. A "muse," of course, is a woman who inspires an artist, rather than an artist in her own right. This list could be extended specifically to include the women artists who became models, mistresses, muses, whatever, for Picasso himself—but for the moment, a mere mention of this aspect of the situation will have to suffice.

Now we are concerned with the other side of this relationship—specifically, the ambivalence of male artists who saw that they, too, sometimes played the role of prostitute in order to function as artists. Under the commodity culture which spawned modernism, even succesful artists could scarcely avoid thinking of themselves in this manner. The greatest of modernists were often as jealous of one another as any prostitute might be of another who was getting a higher rate. Thus we find James Joyce, in a 1920 letter to his friend Frank Budgen, complaining in this vein: "If you see the October *Dial* in any reading room you will find a long film about me. I observe a furtive attempt to run a certain Mr Marcel Proust of here against the signatory of this letter. I have read some pages of his. I can't see any special talent but I am a bad critic" (*Letters,* 148); and in 1927 he complained to his patron, Harriet Weaver, about yet another rival or competitor: "My position is a farce. Picasso has not a higher name than I have, I suppose, and he can get 20,000 or 30,000 francs for a few hours work. I am not worth a penny a line" (*Selected Letters,* 327).

Consider for a moment this brief reference to Proust and *The Dial.* Joyce's relationship with Scofield Thayer, the editor of *The Dial,* was a strange one. In 1919, persuaded by Mary and Padraic Colum, Thayer cabled Joyce the substantial sum of $700, but his magazine was never interested in the seamy side of modernism, which Joyce represented all too clearly for him. *The Dial* really did preach the gospel of Proust, who expressed his gratitude in appropriately fulsome terms: "Au trés cher Dial qui m'a mieux compris et plus chaleureusement soutenue qu'aucune journal, aucune revue. Tout ma reconnaissance pour tout de lumière qu'illumine la pensée et réchauffe le coeur" (Joost, 192). Proust's choice of words is illuminating. A *souteneur* may be one who sustains, but in French he is also specifically a pimp. The language of patronage and the language of prostitution often proved painfully similar to those being patronized. It is clear that Thayer had no intention of "sustaining" Joyce. Although he testified at the *Ulysses* trial on behalf of Joyce's book, he admitted on the witness stand that he would not have published the novel's "Nausicaa" episode in *The Dial.* Given his feeling about Joyce, it is a wonder that Thayer did print Joyce's poem "A Memory of the Players in a Mirror at Midnight" in the July 1920 issue. Written in Zurich in 1917, "Memory" was later included in *Pomes Pennyeach.*

> They mouth love's language. Gnash
> The thirteen teeth
> Your lean jaws grin with. Lash
> Your itch and quailing, nude greed of the flesh.
> Love's breath in you is stale, worded or sung,
> As sour as cat's breath,
> Harsh of tongue.
>
> This grey that stares
> Lies not, stark skin and bone.
> Leave greasy lips their kissing. None
> Will choose her what you see to mouth upon.
> Dire hunger holds his hour.
> Pluck forth your heart, saltblood, a fruit of tears:
> Pluck and devour!
>
> (*Collected Poems,* 57)

This poem, it is fair to say, is the most avoided text in the entire Joycean oeuvre. Joyce's biographers and commentators have virtually nothing to say about it, beyond the fact that it exists. Like many of the other poems that ultimately appeared with it in *Pomes Pennyeach,* these words may have sprung partly from Joyce's reading of Elizabethan or Jacobean drama—or from Baudelaire himself. Certainly, this language has the putrescent flavor that drew T. S. Eliot to some of his raids upon these same sources. But who can doubt that Joyce's poem also has roots in his own broodings on age, lust, and corruption. Without attempting a full-scale reading of the poem on this occasion (I, too, shall avoid it), let me observe that it combines images of the brothel and the charnel house, motifs that haunt the work of Picasso as well as Joyce, both of whom frequented brothels and had bouts with venereal disease in their youth. The poem can even be read as a gloss upon Picasso's *Les Demoiselles d'Avignon,* to which we shall turn our attention shortly. In any case, it is not typical of what Thayer liked to publish in *The Dial,* yet it is the only work by Joyce that he actually did publish.

What Joyce referred to (in his letter to Budgen) as "a long film about me" is in fact a critical essay by Evelyn Scott, which was the first extended discussion of Joyce's work to appear in America and still ranks as one of the best essays written about Joyce by anybody at any time. This should have pleased him, and perhaps it did, since Scott's biographer says that Joyce wrote her a thank-you note, though such a note does not appear in any volume of Joyce's letters (Callard, 39). But why did Joyce call this essay a "film"? Perhaps because it rolled along through his work and only stopped with the latest serialized publications of the unfinished *Ulysses.* As we know, film was frequently on Joyce's mind, and especially in 1917, when "A Memory of the Players in a Mirror at Midnight" (not a bad metaphor for film in itself) was composed. At that time, in addition to being very involved in the theater, Joyce was working on a scheme, with a man who called himself Jules Martin, for making a film (or pretending to make a film): " 'We'll get wealthy women into it,' Martin said, 'women in fur pelts. We'll teach them how to walk and then charge them a fee for being in the film.' The studio was to have a *Kino Schule* as an adjunct" (Ellmann, 423). Martin, who at one time proposed himself for the Joycean role of Richard Rowan in a performance of *Exiles,* was a bohemian confidence man (a metempsychotic version of Alexandre Privat, perhaps) whose real name was Juda de Vries and who ultimately had to be helped out of jail and into a hospital by Joyce. Nevertheless, Joyce, who was a bit of a bohemian confidence man himself, went along with the film project for a while.

Joyce's cinematic inclinations (let us not forget the Volta theater project) encourage me to find a place for him in Louis Malle's cinematic brothel. We shall return to that, but first it should be acknowledged that Joyce's jealousy over *The Dial*'s preference for Proust was well founded, for Scott's article was preceded by a short selection from Proust's massive work in progress, with a fulsome introduction by Richard Aldington in which Joyce was relegated, along with Dorothy Richardson and May Sinclair, to the ranks of Proust's inferior contemporaries. Perhaps by "film" Joyce meant to include Scott's and Aldington's pieces, but my point is that in 1920 *The Dial* provided both the public location for his poem on the horrors of sexuality and the occasion for his jealousy of a rival who was described by Aldington as "more coherent than Mr Joyce, more urbane, less preoccupied with slops and viscera" but nonetheless capable of describing "a public convenience with a precision and verve which would have aroused the jealousy even of Flaubert" (345). Joyce, who was himself no mean describer of public conveniences, must have bitterly resented being called a purveyor of "slops and viscera," and then being positioned as a poor third behind Proust and Flaubert in the public convenience derby.

When it came to brothels, however, which in the modernist era were clearly perceived as a kind of public convenience, Joyce really deserved the palm, though he had one interesting and powerful rival: Pablo Picasso. Let us not forget, in this connection, that Joyce was "kept," as an artist, by Harriet Shaw Weaver, who sent him money regularly for the last twenty years of his life. Both Joyce and Picasso, however, actually knew prostitutes. They almost certainly were both sexually initiated by these professionals and both, at some point, probably contracted venereal disease from the same sources. Recall that chapter 2 of *A Portrait of the Artist as a Young Man* ends with Stephen Dedalus in the arms of a gentle prostitute, herself enough of a child to keep a doll in a chair (with its legs spread suggestively, however), who bends Stephen's head down to hers and by forcing her tongue into his mouth gives him the gift of tongues. At the end of the next chapter, Stephen is kneeling at the altar rail, with his tongue out for the consecrated wafer to be put upon it, containing the body and blood of Jesus Christ.

The young hooker of Joyce's *Portrait* is, like the prostitutes and jugglers of Picasso's blue period, represented with more sentiment than violence. This changed in *Ulysses,* and it changed for Picasso in the text we are about to examine. Picasso's most important early painting, and one of the most important he ever painted, is *Les*

Demoiselles d'Avignon, which he completed in June or July 1907 (fig. 1).[2] In this painting he made his most decisive break with the past, including the work of his own blue and pink periods, and began the move that was to culminate a few years later in analytic cubism. *Les Demoiselles* is a brothel painting—its Avignon being not the Provencal home of the anti-popes but the Nighttown of Barcelona. What do we see on this canvas? Five female figures, unclothed. Some drapery. A table with some fruit. The women's bodies are arbitrarily geometrized. The tones of their flesh are rigid blocks of color. Their faces range from masklike to actual masks. A primitive animality surges through the painting, distorting, dehumanizing, threatening the viewer, who is ineluctably coded as male and who is positioned as the object of many of these fierce female eyes. How are we to account for this? What is going on here?

Since we have literally hundreds of the preliminary sketches Picasso made for this work in sixteen different notebooks, we know a good deal about how the painting evolved. In May 1907 Picasso made a pastel sketch of the painting he was planning (fig. 2). He and his friends half-jokingly referred to the work in progress as *"le Bordel philosophique"* (the philosophical brothel). In it we find seven figures: five women, as in the *Demoiselles,* and two men. The seated man is dressed as a sailor; the other, standing at the left, and carrying an object that is probably a book, is usually identified as a medical student. The pastel is in fact reminiscent of other brothel drawings, such as the monotypes of Degas discussed recently by Charles Bernheimer in a very important chapter of *Figures of Ill Repute,* which takes its own point of departure from Paul Valéry's "Degas danse dessin." Bernheimer takes seriously Valéry's observation that "Degas was passionately determined to reconstruct the specialized female animal as the slave of the danse, the laundry, or the streets; and the more or less distorted bodies whose articulated structure he always arranges in very precarious attitudes . . . make the whole mechanical system of a living being seem to *grimace* like a face" (159).

Eunice Lipton, in *Looking into Degas,* has amplified this case, arguing persuasively that most of Degas' nudes, especially those shown bathing themselves, were in fact prostitutes at work, since they had to bathe more than most people thought was healthy at that time and since they thought nothing of bathing before their clients. Degas apparently made over one hundred brothel monotypes, of which less

Figure 1. *Les Demoiselles d'Avignon.* Pablo Picasso. Oil on canvas, 8′ × 7′8″. Collection of the Museum of Modern Art, New York. Acquired through the Lillie P. Bliss Bequest.

Figure 2. A sketch for *Demoiselles.* Black crayon and pastel on paper, 47.7 × 63.5 cm. Öffentliche Kunstammlung Basel. Gift of the artist to the city of Basel, 1967.

than half are extant, his brother having destroyed more than fifty at the time of the painter's death. Bernheimer points out that Degas made most of these sketches around 1879 and 1880, at "a time when literary versions of the prostitute's life were arriving on the cultural scene in rapid succession (Huysmans' *Marthe* was published in 1876; Edmond de Goncourt's *La Fille Elisa* appeared in 1877; Zola's *Nana* created a sensation in 1880, also the year of Maupassant's 'Boule de suif,' followed in 1881 by his 'La Maison Tellier')" (161). Picasso, of course, was born late in that year and Joyce early in the next. The interest in prostitutes and the rise of modernism, I argue, are aspects of the same cultural process, one that begins with Baudelaire, who links the modern city with the bold women who walk the city's streets in poems like the one from *Spleen et idéal* that begins "Tu mettrais l'universe entier dans ta ruelle / Femme impure" (You would put the whole universe up your alley / Impure woman; *Selected Poems,* 66), so that one scarcely knows whether Baudelaire is talking of the city as whore or the whore as city. Joyce and Picasso have their own angles of approach to this uniquely modern conundrum, for they share a special interest not only in the prostitute but in the brothel itself as a place of degradation and magic.

The monotypes of Degas can help us to place what is—and is not—going on in Picasso's brothel painting (and in Joyce's brothel writing, to which we shall come eventually).[3] In one of Degas' brothel monotypes, for instance, we see naked women sitting casually on display for the gaze of a cigar-smoking client who is fully dressed, including his hat. They look at him as seductively as they can. He looks at them. We look, unobserved, at all. In another scene, titled "The Serious Client," a fully clothed man (complete with umbrella) chooses a woman from among several on display (or, perhaps, he is chosen by one of them). Picasso owned eleven of the fifty or so extant brothel monotypes, and in his ninetieth year he made a series of forty etchings that Bernheimer calls a "remarkable reading" (177) of these visual texts. In one of these etchings Picasso represents Degas himself, positioning him as the medical student in a *Demoiselles* sketch of sixty-five years earlier, confronted by an aggressively delineated group of naked women. In another of these etchings, Picasso shows Degas in a brothel, holding easel and paintbrush and painting another Degas, still in the medical student's place, while the women around him offer themselves.

The point is not necessarily that Degas influenced *Les Demoiselles* (I do not, in fact, know when Picasso first saw these monotypes) but that Degas could so easily be inserted into the situation of *Les Demoiselles* by being given a place already prepared for him in the preliminary sketches of Picasso's painting. The man whose place Degas is given was ultimately erased from *Les Demoiselles*—or, rather, was blended with the woman originally positioned to his left. He was, however, prominent in a number of versions throughout the early sketches and was thought of by Picasso and his friends as a "medical student." In some versions he appears with what is clearly a book, in some with a skull, and in one memorable sketch with both book and skull in hand and a dog playing around his leg (fig. 3). At one time, Picasso did intend to put a dog in the painting and made a number of dog sketches, including several in which the dog is nursing a set of puppies. The dog is a bitch.

What is going on here? A medical student, a sailor, and a dog all appear in or around Bella Cohen's brothel in *Ulysses,* but what are they doing in Picasso's sketches for the painting he thought of as *Le Bordel philosophique*? It seems clear enough, as a number of commentators have pointed out, that Picasso was thinking in symbolic terms as he worked on the early sketches for this painting, inviting us to read this text as an allegory of basic human processes in which primordial lust is surrounded with signifiers of death (the skull), learning or science (the book), animality and birth (the bitch nursing her pups). The medical student seems to have functioned mainly as the carrier of these symbolic objects, but the sailor is there for other reasons. Most of the sketches show him as a gentle, shy youth with downcast eyes. In this respect he is reminiscent of the young Stephen Dedalus comforted by the prostitute at the end of chapter 2 of *Portrait.* In a later sketch, Picasso's sailor has one eye open, and still later he begins to metamorphose or merge with the female figures around him, on the way to being totally subsumed in them. But what is it that he looks away from or glances at with one eye in these sketches?

Opposite him, with her back to the viewer, squats the most sexually provocative of the *demoiselles.* Like the women in a monotype by Degas, which Picasso owned before its donation to the Louvre, she is presenting herself to the sailor as a potential client. In one study, for instance, we see her spreading her legs as far apart as she can and provocatively glancing to her left at the newly arrived medical student,

Figure 3. Study for the medical student from Picasso's notebook of March 1907. Black crayon, 19.3 × 24.2 cm. Musée Picasso, Paris.

who is holding up the curtain in order to enter the theatrical space of the brothel's inner sanctum (she will partly absorb the sailor's features). This moment of presentation is crucial for a prostitute or an artist, since the possibilities of rejection are most acute. The client, equipped with the power of the gaze, has the purveyor—and especially the purveyor of her own flesh or the product of her own imagination—at his mercy. What was most shocking about Manet's *Olympia* (fig. 4), when it was displayed to the clients of the Salon of 1863, was that it put the client of art and the client of sex in exactly the same place—and that the artist dared to look back through the eyes of this painted female body at those clients. The boldness of this painting becomes more obvious when we compare it to one of Cézanne's two versions of this scene, called *A Modern Olympia,* done in watercolors around 1873 (fig. 5).[4] Here the client of flesh has been put back inside the pictured space, leaving the client of the painting safely outside the frame, and the eyes of the woman for sale are turned demurely away from both of these male gazes.

When I say that the artist looks out at the client through the eyes of the naked woman in Manet's *Olympia,* I am not just making a metaphorical statement. The woman who looks at us from that canvas is clearly Victorine Meurent, whose activities ranged from posing for the nude photographs collected as aids to his work by Eugène Delacroix in the 1850s, to painting well enough herself to have her work hung in the Salon of 1876, a year in which Manet's own works were rejected, and again 1879, when her painting *Une Bourgeoise de Nurembourg* hung in the same room as Manet's entries (Adler, 152–53). In *Olympia* Victorine Meurent is on display, but her left hand firmly indicates the limits of that display, and her eyes are those of one who sells her art where and when she chooses. I am suggesting that Manet, in this and other paintings of women who were more or less on sale or on display, broke the traditional molds of such displays because he, at some level, saw in their situation the situation of artists such as himself, just as Baudelaire did. These figures, to some degree, were images of himself as well as paintings done by him.

Picasso also put himself into his brothel painting, imagining, for instance, how, if he were the sailor, the squatting woman would appear to him. That the sailor was sometimes conceived as a surrogate for the painter is apparent in the resemblance between certain sketches for this figure and certain portraits of the artist as a young

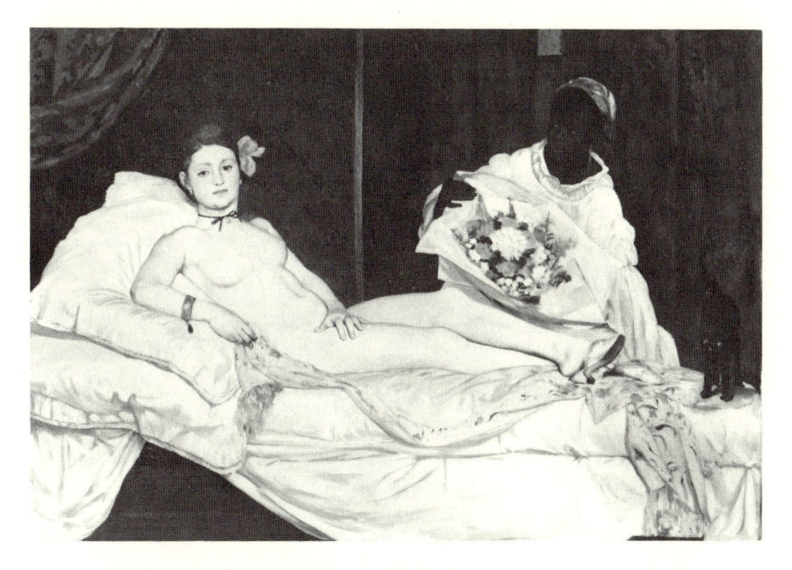

Figure 4. *Olympia.* Édouard Manet. Paris, Musée d'Orsay.

Figure 5. *A Modern Olympia.* Paul Cézanne. Philadelphia Museum of Art.

man of the same period. What the sailor in the brothel saw (or averted his eyes from—depending on which sketch of him we use for our imaginary location) was a woman displaying herself to him, with legs spread, then tilting her head toward the medical student. (As Brigitte Leal puts it in her introduction to an edition of one of Picasso's sketchbooks, "La fille accroupie dans son coin . . . ouvre grand ses cuisses, comme pour vanter sa marchandise.") Displaying herself to the sailor, then tilting her head toward the medical student, this squatting figure became something of a compositional problem for Picasso as, in the course of the painting's evolution, the male figures metamorphosed into their neighboring females (partially masculinizing them in the process). Picasso's solution, as later developments force us to acknowledge, was essentially a cubist one. The squatting prostitute remains as she was but also turns impossibly toward us, forcing us to see her from front, rear, and side at once. She turns toward us because as the male figures were removed their function devolved upon the viewer. She also remains facing away from us because Picasso wanted to capture the turn itself, to transcend the limits of his medium and perhaps of space and time as well. Thus, she absorbs, to some extent, the gaze of the absent sailor and turns it back upon us, the spectators, in the role of client of sex or art.

The point I am trying to make is so crucial that I must take the liberty of repeating it: these modernist artists were fascinated by prostitutes because they saw in them an image of themselves. Just as Baudelaire, in his prose poem about an old acrobat, or *saltimbanque* (*Petits Poèmes en prose,* no. 14), saw in this wretched creature the image of a writer who had outlived his generation, Picasso and Joyce saw themselves as combining the almost magical power over men of a Circe or Medusa with the degrading status of a human commodity exemplified by the whores of Avignon and Nighttown. As early as 1904, Joyce had represented himself in this way in "The Holy Office":

> But all those men of whom I speak
> Make me the sewer of their clique.
> That they may dream their dreamy dreams
> I carry off their filthy streams
> For I can do those things for them
> Through which I lost my diadem,
> Those things for which Grandmother Church
> Left me severely in the lurch.
>
> (*Critical Writings,* 151)

It is true that Joyce represents himself here as performing mainly a cloacal function, but this was precisely the way that prostitutes were represented in the public discussions of the nineteenth century (see Bernheimer's first chapter for a fascinating discussion of this connection). Joyce, in his Irish Catholic way, saw his cloacal function as a "Holy Office," but the point is that both he and Picasso were obsessed by the extreme tension between some grand religious or mystical function for themselves as artists and the vision of themselves as street entertainers, prostitutes, or public conveniences. Their modernism is a Romanticism that has passed through naturalism.

Picasso's philosophical brothel, as the painting developed, also became a locus for the artist's growing interest in primitive artifacts. The way primitive painting penetrated the superficial surface of life in order to symbolize elemental forces appealed to Picasso and to many other modern artists and writers. Joyce's primitivism tended toward the early Celtic and Viking heritage of Ireland, as we might expect, finding expression early in the Cyclops chapter of *Ulysses* and later throughout *Finnegans Wake.* But Picasso turned readily to early Iberian art and the art of Africa and Oceania. In this respect (as has been pointed out by Maurizia Boscagli and Marianna Torgovnick) he is joined by that other male modern master of verbal art, D. H. Lawrence. This is visible in such episodes as the section of *Women in Love* (written in 1916) in which Rupert Birkin and Gerald Crich, along with the allegorically named Russian, Libidnikov, visit Julius Halliday's Picadilly Circus apartment. With them goes the pregnant Minette Darrington, who might easily find her place among the *demoiselles,* as Lawrence describes her: "like some fair ice-flower in dreadful flowering nakedness" (Lawrence, 62)–except that Minette is a born victim, more like a character from a Jean Rhys novel than like Olympia or Picasso's Catalunian hookers. Many prostitutes are no doubt victims, but Picasso's *demoiselles* have been metamorphosed into dreadful ice-flowers by the primitivism that energizes the final versions of their faces and bodies. This primitivism is also present in Halliday's London apartment, which contains two new pictures "in the Futurist manner" as well as "several statues from the West Pacific, strange and disturbing" (67). The pregnant Minette's seduction of Gerald (or hers by him) is presented so as to merge her personality, at least temporarily, with that of one of the primitive statues: "a woman sitting naked in a strange posture, and looking tortured, her abdomen stuck out" (67).

The statue is a representation of a woman in labor, whose face appears to Birkin as "dark and tense, abstracted in utter physical stress. It was a terrible face, void, peaked, abstracted almost into meaningless by the weight of sensation beneath. He saw Minette in it" (71).

For those of us coming from literature toward modern visual art, it may help to see Picasso as combining Joyce's drive toward formal (almost geometrical) experimentation with Lawrence's complex response to the primitive, a response that combines fascination, hope, and fear. What is interesting here is the peculiarly modernist way in which the bohemian and the primitive mix to generate a new configuration for the female in the imaginations of these male modernists. No longer is the Christian division into the Virgin or the Magdalen dominant; rather, it is a new configuration in which the prostitute represents a pre-Christian, primordial level of existence, at once more bestial and more authentic than either Virgin or Magdalen could be—and represents as well a degraded, possibly diseased female commodity that captures the essential quality of modern urban existence. In Lawrence's *Women in Love* the poor pregnant bohemian girl and the powerful image of the primitive woman in labor can merge only in the imagination of Birkin.

Try as he might, Lawrence tended always to give his male characters (human or equine) the primordial power represented here in the female Oceanic statue, while forcing his females to remain bourgeois or bohemian, dependents on a masculinity that obsessed and sometimes destroyed them. (In its purest form we find this in "The Woman Who Rode Away," in which a modern woman becomes the human sacrifice of primitive men.) But Picasso was able, in *Les Demoiselles* in particular, to bring the modern, the female, and the primitive together in a genuinely new way, of which the subsumption of the two male figures within the five females is the plainest indicator. This move was hinted at even earlier in his work—for instance in his 1901 parody of Manet's *Olympia* (fig. 6). In this painting Victorine Meurent has been replaced by the black serving woman, who is clearly a primitive Venus, shaped like an ancient figurine, and thus undoubtedly a parody of Baudelaire's black Venus. The cat has been supplemented by a dog, and two clients have been put inside the frame, one of whom is a thoroughly emasculated portrait of the artist himself. The connection between this and the later *Demoiselles* can be read in the reappearance in the later painting of the bowl of fruit from this crayon sketch.

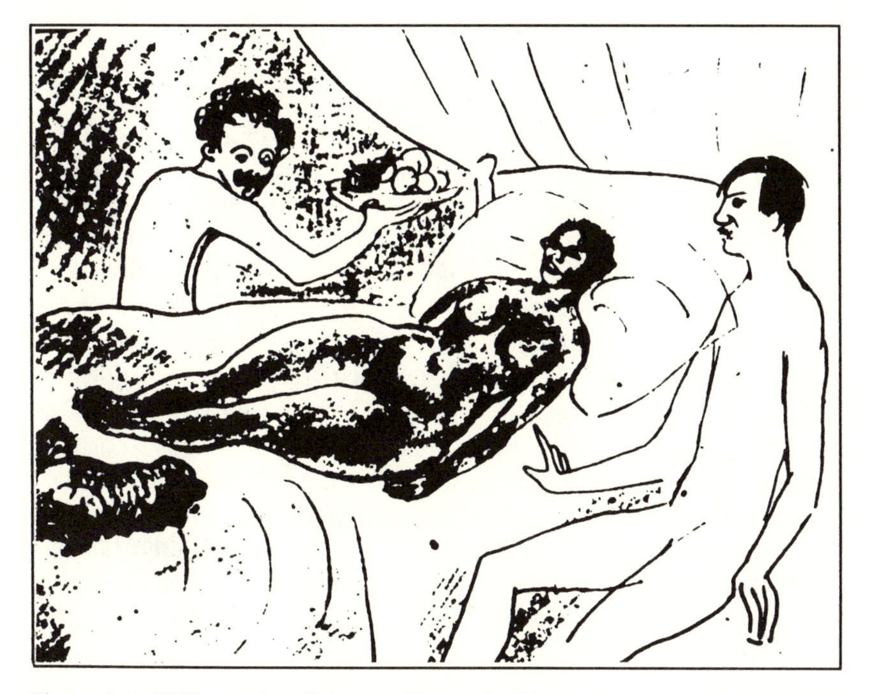

Figure 6. A 1901 parody of Manet's *Olympia* by Picasso.

In the Circe chapter of *Ulysses,* Joyce also managed a similar feat of modernist legerdemain. This chapter, as Michael Groden argues convincingly in *"Ulysses" in Progress,* was the point at which Joyce's art entered a new phase: "His work on 'Circe' was crucial; he seems to have begun it as an episode similar in scope and length to the previous three, but by the time he finished it he had left the middle stage behind for new developments" (52). The writing of "Circe" led to elaborate revisions of the earlier chapters, along with a shift of emphasis from the interor monologue and stylistic parody to what Groden calls a "complex intermixture of realism and symbolism" (204). In September 1920, when he was working on this chapter, Joyce wrote to Carlo Linati: "I am working like a galley slave, an ass, a brute. I cannot even sleep. The episode of Circe has changed me too into an animal" (*Letters,* 146). What is abundantly clear is that working on their two brothel scenes changed both Joyce's and Picasso's art in the most profound ways. *Les Demoiselles* pointed the way to cubism, just as "Circe" led inexorably toward *Finnegans Wake.* Let us now consider more specifically what happened in Joyce's writing of "Circe" and then return to the question of why the brothel should be so situated at the creative center of modernist art.

In *The Odyssey* Circe's island is a place of magic in which men are turned into animals by a powerful enchantress. The link between magical power, transformation, and animal degradation are shared by Joyce's chapter and Picasso's painting. "Circe" is set in a space clearly delineated as theatrical by its formal properties of stage direction and dialogue, but it is no more theatrical than *Les Demoiselles,* with its stage curtains held open by the entering figure from the left (whether medical student or primordial female), giving the viewer access to what lies beyond the proscenium. Many of Joyce's stage directions, however, would defy the most resourceful theatrical impresario: "The beagle lifts his snout, showing the grey scorbutic face of Paddy Dignam. He has gnawed all. He exhales a putrid carcasefed breath. He grows to human size and shape. His dachshund coat becomes a brown mortuary habit. His green eye flashes bloodshot. Half of one ear, all the nose and both thumbs are ghouleaten" (*Ulysses,* 385). Even supposing film rather than stage drama, the most technically adept special effects team would have trouble with that putrid breath (though experiments along olfactory lines are still being undertaken). My point is simply that the brothel and its environs offered Joyce and Picasso a space already devoted to theatrical deceptions and the aesthetic organization of primal needs, which they could adapt to their own surrealistic ends.

These two artists populate their stages with creatures that are not mere human actors and actresses but transgressors of the border between human and animal, normal and freakish. The following stage direction of Joyce's degrades the human form at least as much as Picasso's bodily distortions: "In an archway a standing woman, bent forward, her feet apart, pisses cowily. Outside a shuttered pub a bunch of loiterers listen to a tale which their brokensnouted gaffer rasps out with raucous humour. An armless pair of them flop wrestling, growling, in maimed sodden playfight" (*Ulysses,* 367). The ideal integrity of the human form, privileged for so long in art and in Romantic aesthetics, has become an object of programmatic destruction in both these works, which are driven in part by an anger against aesthetic pretensions.

They are also, however, driven by a peculiarly modernist anxiety to achieve formal innovations that stamp this work as different from everything that had been done before. Both artists knew that brothels had previously been presented naturalistically. To go beyond naturalism for them meant making their brothels philosophical. Thus the medical student Lynch, who had been the auditor of Stephen's lecture on aesthetics in *Portrait,* responds to Stephen's latest aesthetic installment in "Circe" with this denunciation: "Pornosophical philotheology. Metaphysics in Mecklenburgh Street." This is said as the two young men go toward the bawdy house, or, in Stephen's words, "to *la belle dame sans merci,* Georgina Johnson, *ad deam qui laetificat iuventum meam*" ("to the goddess who gladdens my youth"—which is the response of an altar boy serving at Mass to the priestly words spoken by Buck Mulligan at the opening of *Ulysses—"Introibo ad altare Dei"*—but with the gender changed so that the reference is not to God but to a goddess [353]).

Picasso began with five women and two men. Joyce's central stage contains a similar number: the whores Zoe, Kitty, and Florry, along with the madam, Bella Cohen; Lynch, the medical student; Stephen, the homeless wanderer in place of Picasso's young sailor; and Bloom, who is "unmanned" and auctioned off as a whore by Bella, now transformed into the masculine Bello: "My boys will be no end charmed to see you so ladylike . . . when they come here the night before the wedding to fondle my new attraction in gilded heels. First I'll have a go at you myself. . . . Swell the bust. Smile. Droop shoulders. What offers? (*he points*) For that lot. Trained by owner to fetch and carry, basket in mouth. (*he bares his arm and plunges it elbowdeep in Bloom's vulva*) There's fine depth for you! What, boys? That give you a hardon? (*he shoves his arm in a bidder's face*) Here wet the deck and wipe it round!" (440). There is just as much of the violence and degradation of prostitution in Joyce's text as in Picasso's. These words, it is worth noting, were added by Joyce to the text on the printer's proofs, indicating that in *Ulysses* as well as in *Les Demoiselles,* a brutal bestiality was the end toward which these works in progress moved. In this ultimate addition to "Circe" Bloom is not only transformed into a woman (as the sailor and medical students in Picasso's painting were absorbed into the female figures around them), he is also degraded to the level of an animal, like the *demoiselles* whose faces become inhuman masks. In her guise as Circe, Bello transforms Bloom into a female pig (also a dog and a horse): "Very possibly I shall have you slaughtered and skewered in my stables and enjoy a slice of you with crisp crackling from the baking tin basted and baked like suckling pig with rice and lemon or currant sauce. It will hurt you" (434).

These are stagings of the lower psychic depths, produced at times in their lives when Joyce and Picasso were concerned with their own health and driven by a ferocious alienation from their fellows. Joyce, seeing himself in a mirror at midnight, thought, "This grey that stares / Lies not, stark skin and bone. / Leave greasy lips their kissing. None / Will choose her what you see to mouth upon." And he advised himself to "Lash / Your itch and quailing, nude greed of the flesh." One of Picasso's friends (André Derain), reacting to the finished *Les Demoiselles,* said that the painter would probably soon be found hanged behind it. Driven by their own flesh and by the promptings of no ordinary ambition, it is no wonder that these two artists found their most powerful expressive forms in these pornosophical, philo-theological bordellos. But the brothel of modernism was also a sanctuary, a relic of a time when the flesh at least counted for something—so that artists could seek to contain and control their own commodification by joining forces with members of that ancient guild, incorporating images of prostitution within their works in a last doomed attempt to sustain what Walter Benjamin called the "aura" of art. The threat faced by all modern artists is the one that overtakes E. J. Bellocq in *Pretty Baby.*

After World War I, Storyville is cleaned up and closed down by the moralizing bourgeoisie. The jazz musician (modeled on Jelly Roll Morton) must find another place to play. We know he will end up as a recording in someone's collection. The photographic artist marries his baby hooker and tries to continue his work, but her mother, earlier removed from the bordello by a wealthy cement contractor from St. Louis, comes back to rescue her daughter, so she, too, can grow up as a good bourgeoise. Did Victorine Meurent imagine herself as a "Bourgeoise of Nuremburg" when she exhibited a painting with that title? In *Pretty Baby* the artist is separated from his model, and the film closes with the cement contractor lining up his new family at the railroad station, so that he can snap their picture with a Kodak box camera. (The Kodak slogan then was, "You press the button, we do the rest.") In the brothel two of the major modernists found, in the very squalor and degradation of the place, a powerful embodiment of the human psyche that lent itself to a corresponding disembodiment of form—in which that power was explosively released. The brothel was the last sanctuary of the "aura" of art, a refuge from the mechanical reproduction that threatened to end the Romantic reign of art. This is why Louis Malle's film, constructed from within the mechanical, can ultimately portray the brothel of modernism only in a mood dominated by nostalgia.

For the male artists who dominated modernism, the brothel constituted a theatrical space in which to reenact those moments when they were clients for fleshly commodities and to envision their own positions as caterers to public whims and victims of market forces. In the figures of prostitutes these artists could embody a primordial natural energy they admired—and a bestiality that, to varying degrees, they were forced to acknowledge in themselves. They could also represent the situation of human beings forced to be commodities in their own flesh, alienated from themselves in the most intimate way. Thus, in the magical power of these figures and in the gazes of their terrible eyes, Joyce and Picasso could see both what they feared and what they were. They looked at and through these eyes; they were both seers and seen. What we, as the ultimate clients of these texts, should also see is how those gazes are meant for us, to remind us that we, too, maintain our subjectivity only by turning others into objects. The Medusa eyes of Picasso's *demoiselles* and the Circean power of Bella Cohen remind us how in our world the most elemental drives take the structure of commodities and art itself is neither safe nor pure. We cannot touch it and pretend that we are undefiled. The mythical Medusa's eyes turned their objects to stone. Circe changed men into beasts. Stone or beast, these works are telling us. Take your choice. You must be one or the other. There is no escape.

In this modernist cultural situation, the brothel offered an ideal textual space. Here the drive for perpetual formal innovation could be combined readily with the need to represent the full degradation of modern life. Here, too, the mythic and archetypal connections that kept modernism from falling into the merely naturalistic were also readily available for those who could find them. Here the artist as Minotaur could meet his object as Medusa, and Daedalus/Icarus/Telemachus could meet Odysseus on Circe's island. However, this textual space—and this cannot be emphasized too much—was structured like that modern medium par excellence, the cinema—structured, that is, voyeuristically in terms of male subjectivity and female objectivity, so that wherever female subjectivity appeared, it could be appropriated for the artists themselves, who were inevitably male.

There is also a practical side to this. If, as I have argued, the brothel was a privileged place for male modernists, it was also a place that, for the most part, excluded women who were not themselves prostitutes. The list of women artists and writers who produced brothel texts scarcely exists at all. If we borrow a textual move from Virginia Woolf and try to imagine one of Joyce's sisters becoming a modernist writer; we can readily see how a certain crucial experience of prostitutes and brothels was simply impossible for her, while it was almost inevitable for her brother. However, the list of male artists and writers who situated works in brothels, from Baudelaire and Manet through Joyce and Picasso, is long and distinguished. We have a subject matter here that clearly divides women writers from men, and it is also a subject matter uniquely associated with modernist formal innovation and the other features of modernist writing. I believe that modern*ism*—as distinguished from modern writing and painting, or writing and painting in the modern period—has a distinctly masculist structure that is embodied most clearly and powerfully in its images of the brothel: a structure in which extremes of formal innovation are linked with this specific cultural site, with its powerful division of sexual roles. This is why *Pretty Baby,* which aligns modernism and photography so beautifully, inserts its photographer into the brothel as a figure of male subjectivity, bringing together the voyeuristic structure of film—and of modernist textuality in general—so plainly and simply that we cannot miss it. When Brooke Shields leaves Storyville, she will become a bourgeois subject, go to an Ivy League college, and modernism will be over. We need shed no tears over this.

Notes

1. The French text of "Loss of Halo" appears in *Twenty Prose Poems* (trans. Michael Hamburger. San Francisco: City Lights, 1988).

2. *Les Demoiselles d'Avignon* hangs in the Metropolitan Museum of Art. The sketches referred to in this discussion may all be found in *Les Demoiselles d'Avignon,* vol. 1 (Paris: Éditions de la réunion des musées nationaux, 1988). Some of the sketches may also be found, with a short introduction by Brigitte Leal, in *Les Demoiselles d'Avignon: Carnet de Dessins* (Paris: Éditions de la réunion des musées nationaux, 1988).

3. The Degas brothel monotypes discussed here may be found in Janis, *Degas Monotypes.*

4. Cézanne's versions of Manet's *Olympia,* both called *A Modern Olympia,* may be found in Dunlop and Orienti, *The Complete Paintings of Cézanne,* and in Adler, *Manet.*

Works Cited

Adler, Kathleen. *Manet.* Topsfield, Mass.: Salem House, 1986.

Aldington, Richard.

Baudelaire, Charles. *Petits Poèmes en prose.* Translated by Edward K. Kaplan as *The Parisian Prowler.* Athens: University of Georgia Press, 1989.

——. *Selected Poems.* New York: Penguin, 1975.

Benjamin, Walter. *Reflections.* New York: Harcourt Brace Jovanovich, 1979.

Bernheimer, Charles. *Figures of Ill Repute.* Cambridge: Harvard University Press, 1989.

Boscagli, Maurizia. "The Eye on the Flesh: Gender, Ideology, and the Modernist Body." Ph.D. dissertation, Brown University, 1990.

Buck-Morss, Susan. *The Dialectics of Seeing.* Cambridge: MIT Press, 1989.

Callard, D. A. *"Pretty Good for a Woman."* New York: W. W. Norton, 1985.

Clark, T. J. *The Painting of Modern Life.* Princeton: Princeton University Press, 1984.

Dunlop, Ian, and Sandra Orienti. *The Complete Paintings of Cézanne.* New York: Penguin, 1970.

Ellmann, Richard. *James Joyce.* New York: Oxford University Press, 1959.

Groden, Michael. *"Ulysses" in Progress.* Princeton: Princeton University Press, 1975.

Janis, Eugenia Perry. *Degas Monotypes: Essay, Catalogue, and Checklist.* Greenwich, Conn.: New York Graphic Society, 1968.

Joost, Nicholas. *Scofield Thayer and "The Dial."* Carbondale: Southern Illinois University Press, 1964.

Joyce, James. *Letters,* ed. Stuart Gilbert. Viking, New York: 1957.

——. *Collected Poems.* New York: Viking, 1957.

——. *Critical Writings.* New York: Viking, 1959.

——. *A Portrait of the Artist as a Young Man.* New York: Viking, 1968.

——. *Selected Letters,* ed. Richard Ellmann. New York: Viking, 1975.

——. *Ulysses.* New York: Random House, 1986.

Kenner, Hugh. "The Making of the Modernist Canon," in *Canons,* ed. Robert von Hallberg. Chicago: University of Chicago Press, 1984, pp. 363–75.

Lawrence, D. H. *Women in Love.* New York: Viking, 1965.

Leal, Brigitte, ed. *Les Demoiselles d'Avignon: Carnet et Dessins.* Paris: Éditions de la réunion des musée nationaux, 1988.

Lipton, Eunice. *Looking into Degas.* Los Angeles: University of California Press, 1987.

Newhall, Beaumont. *The History of Photography.* New York: Museum of Modern Art, 1982.

Seigel, Jerrold. *Bohemian Paris.* New York: Penguin, 1986.

Torgovnick, Marianna. *Gone Primitive.* Chicago: University of Chicago Press, 1990.

Valéry, Paul. "Degas danse dessin," in *Oeuvres,* ed. J. Hytier, 2 vols. Paris: Pléiade, 1960.

Index

Permission to reprint these essays is gratefully acknowledged:

"Stephen Dedalus: *Eiron* and *Alazon*" first appeared in *Texas Studies in Literature and Language* 3, no. 1 (Spring 1961): 8–15. Reprinted by permission of the University of Texas Press.

"Some Observations on the Text of *Dubliners*" first appeared in *Studies in Bibliography* 15 (1962): 191–205. Reprinted by permission of the Bibliographical Society of the University of Virginia.

"Further Observations on the Text of *Dubliners*" first appeared in *Studies in Bibliography* 17 (1964): 107–22. Reprinted by permission of the Bibliographical Society of the University of Virginia.

"Review of a New Edition of *A Portrait of the Artist as a Young Man*" first appeared in *Philological Quarterly* 44, no. 2 (April 1965): 278–82. Reprinted by permission of the publisher.

"Joyce and the Epiphany: The Key to the Labyrinth?" first appeared in the *Sewanee Review* 72 (1964): 65–77. Copyright 1964 by the University of the South. Reprinted by permission of the editor.

"Stephen Dedalus, Poet or Aesthete?" first appeared in *PMLA* 79, no. 4 (September 1964): 484–89. Reprinted by permission of the Modern Language Association of America.

"James Joyce, Irish Poet" first appeared in *James Joyce Quarterly* 11, no. 4 (Summer 1965): 255–70. Reprinted by permission of the publisher.

"Joyce and Symbolism" combines a portion of "Design: Juxtaposition and Repetition in the Structure of Fiction" and "A Commentary on 'Clay'" from *Elements of Fiction,* Robert Scholes (New York: Oxford University Press, 1968), pp. 38–40, 66–77. Reprinted by permission of the publisher.

"Counterparts" first appeared in *James Joyce's "Dubliners": Critical Essays,* ed. Clive Hart (London: Faber and Faber, 1969), pp. 93–99. Reprinted by permission of the publisher.

"*Ulysses:* A Structuralist Perspective" first appeared in *James Joyce Quarterly* 10, no. 1 (Fall 1972): 161–71. Reprinted by permission of the publisher.

"In Search of James Joyce" first appeared in *James Joyce Quarterly* 11, no. 1 (Fall 1973): 5–16. Reprinted by permission of the publisher.

"Semiotic Approaches to a Fictional Text: Joyce's 'Eveline'" first appeared in *James Joyce Quarterly* 16, nos. 1/2 (Fall 1978/Winter 1979): 65–80. Reprinted by permission of the publisher.

"x/y Joyce and Modernist Ideology" first appeared in *Coping with Joyce,* ed. Morris Beja and Shari Benstock (Columbus: The Ohio State University Press, 1988), pp. 91–107. Reprinted by permission of the publisher.

A Note on the Author

ROBERT SCHOLES, a Joyce scholar for more than three decades and an important contributor to the rise of literary theory, is Andrew W. Mellon Professor of Humanities at Brown University. He is the author or editor of over two dozen books, among them *Structuralism in Literature, Semiotics and Interpretation, Textual Power,* and *Protocols of Reading.*